FOLLOW THE BUZZARDS

FOLLOW THE BUZZARDS

Pro Wrestling in the Age of COVID-19

KEITH ELLIOT GREENBERG

This book is also available as a Global Certified Accessible™ (GCA) ebook. ECW Press's ebooks are screen reader friendly and are built to meet the needs of those who are unable to read standard print due to blindness, low vision, dyslexia, or a physical disability.

Purchase the print edition and receive the ebook free. For details, go to ecwpress.com/ebook.

Published by ECW Press
665 Gerrard Street East
Toronto, Ontario, Canada M4M 1Y2
416-694-3348 / info@ecwpress.com

Editor for the Press: Michael Holmes
Copy editor: Rachel Ironstone
Cover design: Made by Emblem

LIBRARY AND ARCHIVES CANADA CATALOGUING IN PUBLICATION

Title: Follow the buzzards : pro wrestling in the age of COVID-19 / Keith Elliot Greenberg.

Names: Greenberg, Keith Elliot, 1959- author.

Identifiers: Canadiana (print) 20220226474 | Canadiana (ebook) 20220226520

ISBN 978-1-77041-598-0 (softcover)
ISBN 978-1-77090-741-6 (ePub)
ISBN 978-1-77852-000-6 (PDF)
ISBN 978-1-77852-001-3 (Kindle)

Subjects: LCSH: Wrestling. | LCSH: COVID-19 Pandemic, 2020—Influence.

Classification: LCC GV1195 .G74 2022 | DDC 796.812—dc23

PRINTED AND BOUND IN CANADA

PRINTING: MARQUIS   5 4 3 2 1

Dedicated to my father,
Abe Greenberg
December 21, 1926, Wilkes Barre, Pennsylvania–
July 13, 2021, Queens, New York

"The plague full swift goes by;
I am sick, I must die.
Lord, have mercy on us!"
    — "A Litany in Time of Plague," Thomas Nashe, 1593

"That's all I hear about now. That's all I hear. Turn on television. 'COVID, COVID, COVID, COVID, COVID, COVID.' A plane goes down, 500 people dead. They don't talk about it. 'COVID, COVID, COVID, COVID.'"
    — President Donald J. Trump, October 24, 2020

"And Jacob was left alone; and there wrestled a man with him until the breaking of the day."
    — Genesis 32:24

CHAPTER 1

THE CARS PULLED into the parking lot of the Chase Center on the Riverfront in Wilmington, Delaware. Inside the vehicles, drivers exuberantly honked horns and passengers rolled down windows to wave flags, signs and mylar balloons festooned with the images of former vice president Joe Biden and California senator Kamala Harris.

Earlier in the day, following a long, bitter campaign, conducted in the midst of an international pandemic, the final projections came in, verifying that Biden would become the next president of the United States. To the television networks, Biden's triumph was a shoot — pro wrestling parlance for something authentic. But as the victor's supporters jubilantly surged into the streets, the sitting president — real estate developer, reality TV star and World Wrestling Entertainment (WWE) Hall of Famer Donald J. Trump — holed up in the White House, brooding, vengeful, refusing to concede. For the next two months — until his account was permanently suspended by the social media giant — Trump would take to Twitter, weaving conspiracies about voter fraud.

There were tales about dead people casting ballots, Republican poll watchers being banned from monitoring the count and voting machines somehow reprogrammed to log Trump votes for Biden.

To hear Trump tell it, the election was a work — the wrestling term for a con — the biggest double cross since Stanislaus Zbyszko went against the script and pinned champion Wayne Munn in 1925, allowing the referee no option but to award the title to the Polish strongman.

As I watched the broadcast of the president-elect's motorcade rolling down I-95 to the celebration in Wilmington, I was monitoring another auspicious event on my laptop. This one emanated from Jacksonville, Florida, and, like the Biden fete, was a long time in the making.

In the sports world, billionaire Shahid Khan's assets included England's Fulham Football Club, the NFL's Jacksonville Jaguars and All Elite Wrestling (AEW) — the brainchild of his 38-year-old son, Tony, who grew up loving pro wrestling with the same voraciousness as anyone who'd spot this book in a store and immediately walk it over to the cashier's counter. The Khans also owned the Jaguars' home stadium, TIAA Bank Field, as well as an adjacent amphitheater, Daily's Place, named after the local chain of convenience stores. It was there on this night, November 7, 2020, that AEW's pay-per-view *Full Gear* was being held.

Just as Biden's victory had great import, the scene in the ring at Daily's Place would spin off into an assortment of dramas. Kenny Omega and "Hangman" Adam Page had been partners in the Bullet Club, the faction that developed a cult following in the Ring of Honor (ROH) and New Japan promotions, then its splinter group, the Elite, whose members formed the backbone of the AEW roster upon the company's founding in 2019. In New Japan, Omega was called "The Cleaner" and the "Best Bout Machine," the man considered the industry's premier night-to-night performer. Eight years younger, Page was being groomed to be a future champion — an achievement he'd realize exactly one year later at the same pay-per-view, when he'd topple The Cleaner for the AEW crown.

In January 2020, Omega and Page had dethroned the company's inaugural tag team champions, SoCal Uncensored (Frankie Kazarian and Scorpio Sky). But the personality clash between the pair was always evident. Omega was disapproving when Page would imbibe immediately after title defenses. In August, Hangman was kicked out of the Elite and derided for his drunkenness when he prevented fellow members, the Young Bucks, from scoring a win over the team of Best Friends (Chuck Taylor and Trent Beretta). The next month, Omega stormed out of Daily's Place, leaving Page behind, after they dropped the championship to FTR (Cash Wheeler and Dax Harwood).

Each had reached the finals of a tournament to determine a number one contender for the AEW World Championship, so there was subtlety in the storytelling. While Omega and Page didn't hate each other — at least not yet — they didn't like each other either. Still, there was an air of sadness over such a talented team bringing it all to an end.

Just prior to the match, fans at home, as well as the 1,000 COVID-tested spectators permitted to spread out at the open-air arena in Jacksonville, watched a bittersweet video montage of Omega and Page's finer moments — set to the hair metal strains of Cinderella's "Don't Know What You Got (Till It's Gone)."

Predictably, the clash was fast-paced and peppered with hard strikes and chops. Page delivered a springboard clothesline and series of power-bombs, Omega a snap hurricanrana and moonsault. The Cleaner had just put away Page with a One-Winged Angel when, in Wilmington, the future vice president, Kamala Harris, crossed the stage outside the Chase Center, exuberant and clad in white like the late Tim "Mr. Wrestling" Woods.

The daughter of immigrants from India and Jamaica, Harris had spent much of the campaign denouncing what she viewed as Trump's insensitivity on race, negligence in addressing the coronavirus and indifference to climate change. As horns honked approvingly from supporters who chose to insulate themselves from the virus by staying in their cars, she said, "When our very democracy was on the ballot in this election, with the very soul of America at stake, and the world watching, you ushered in a new day for America."

It's a New Day. Yes, it is . . .

At 8:39 p.m., Eastern Standard Time, while Orange Cassidy and John Silver of the Dark Order were struggling at the top of the turn-buckles in Florida, Biden jogged down the ramp to join his VP pick. Just 13 days shy of his 78th birthday, he was poised to become the oldest president in U.S. history, and the trot was an effort to showcase his vitality the way Hulk Hogan still flexed his pythons even as his career was winding down. Placing the side of his hand across his brow, Biden squinted into the crowd and seemed to point to a number of familiar faces, conjuring up memories of a wrestler wearing a local sports jersey for a cheap pop.

His speech continued through Cassidy's victory. By the time Cody Rhodes entered the ring — en route to an AEW TNT Championship loss to Darby Allin — Biden was in the midst of a babyface promo, talking about reaching out to Republicans to end division and demonization: "The Bible tells us to everything there is a season, a time to build, a time to reap and a time to sow. And a time to heal. This is the time to heal in America."

After the speech, and a fireworks show that featured drones lighting up with sky with a map of the United States and the term "President-Elect," I turned off my television and focused solely on the broadcast of *Full Gear*. In the main event, Jon Moxley defended his AEW World Championship against his old running buddy from the independent circuit, Eddie Kingston. Like Biden, Mox had seemed destined to grab the gold earlier in his career. But just as Biden failed to win the Democratic nomination on two prior occasions, Moxley — as Dean Ambrose in WWE — took a secondary position while partners Roman Reigns and Seth Rollins each snared the top prize.

For both Biden and Moxley, 2020 would be different. On the same day Biden turned the tide of the Democratic primary season by decisively defeating Bernie Sanders in South Carolina, Moxley dethroned Chris Jericho for the AEW World Championship at the *Revolution* pay-per-view.

Now, he was defending against Kingston, who, like Trump, seemed out of his element in the main event. Although he was unwavering in his determination — arguably cutting the best promos in the business in 2020 — the Bronx-born brawler was coarse, spiteful, held personal grievances too close and couldn't shut his big mouth. But he'd clawed his way past better groomed and prettier contenders and, in this special "I Quit" match, was primed to give Moxley the fight of his life.

The bout was a festival of inhumanity, with thumbtacks, blood, even some rubbing alcohol to pour into the cuts. At the end, Moxley wrapped a piece of barbed wire around his forearm, got behind Kingston and clamped on a vicious bulldog choke. Kingston trembled and resisted until referee Bryce Remsburg frantically called for the bell.

Did Kingston ever utter, "I quit"? Remsburg said he did. The announcers said he did. And the websites listed Moxley as the undisputed winner. But was it true? Or had the outcome been no different than the outrages Trump claimed were being perpetrated in Pennsylvania and Michigan and Georgia?

Was Moxley still the champion? Or was this fake news?

So this is the book I've chosen to write. It's a natural follow-up to *Too Sweet: Inside the Indie Wrestling Revolution*, which you could probably buy at Goodwill with a PlayStation 2 for under $20. I ended that story in 2019 as AEW's flagship TV show, *AEW Dynamite*, was about to debut. My intention was always to chronicle pro wrestling in 2020 against a backdrop of real-world events. When I signed the contract, though, I never expected those actual events to insinuate themselves into everything, including the very diversion fans have traditionally relied upon to avoid the gloom on the other side of the living room window. But during the COVID era, the shoot and the work were so intertwined that, at times, it was impossible to distinguish what was life and what was wrestling.

As an author, I tried keeping pace — which wasn't always easy, since history was unfolding as I was writing. This was an advantage in some ways, since I was describing events not from memory, but when I was actually feeling their aftershock. Still, I'm certain that I missed a few things too; even with all the COVID shutdowns, the wrestling galaxy is so wide, there were certainly occurrences and promotions I overlooked. The objective was never to include every detail of pro wrestling in the COVID era. But I am confident that, if readers open this book a decade from now, they will have a pretty good sense of what it was like.

On this, most industry observers agree: 2020 was supposed to be the best year to be a wrestling fan in a very long time. To be honest, I'm still not sure it wasn't.

With the emergence of AEW as a viable competitor to WWE and the prominence of healthy secondary promotions like Ring of Honor and Major League Wrestling (MLW), "the wrestling landscape was on fire for the first time in, I'd say, forever," Tommy Dreamer, the hardcore legend once known as "The Innovator of Violence" told me. "Wrestlers had leverage. They could choose where they wanted to work."

In addition to the Khan family recognizing the value of professional wrestling, New Japan had planted its flag on American shores in 2019 when a combined show it staged with ROH sold out New

York's fabled Madison Square Garden. And, following its purchase by Smashing Pumpkins lead singer Billy Corgan in 2017, the National Wrestling Alliance (NWA) — the world's most dominant promotion from the advent of television to the time Jimmy Savile stepped down as the weekly host of *Top of the Pops* — was experiencing a re-emergence. "Pro wrestling was at its peak," noted Dave LaGreca, Dreamer's co-host on the popular *Busted Open* radio show.

But it all changed so quickly.

COVID-19, the lethal disease caused by one of a family of coronaviruses — named for their distinct spiked crown — rapidly spread around the world, even making its way to Antarctica, where 36 people at a research base fell ill. The outbreak was called the worst health crisis in a century. In the United States, 2020 was the deadliest year in recorded history, with a 15 percent increase in fatalities due to the pandemic. According to the World Health Organization (WHO), as of June 2022, more than 528 million people in 222 countries and territories had been infected, resulting in excess of 6.2 million deaths.

"This is crazy," Mexican star Místico said on Instagram after his diagnosis. "Bags under my eyes, headaches, my bones hurt, chills, weight loss." Confided the Consejo Mundial de Lucha Libre (CMLL) World Tag Team Championship coholder, "I am scared knowing that this virus that has killed many people is now in my body."

In an online post, WWE Hall of Famer Mick Foley claimed the illness kept him up all night. "Brain fog," he said. "You can't think clearly, easily fatigued, and perhaps worst of all . . . the loss of strength is incredible."

Among other members of the wrestling community affected by the virus were Roman Reigns, Seth Rollins, Kenny Omega, Jake "The Snake" Roberts, Charlotte Flair, Terry Funk, Bill Goldberg, Drew McIntyre, AJ Styles, Randy Orton, Tommy Dreamer, Bill "Demolition Ax" Eadie, Rey Mysterio, Kazuchika Okada, "Hangman" Adam Page, "Switchblade" Jay White, Bandido, L.A. Park, Konnan, Dr. Wagner Jr., Lance Archer, Chris Jericho, Arn Anderson, Keith Lee, Jeff Hardy, both members of the Young Bucks, Booker T, Kevin Nash and The Rock.

In the larger sports world, seven-time champion Jimmie Johnson was forced to skip his first NASCAR Cup series event in 663 starts — a record among active drivers — because of the illness. After a trip to the Spanish Mediterranean island of Ibiza with several other Paris Saint-Germain players, Brazilian soccer superstar Neymar missed the start of France's Ligue 1 season. And Portuguese great Cristiano Ronaldo, the first player to ever score 100 international goals, tested positive two days after competing against France.

As evidence that the virus did not discriminate, Prince Charles was infected twice, while his mother Queen Elizabeth, son Prince William and cousins Prince Albert of Monaco and Prince Joachim of Belgium were also impacted.

In the political arena, British prime minister Boris Johnson, Brazilian president Jair Bolsonaro and French president Emmanuel Macron came down with the sickness, along with the leaders of Canada, Mexico, Poland, Guatemala, Pakistan, Algeria, Bolivia, Belarus and Honduras. After I started this project, I began keeping a file on American governors and senators exposed to COVID-19. But they were soon eclipsed by more than 50 people listed as members of Trump's inner circle. Along with the commander-in-chief, known for gatherings in which mask-wearing seemed to be outright discouraged, the infected included his wife, Melania; sons Barron and Donald Jr.; Donald Jr.'s girlfriend, former Fox News personality Kimberly Guilfoyle; Trump's attorney Rudy Giuliani and former New Jersey governor Chris Christie, who helped the president prepare for his first debate with Biden.

In the most contagious parts of the United Kingdom, the government, for all intents and purposes, cancelled Christmas. The decision impacted 18 million citizens in London and the southeastern part of the country, but it was not without precedent. Back in 1643, British subjects were told to forego Christmas feasts and treat the season "with solemn humiliation" while contemplating sin. For the next 17 years, Christmas celebrations were literally illegal. While this time around there were no pro-Christmas riots in Covent Garden or Camden Town, earlier in the year, across the pond, a paramilitary group called the Wolverine Watchmen was accused of plotting to kidnap Michigan governor Gretchen Whitmer in retribution for her lockdown measures.

And you thought Edge's 2010 abduction of Paul Bearer was injurious to the public welfare.

With an international pandemic coloring every life choice and experience, the wrestling business endured cancellations, pay-per-views in empty venues and, in the WWE organization, terminations of longtime employees who might not have been prepared to function in an environment where people didn't regularly use terms like "Gorilla position" and "hardway juice." Remarkably, companies discovered that, even without live events, fans would still impulse purchase merchandise, resulting in a reassessment of whether wrestling needed to run arena shows as frequently as before the outbreak.

On March 11, 2020, Chris Jericho was walking to the ring in Salt Lake City when the world transformed forever. Earlier in the day, the WHO had declared the coronavirus a pandemic. As Jericho stepped through the ropes, he contemplated upcoming editions of of *AEW Dynamite*, scheduled for Rochester, New York, and Newark, New Jersey — firsts in that corner of the northeast and orchestrated to push the company forward. "[I was thinking] if we could just make it to that, then things have to shut down, then we'll deal with it," he told Kenny McIntosh in *Inside the Ropes Magazine*. "Well, I went to the ring at 9:40 and came back at 10 and, in that 20 minutes, Rochester had been cancelled, Newark had been cancelled, the NBA had been cancelled and Tom Hanks was diagnosed with COVID. So it was like, 'Alright. I guess we're fucked.'"

And COVID wasn't the only outside force rattling pro wrestling. In June, a handful of online posts alleging sexual improprieties perpetuated by male talent turned into the #SpeakingOut movement. Long-simmering racial tensions would spark protests around the world, forcing the wrestling industry to reevaluate the way people of color have traditionally been treated backstage and depicted onscreen. During one month in 2021, approximately 4.5 million Americans quit their jobs. While some of the "Great Resignation" could be blamed on retirement, many simply decided to take their careers in another direction. At the same time, WWE was also reconsidering the way it did business, laying off an astonishing 80 in-ring performers in 2021.

Oh, and in case you missed wrestling that week, Randy Orton set Bray Wyatt on fire.

With the economy challenged by shutdowns around the globe, it felt as if western society was going to buckle. And yet, the adversity brought out some of pro wrestling's most cherished moments. The cinematic match — with aspects directed in advance, away from live fans — had existed at least since 1996 when Goldust battled Rowdy Roddy Piper in a Hollywood Backlot Brawl at *WrestleMania XII*, and Mankind fought the Undertaker in a boiler room at *SummerSlam*. But in 2020, it became an indispensable part of the industry due to WWE's ingenuity in making up for the scarcity of spectators at *WrestleMania 36*. After trying a number of devices to compensate for the privation of crowds on television, the company unveiled the ThunderDome, featuring an enthusiastic, virtual audience. Roman Reigns's long-overdue heel turn — his coming out as a villain — converted him into a guy even the most subversive fan loved to watch. Drew McIntyre reversed the setbacks from earlier in his career to win the *Royal Rumble*, as well as the WWE Championship on two separate occasions. On Wednesday nights in the U.S., AEW and WWE's third brand, NXT, went head-to-head to the benefit of fans — and Chris Jericho, who christened himself the "Demo God" while taking credit for AEW's consistent supremacy in the 18-to-49 demographic. Simultaneously, All Elite Wrestling widened its indie credentials by highlighting — and sometimes hiring — talent who'd normally be taking bumps at county fairs and flea markets.

Rather than following the pattern of WWE, which often isolated itself from the wider wrestling universe by pretending that no other promotion existed, AEW expanded its global presence by working with groups like AAA, New Japan, the NWA and Impact, allowing viewers to fantasize about dream matches that would have been impossible when only one operation was lording over the scene.

And through it all, there was eminent wrestling manager, promoter and historian Jim Cornette, reminding everybody that, as much as you might have enjoyed a silly angle or preposterous exchange you'd never see in a real fight, Frank Gotch, Jim Londos and Lou Thesz would be collectively appalled.

CHAPTER 2

AT 5:01 A.M. on New Year's Day 2020, I boarded a Jet Blue flight at New York's JFK airport, then took a nap and woke up in Fort Lauderdale. There, I transferred to a plane bound for Jacksonville and the first *AEW Dynamite* taping of the year. My mood was soaring. I was finishing up *Too Sweet* and writing a profile on future AEW Women's World Champion Nyla Rose for the *Daily Beast*.

Let them call me a mark. At least I'm paying my bills . . .

As I waited outside Daily's Place for my press credentials, I engaged in several animated conversations with fans, including two guys from Georgia whose names now escape me. But I remember that I liked them and they liked me. We spoke about the performers who hooked us on wrestling, high-profile talent we'd first seen on the indies, and the "Wednesday Night Wars" between AEW and NXT.

None of us were aware that, already, the first cases of COVID-19 — the number was chosen by the WHO to designate the year that this particular version of the coronavirus was identified — had been reported in Wuhan, China. (In the ultimate case of kayfabe, Chinese news anchors would read a government-vetted script that day, reporting, "Eight people were punished for spreading rumors about an unknown pneumonia.") But what did that have to do with us? We were wrestling fans in America, and, like the SARS outbreak of 2002 and the 2009 swine flu pandemic, the sickness would probably be over before we even realized it arrived. The *Royal Rumble* was coming up and, after that, *WrestleMania 36*. AEW had a *Dynamite* scheduled for Atlanta, the centerpiece of World

Championship Wrestling (WCW), WWE's chief rival until the monolith absorbed it in 2001. And then, Tony Khan and his father were going to sling on their muskets and march on the Northeastern United States, the place where WWE boss Vincent Kennedy McMahon's grandfather Jess began promoting wrestling in 1915.

Mike Weber, chief operating officer for FITE TV, the international streaming service specializing in combat sports, was also feeling the excitement. In the few months since *Dynamite* debuted, talent like Darby Allin, Maxwell Jacob Friedman (MJF) and Dr. Britt Baker had become stars. "It's not like TNA [Total Nonstop Action], when the older [former WWE] guys were so dominant, it was very hard for the younger talent to break through," Weber said of the promotion where he'd been the vice president of marketing.

With the exception of the U.S., Canada, Germany and France, fans could watch live broadcasts of AEW on FITE for US$4.99 a month. "Two-thirds watch it live," Weber pointed out, "even if it's at one in the morning in their time zone. We have a live chat feature, and people comment on the matches as they're airing. So we look at that and can see that a lot of those personalities are sticking."

Jeff Cobb, the flag bearer for Guam in the 2004 Olympics, was seen as a future king of the industry after winning the New Japan NEVER Openweight title, ROH Television crown and the top honors in Pro Wrestling Guerilla (PWG), the L.A.-based independent promotion that many considered the best on the planet. When he let his Ring of Honor contract expire on the first day of 2020, he said, "I wanted to see what the world was offering."

He told me that WWE, AEW and New Japan all expressed interest. "I was very optimistic. This was going to be the best year of my career."

Similarly, twin brothers Sterling and Logan Riegel, a high-flying tag team out of Kansas City, sensed that — after laboring on the indies and experiencing accolades, as well as disappointments — their fortunes were about the change. Instead, as the world started locking down, the pair found themselves separated by the Atlantic Ocean, with Sterling in England and Logan home in Missouri.

"I'm sorry," Logan said, apologizing for jumping from one wrestling topic to another when we spoke in August. "It just feels so good to be talking about wrestling again.

"We were finally getting to where we wanted to be until the coronavirus."

In Sterling's case, his regret about the timing of it all was aggravated by his uncertainty about the future. "Wrestling as we know it may have changed forever," he said. "Who knows?"

If there was one major wrestling event where the Riegels pictured themselves, it was *Wrestle Kingdom*, staged in the Tokyo Dome each January 4 since 1992 by New Japan Pro-Wrestling. It's the equivalent of *WrestleMania* for Asia's premier promotion and has featured such memorable classics as Kenny Omega vs. Chris Jericho at *Wrestle Kingdom 12*, Kazuchika Okada vs. Hiroshi Tanahashi at *Wrestle Kingdom 10*, Shinsuke Nakamura's battles with both AJ Styles and Kota Ibushi at *Wrestle Kingdom 9* and Okada's epic with Omega at *Wrestle Kingdom 11* — which received an unprecedented six stars from Dave Meltzer's *Wrestling Observer Newsletter*.

As New Japan's Dutch-born president Harold Mejj was building the company's name outside Japan, the promotion broke with tradition and expanded *Wrestle Kingdom 14* to two nights in 2020. Of the 40,000 or so attendees, 8,300 came from outside the country on night one, while 6,500 were gaijin — or foreigners — on night two. In addition to including the retirement of international superstar Jushin "Thunder" Liger — who'd been associated with New Japan since 1984 — *Wrestle Kingdom 14* saw Tetsuya Naito emerge with both of the promotion's main titles, the IWGP (International Wrestling Grand Prix) Intercontinental and Heavyweight belts, following wins over New Zealander "Switchblade" Jay White and Okada.

As Naito was addressing the crowd after unifying the championships, he was attacked by KENTA — Kenta Kobayashi— following a lengthy stint as Hideo Itami in WWE, which the former kickboxer called his "humiliation in America."

An even more significant story may have been the burgeoning relationship between New Japan and AEW. While the affiliation was said to be tenuous — New Japan already had a partnership in the U.S. with ROH — two major AEW stars appeared at *Wrestle Kingdom 14*. On night one, Jon Moxley regained the IWGP United States Heavyweight Championship in a Texas Death Match with Lance Archer, then successfully defended the strap against Juice Robinson a day later. On the same card, Jericho wore his AEW World Championship to the ring for his bout with Tanahashi. Although Jericho won the non-title affair, announcers were permitted to push the idea that Tanahashi would be granted a shot at the gold if he won in Tokyo.

Two weeks later, both Moxley and Jericho took part in another event that, for a certain type of wrestling fan, seemed well on its way to becoming an annual pilgrimage: Jericho's second-annual Rock 'N' Wrestling Rager at Sea. The cruise, co-hosted by the AEW World Champion and comedian Gabriel Iglesias, included concerts, podcasts, standup and a series of matches taped for the January 22 edition of *AEW Dynamite*.

Moxley viewed the experience as an example of how wrestlers and fans — once kept apart by the barrier of kayfabe — were becoming closer than ever before. "The energy and passion and excitement we get from the fans, whether it's at an arena or a fuckin' boat in the middle of the ocean, they are all there for us," he told Scott Fishman at *TV Insider*. "This is what is driving this whole thing forward. That last show of the cruise, everyone was just hanging out and hugging and high-fiving. It really felt like we were on the same team . . . because we love this crazy thing called wrestling."

What no one — with the exception of the scientists contemplating the genome sequence of the new coronavirus outbreak — could have realized was that, for a time in the very near future, hugging and high-fiving, even with other members of the wrestling family, would be strictly off-limits.

One day after the broadcast, Wuhan became the first city in the world to impose a quarantine on its citizens. Not bound by the same liberties as elsewhere, Chinese authorities confined most of Wuhan's 11 million residents to their apartments for more than two months. Bus, subway, ferry and air travel were suspended. Highway exits were closed.

In some cases, metal bars were welded across front doors, the entrances sealed save for small gaps to allow food to be passed inside.

January's *Royal Rumble* marks the official start of *WrestleMania* season, and, even during years when cynical followers are less than smitten with WWE, the main event is consistently rousing. The format is a simple one. Before the contest, according to the storyline, wrestlers draw numbers. The pair who pick numbers one and two start the match, and are joined by a fresh participant — to the accompaniment of entrance music — either every 90 seconds or two minutes. In total, 30 gladiators fill the ring, although not necessarily at the same time, since combatants are being regularly eliminated via the top rope. The action is easy to follow and watch with friends who are not necessarily fans. As the various competitors are sent sailing onto the arena floor, even those who claim to disdain wrestling find themselves choosing a personal favorite to outlast the others. During the 2010s, while WWE's "women's revolution" expanded, the *Rumble* also evolved; in 2018, an all-female *Royal Rumble* was added to complement the men's version.

The surprise of the 2020 *Royal Rumble* was the return of Adam "Edge" Copeland, who'd been forced to retire in 2011 because of neck injuries. After briefly aligning himself with Randy Orton — with whom he'd won the WWE World Tag Team Championship in 2006 — in the free-for-all, Edge suddenly surprised the Viper and eliminated him.

It was supposed to be all in good fun and healthy competition. But was it?

The next night on WWE's traditional flagship show, *Monday Night Raw*, Edge told the fans that he was returning to the sport of kings. "I got in the best shape of my career at 46 years old so I can get back in here and end my career on *my* terms," the Hall of Famer said while standing in the center of the ring.

He was soon joined by Orton, who appeared not to have been bothered by what transpired the night before. After hugging the Rated-R Superstar, Orton suggested reuniting as a duo. As the audience loudly shouted its approval, the Apex Predator suddenly hit Edge with the RKO — an idiosyncratic neckbreaker recurrently featured in memes.

Given Edge's real-life medical issues, the attack startled the crowd.

Sliding to ringside, Orton snatched a folding chair, brought it through the ropes and smashed Edge across the back. Placing Edge's head in the cavity between the seat and back of the chair, Orton climbed to the second rope, sat down and contemplated what he was going to do next. Returning to the mat, Orton appeared to have let his conscience dissuade him from inflicting further damage. A moment later, though, he grabbed another chair. With Edge's head against the object already in the ring, Orton swung and brought the second weapon down onto the skull of his old friend.

The show ended with Edge convulsing on the mat.

WWE now had a hot, credible angle leading into *WrestleMania 36* and focused on building Orton into a merciless monster. While Edge was supposed to be laid up, with his future in jeopardy, Matt Hardy would be the next performer to experience Orton's cruelty.

At 45 years old, Hardy was a true legend. He and his brother Jeff had comprised one of the most daring tag teams in history, engaging in wild — and, some would argue, careless — tables, ladders and chairs matches during WWE's "Attitude Era" in the late 1990s. Unable to sustain that level of combat, Matt worked hard to reimagine his gimmick. In 2016, while wrestling for TNA, Hardy began appearing on YouTube as a character unlike any seen before in pro wrestling. Sporting a blond streak through half of his long, dark hair, the native North Carolinian spoke in a bizarre, patrician accent — drawing out terms like "sensational," "magnificent," "exquisite," "wonderful," "splendid" and "delightful." In times of desperation, Matt's drone, Vanguard 1, would intercede on his behalf, as well as cultivate its own following on Twitter. Calling himself "Broken" Matt Hardy, he referred to Jeff as "Brother Nero" — Jeff's middle name actually *is* Nero — and curiously blamed him for the metamorphosis. Like *Death Note* manga/anime character Teru Mikami, Hardy repeatedly vowed to "delete" his enemies, running his hand across the throat to underscore the word.

Several unusual TNA events were telecast from what's become known as the Hardy Compound — preludes to the cinematic matches that would become so popular during the age of COVID-19. In one, Matt's toddler son, King Maxel, accompanied by his mother, former wrestler Reby Sky, defeated Rockstar Spud — the future Drake Maverick in WWE.

In 2017, the brothers parted ways with TNA. That same week, the Hardyz took their gimmick to Ring of Honor and captured the group's tag team titles from the Young Bucks, Nick and Matt Jackson. A month later, the Hardyz dropped the belts back to the Bucks at a show deliberately booked on *WrestleMania* weekend — when fans from all over the world were in town, and curious about sampling other products.

The next night at *WrestleMania 33*, the Hardyz were surprise entrants in a four-way ladder match for the *Raw* Tag Team Championship — for those who've been negligent in their viewership, both of WWE's main television shows, *Raw* and *SmackDown*, had their own titles at the time — enthralling the announced audience of 75,245 at Camping World Stadium in Orlando, Florida, by reacquiring the gold.

The circle of the Hardyz's long, distinguished career should have closed at that point. But, even though he spoke in his normal voice at first, Broken Matt Hardy was anxious to come out. WWE was willing to accommodate to an extent, with a few alterations. For one thing, Hardy was now "Woken," not "Broken."

According to Matt, the idea came from Vince McMahon. "When we first did 'Woken' Matt Hardy, Vince was the one that initiated it," he told *Busted Open*. "We'd talk about it . . . I think there was a possibility there. But it's a very different concept. I don't think he understood it."

Still, even if it was a Titanized — the term is derived from the years when WWE's corporate name was Titan Sports — version of a shtick that came from the depths of Matt's soul, he was given an ideal foil in Bray Wyatt, scion of a wrestling family that included grandfather Blackjack Mulligan, uncles Barry and Kendall Windham and father Irwin R. Schyster. (Bray once told me that, as a child, when he saw his grandmother leave for work, he just assumed that she was going off to wrestle somewhere.) Few characters in the modern version of WWE had reinvented themselves as successfully, and much of it had to do with the depth of Wyatt's creativity and understanding of squared circle storytelling. And, unlike other talent who were forced to rely on script writers, Wyatt's instincts were so highly venerated that he was reportedly given a wide rein to chart the course of his gimmick.

Already, Wyatt had been portrayed as a swamp creature who headed a small but insidious cult. So when he met Woken Matt on the Hardy Compound for an Ultimate Deletion match in 2018, fans could effortlessly suspend disbelief; if Hardy and Wyatt were going to pick a place to fight, this would be it. The skirmish ended with Hardy delivering his finisher, the Twist of Fate, to his antagonist into the "Lake of Reincarnation."

After Wyatt failed to surface, Hardy crowed on Twitter, "Bray won't see the sun AGEEN."

Which wasn't true, of course. Wyatt *did* return; he tended to die and come back sometimes. Only now, the mud bog guru was under Matt Hardy's spell. The duo had a cool name, The Deleters of Worlds — Bray had previously referred to himself as the Eater of Worlds — and won a tournament for the vacant *Raw* Tag Team Championship in King Abdullah International Stadium in Jeddah, Saudi Arabia, as members of the country's elite reclined on couches at ringside — the way women in evening gowns and men in suits dined in the Khorassan Room of St. Louis's Chase Park Plaza Hotel during episodes of *Wrestling at the Chase* in the 1960s.

But Hardy said that WWE eventually lost interest in the unit. "In all honesty, I think the reason why Bray and I were pulled off of TV . . . was because they were tired of us suggesting ideas about how we should use the Hardy Compound," he said to *Busted Open*. "I think that the whole scenario between myself and Bray could have been so much more if we could have gotten people to listen to our ideas."

On the February 17, 2020, edition of *Raw*, Orton would punish a lonely, directionless Hardy with a flurry of chair shots. Afterwards, commentators reported that the victim had been taken to a medical facility and fitted with a neck brace. Online, fans speculated that Hardy, whose contract was due to expire on March 1, had been written out of the company's storylines. Who would have the last word, though, remained to be seen.

"Sitting on my #ChairOfWheels at the hospital & just realized I've seen this exact moment before in a PREMONITION," Matt tweeted in his distinct vernacular. "One ESSENCE must PERISH for a new ESSENCE to be RESURRECTED."

Fans didn't have to scrutinize the posting too closely to draw the conclusion that Broken Matt was going to reappear elsewhere. "When tragedy FRACTURES you, SHATTERS you," he wrote, "pick up the pieces & recreate yourself into something GREATER. The #BROKEN pieces won't be lost in limbo forever. NEVAH LOSE FAITH."

CHAPTER 3

"I WOULD LIKE you to do us a favor, though."

The words spilled out of President Donald Trump's mouth painlessly. Since the 1980s, he'd been touting his abilities at the "art of the deal." Now, another world leader needed a courtesy, a shipment of 150 Javelin anti-tank missiles. Trump was not averse to making the guy happy. But as "Million Dollar Man" Ted DiBiase used to say, "Everybody has a price."

The price for Ukrainian president Volodymyr Zelensky, a 41-year-old former comedian who, like Trump, assumed the reins of government by exploiting his outsider status, appeared to be providing information about Joe Biden and his son. When Trump and Zelensky spoke on July 25, 2019, the field of candidates contending for the 2020 Democratic Party nomination was vast. Yet, the sitting U.S. president accurately assumed that Biden would prevail. During the Obama administration, while Biden served as vice president, his sometimes-troubled son, Hunter, scored a $50,000-a-month gig, sitting on the board of Burisma, a Ukrainian gas company of dubious reputation. That Burisma hoped to ingratiate itself with the senior Biden was obvious. But did Vice President Biden intervene in Ukraine's internal affairs for the sole purpose of helping the money marks providing a payday for his kid? Despite no solid evidence, Trump seemed to believe so.

"I heard you had a prosecutor who was very good, and he was shut down and that's really unfair," Trump ventured. He was talking about Viktor Shokin, whose 2016 ouster had come after Biden, and much of the international community, applied pressure on the Ukrainian government. But what Trump didn't say — or didn't know — was that Shokin was perceived as an impediment to anti-corruption efforts and, by the time he left, his office's investigation into Burisma was inactive.

In other words, Burisma seemed to be better off with Shokin as prosecutor than without him.

Now, Trump wanted Zelensky to work with Rudy Giuliani — the former New York City mayor who'd become the president's attorney — and U.S. Attorney General William Barr to probe the conspiracy; Barr would deny knowing that his name was being thrown around this way. "There's a lot of talk about Biden's son, that Biden stopped the prosecution, and a lot of people want to find out about that. So whatever you can do with the Attorney General would be great. Biden went around bragging that he stopped the prosecution, so if you can look into it . . . it sounds horrible to me."

While Trump may have been legitimately concerned about graft in the former Soviet Union, the fact that he wanted a foreign leader to use his authority to provide intelligence on a future political rival was — at least to his adversaries — a little bit curious.

Was he really supposed to be asking for things like that?

Trump later told political nemesis Nancy Pelosi, the speaker of the U.S. House of Representatives, that his call was "perfect." "Perfectly wrong," she apparently replied.

In December, the Democrat-controlled House voted to impeach Trump for abuse of power and obstructing the investigation. Trump, who faced removal from office if convicted, countered that the move was yet another "witch hunt" waged by those who begrudged the very fact that someone like him had been elected to office. But even if he had engaged in a "quid pro quo," one of his lawyers asserted, it wasn't impeachable, since politicians regularly viewed their political interests and national aspirations as one and the same.

As the weeks stretched on, both Democratic and Republican politicians cut promos on each other on the 24-hour news networks and engaged in stunts that seemed to be scripted by the very *Monday Night Raw* writers former WWE standouts scorned after exiting the company. Prior to Trump's State of the Union speech, one day before the verdict, he refused Pelosi's handshake, all but running his fingers through his hair in mockery. When it was over, the speaker — dubbed "Nervous Nancy" by the president — stood, straightened her copy of the speech and dramatically tore it in half.

Representative Tim Ryan of Ohio raised additional heat by tweeting, "I just walked out of the #StateOfTheUnion. I've had enough. It's like watching professional wrestling. It's all fake."

The backlash was instantaneous. "You leave wrestling out of this!!!" tweeted the first NXT Women's Champion Paige, who'd made her in-ring debut at 13 for her parents' World Association of Wrestling (WAW) promotion in the British city of Norwich.

"Don't lump my profession into yours," wrote AEW announcer — and WWE Hall of Famer — Jim "J.R." Ross. "Your 'profession' has become embarrassing on both sides of your beloved aisle. Public Servants? That's laughable."

Even Glenn "Kane" Jacobs, the Undertaker's gimmick half-brother who became mayor of Knox County, Tennessee, as his in-ring career was winding down, added, "Sir, your statement is emblematic of the out-of-touch elitism, so typical of Washington, that has alienated countless everyday Americans. Professional wrestling brings joy to millions around the world. Politicians like yourself usually bring nothing but misery."

The only Republican senator who voted to convict Trump was 2012 presidential nominee Mitt Romney. In a dramatic speech, Romney argued that the president's behavior was "so extreme and egregious" that it met the criteria as "a high crime and misdemeanor." "The president asked a foreign government to investigate his political rival. The president withheld vital military funds from that government to press it to do so . . . The president's purpose was personal and political."

But, like Jesse "The Body" Ventura attempting to convince his fellow performers in the World Wrestling Federation (WWF) — the name the company used before the lawsuit with the World Wildlife Fund that led to its rebranding as World Wrestling Entertainment — to unionize in 1986, Romney was shouting into a void. Republicans held the majority in the U.S. Senate, and every other GOP member of Congress's upper chamber voted to acquit.

Trump walked. "It was evil," he said of the impeachment during an event in the East Room of the White House. "It was corrupt. It was dirty cops. It was leakers and liars."

More than a year later, Romney was still being accosted by Trump supporters, accused of serving as a stooge for the Democrats. Yet, he remained resolute in his decision, claiming that he drew on his Mormon faith and "oath before God" to vote guilty on the abuse of power charge and endure the flagellation of his fellow Republicans.

On the same night as the acquittal on *AEW Dynamite*, Cody Rhodes would experience a similar trial.

As a precondition for engaging in a one-on-one battle with former friend MJF, Rhodes agreed to allow the brash Long Islander to lash him 10 times. MJF lit into the American Nightmare, imploring him to quit before the beating was over. But Rhodes refused to sacrifice his principles and lay on the mat, grasping and kissing his wife Brandi's hand, as MJF meted out the punishment.

Both Cody and Romney were second generation in their respective professions, and willing to take a blow for both cause and legacy.

As Romney explained the motives behind his vote to Fox News's Chris Wallace, one could envision the same words springing forth from either Cody or his father, the late "American Dream" Dusty Rhodes: "I will tell my children and their children that I did my duty to the best of my ability, believing that my country expected it of me."

If you wiiill.

At this stage of the election, though, it seemed like Trump might have erred by going after Biden. When the Iowa caucus — one of the first major events of the presidential primary season — was held on February 3, Senator Bernie Sanders and former South Bend, Indiana, mayor Pete Buttigieg split the lead for the Democrats. Next came Massachusetts senator Elizabeth Warren, followed by Biden.

The process did not go smoothly. According to the Iowa Democratic Party, there was a coding error in the app used to report precinct results.

"The app is fucking up," a senior aide to one of the campaigns was heard to complain.

But the Trump team pounced on the issue to fuel misgivings about the system that would later determine that — regardless of his furious protestations — the president had lost the general election. Tweeted Trump's campaign manager Brad Parscale, "Quality control = rigged?"

At the same time that the votes were being tabulated in Dubuque and Des Moines, WWE was using *Monday Night Raw* to build interest both in *WrestleMania 36* and *Super ShowDown*, yet another lucrative event in the kingdom of Saudi Arabia. According to rumor, Crown Prince Mohammed bin Salman had been a fan as a kid in the 1990s and loved watching the superstars from that era. A popular myth among wrestling fans had the prince — who, despite a disconcerting record on human rights abuses, pointed to the presence of women in the stadium at WWE shows as proof that the country was moving forward — requesting Yokozuna and the Ultimate Warrior for a particular card, only to be told that both former champions were deceased. Still, *Super ShowDown* would be highlighted by Bill Goldberg and a surprise appearance by the Undertaker — both of whom were in their fifties and won their matches within minutes of their introductions.

By then, the possibilities of more of these international spectacles were narrowing. While North American and European fans had their attentions elsewhere, Japanese women's promotion Stardom cancelled a series of upcoming shows as precautions against the coronavirus. Stardom was owned by Bushiroad, the same parent company as New Japan, which emphasized that, even though it still planned to continue with its schedule, meet and greets with the talent were being called off.

In North America, though, those types of restrictions were still difficult to conceive. Two days after *Super ShowDown*, AEW staged its *Revolution* pay-per-view from Chicago's Wintrust Arena. Despite the company's newcomer status, Jon Moxley, who challenged Chris Jericho for the AEW World Championship in the main event, maintained that the promotion's major shows felt distinct from their WWE counterparts. "The difference for us is we don't have to have 37 pay-per-views a year and 600 network specials," he told *TV Insider*. "We have *Dynamite* every week, but four or five pay-per-views a year. We can keep those high quality . . . a big fight feel. I think some of that has been missing over the last few years when you have to rush through stories."

The card saw Kenny Omega and "Hangman" Adam Page retain the group's tag team belts in an animated encounter with the Young Bucks. For Omega, who'd been as decorated a singles star as anyone in the business, the ability to perform at the highest level of the tag team division was evidence of his adaptability. "It doesn't mean I'm not the same guy," he told *The Sporting News*. "I'm part of a very successful tag team with 'Hangman' Adam Page, a guy that I have a lot of chemistry with . . . and showing that it takes more than just having a good, long singles match to be called the best in the world."

In addition to working backstage as an executive vice president (EVP) at AEW, specializing in the organization's women's division, Omega boasted of being at his "creative peak" between the ropes. "You got to be a good tag team wrestler. You have to be a good six-man tag team wrestler. You have to be good at your gimmick matches. You have to be able to appeal to the non–wrestling fan." By layering his approach, he hoped to be regarded as more than "one guy that has the same kind of match over and over again."

In addition to the athleticism displayed by Omega and his peers, the company was trying to keep pace with WWE by adding a certain crossover flavor to its pay-per-views.

This was accomplished when, prior to the main event at *Revolution*, a choir appeared at the top of the entrance ramp and moved the crowd with an a cappella version of Jericho's theme song, "Judas." The audience loudly sang along. As the rendition was ending, the familiar heavy metal version — recorded by Jericho's band, Fozzy — blasted through the speakers, a cue for the titlist to parade down the aisle, accompanied by two members of his Inner Circle faction, Santana and Ortiz of the tag team Proud-N-Powerful.

Although Le Champion, as Jericho had taken to calling himself, was supposed to be the heel in the match, the spectators were ecstatic.

The experience stirred deep emotions in choir member Liz Rose, who'd lost her brother, Greg, to a car accident 17 years earlier. Greg's favorite wrestler had been Chris Jericho, and, whenever she happened to catch wrestling on television, Liz paused to remember her departed sibling.

"For me to think of my brother, knowing that I was a part of that moment in wrestling," she told the BBC, "I felt close to him in a way I had not felt since he was alive."

There was a good backstory leading into this match. Weeks earlier, in their zeal to protect Jericho's title, the Inner Circle had ganged up on Moxley and jabbed a spike into his eye — in 1988, the Road Warriors had done the same thing to Dusty Rhodes, and, in both cases, the angle went over strong. At the weigh-in before the match, though, Moxley swaggered in wearing an eye patch, then surprised the titlist with a head-butt out of nowhere, busting him open.

Almost as soon as the bell rang, Moxley bit at Jericho's stitches, commencing blood flow. Jericho fought back, and the contender was soon bleeding as well. When referee Aubrey Edwards banished Santana, Ortiz and Inner Circle enforcer Jake Hager for interfering, another member of the unit, "The Spanish God" Sammy Guevara, snuck up to the ring and cracked Moxley with the belt. Jericho then went after Moxley's good eye. But the challenger would eventually lift his eye patch and reveal that the bad eye worked fine. After delivering back-to-back versions of his finisher, the Paradigm Shift, Moxley was the new champion.

Although, officially, AEW said there was no war with WWE, it was obvious that the upstart promotion wanted to grab those fans who'd drifted away from the corporate giant. As a former WWE headliner, Moxley had much of the same magnetism as champion Jericho, appealing to followers' sense of the past as well as the future.

Joe Biden had started the day trailing Democratic-Socialist Bernie Sanders in total votes and delegates. By the time *AEW Revolution* began, the former vice president was in the lead. While the wrestlers were back-stage in Chicago, stretching and going over their matches, the South Carolina primary had been taking place. When the contest was over,

Biden defeated Sanders by a margin of 28 percentage points, fueled largely by African-American constituents, who gave Biden 61 percent of their vote.

Within 48 hours, three early Democratic contenders, Buttigieg, Texas representative Beto O'Rourke and Minnesota senator Amy Klobuchar announced that they were now endorsing the former vice president. On Super Tuesday, on March 3, Biden took more than half of the 14 states that were up for grabs — winning the support of yet another vanquished foe.

"I've always believed that defeating Donald Trump starts with uniting behind the candidate with the best shot to do it," said former New York City mayor Mike Bloomberg, a billionaire who some experts had pegged to be the dark horse in the primary.

For his part, Sanders claimed his home state of Vermont as well as Utah, Colorado and the biggest prize of Super Tuesday, California, and vowed to stay in the race.

The night before Super Tuesday, WWE Champion Brock Lesnar had lumbered to the ring on *Monday Night Raw*, with his advocate, Paul Heyman. When outsiders belittled pro wrestling as "fake," they weren't talking about Brock Lesnar. A former National Collegiate Athletic Association (NCAA) and Ultimate Fighting Championship (UFC) heavyweight titlist, Lesnar would have been a valuable asset in the mid-20th century to promoters, who always wanted a legitimate shooter — a guy who could break bones and torture people with holds — to protect their belt from contenders harboring notions of a double cross. Yet, even though Lesnar lived up to his nickname "The Beast Incarnate" in every conceivable way, he was a shrewd professional wrestler, willing to dramatically sell the skills of opponents he respected.

As Heyman bloviated on the mic, the pair were joined in the ring by Drew McIntyre, who'd positioned himself for a title shot at *WrestleMania 36* by winning the *Royal Rumble* and tossing Lesnar over the top rope at one point of the match.

McIntyre's career had been characterized by spurts and stops. The strikingly handsome Scotsman had captured the WWE Intercontinental title in 2009 and was coholder of the WWE Tag Team Championship with Cody Rhodes a year later. Yet, starting in 2013, he was part of a unit called Three Man Band (3MB) with Jinder Mahal and Heath Slater — a comedy team generally programmed to lose. Parting ways with WWE, he found his way to TNA, performing as Drew Galloway and winning the organization's World Heavyweight Championship. In 2017, he was back in WWE. Forsaking *Raw* and *SmackDown*, he immediately joined NXT, the division that, despite its reputation among dedicated fans as the company's most exciting brand, was seen as a developmental league for recent arrivals from the indies. McIntyre was re-energized. He captured the NXT Championship and appeared primed to establish supremacy on the main roster.

On *Raw*, Heyman turned the topic to *WrestleMania 36*. Just because McIntyre managed to hurl Lesnar to the arena floor in the *Rumble*, Heyman emphasized, didn't mean that he could beat The Conqueror and procure the gold on the Grandest Stage of Them All. As Lesnar went to exit the ring, though, McIntyre made an authoritative point, flooring the champ with a signature Claymore Kick, then delivering a second one before the stunned titlist could backpedal to the dressing room.

On the same show, Orton confronted Edge's wife, WWE Hall of Famer Beth Phoenix, and suggested that the attack on her husband had been something charitable. Orton explained that he'd taken out his former tag team partner because his medical condition made him vulnerable to a crippling injury. By assaulting him after the *Rumble*, Orton rationalized, he was teaching Edge a valuable lesson that would force the Rated-R Superstar to retreat back into retirement — and allow his children to grow up around a healthy father. If Phoenix objected to this perspective, Orton continued, it was because she was a lousy mother, an "enabler" with no sense of what was good for her family.

The Glamazon was not persuaded. She slapped Orton, then kicked him in the stomach — triggering an RKO from the Viper that left her lying in the middle of the ring.

The momentum was building. A week later, a vigorous Edge returned to *Raw*, using Orton's signature finisher against him. The Rated-R Superstar's neck had endured a violent con-chair-to — a wrestling term for having one's head squashed between two chairs — and Edge had come out of it ready to reduce the Viper to a mangled mess.

The table was almost set for *WrestleMania 36*, slated to take place in front of 65,000 fans at Tampa's Raymond James Stadium. But as the day crept closer, so did the coronavirus. And for the first time since the Showcase of the Immortals began in 1985, forces outside the wrestling business would actually be calling the spots.

CHAPTER 4

ON JANUARY 19, 2020, a 35-year-old man appeared at an urgent care clinic in Snohomish County, Washington. He had a fever and said that he'd been coughing for four days. When doctors examined him, they learned that, around the time that the illness started, he'd just stepped off a plane from a family visit to Wuhan, China.

The first case of COVID-19 had been diagnosed in the United States.

"It's just one person coming in from China," President Trump told CNBC from the World Economic Forum in Davos, Switzerland. "We have it under control. It's going to be fine."

As the weeks went on, Trump's advisors warned him that the coronavirus could be like the Spanish flu that struck in four successive waves between 1918 and 1920, infecting an estimated third of the world's population. But, in public, the president would minimize the threat. "I wanted to always play it down," he told legendary journalist Bob Woodward in March. "I still like playing it down because I don't want to create a panic."

Coronavirus worries would force Joe Biden and Bernie Sanders to cancel competing campaign rallies in Cleveland on the night of March 10. Biden was spotted shaking hands with union workers that morning, sometimes doing a fist bump instead and applying hand sanitizer. Ultimately, because of the health emergency, the Democratic primary in Ohio was postponed.

In a tighter election, these kinds of disruptions might have had a greater impact. But the energy had shifted to Biden. By April, trailing the former vice president by 300 Democratic delegates, Sanders suspended his campaign and appeared with Biden, via split screen, in a webcast. "I am asking all Americans," the Democratic-Socialist said, joining the list of former rivals now throwing their support to Biden, "to make certain that we defeat somebody who I believe . . . is the most dangerous president in the modern history of this country."

While Trump was eager to travel the continental U.S. and stir up his disciples at tightly packed rallies, Biden held back, social distancing as he used Trump's bravado in a time of crisis against him.

In the UK, there were fears that COVID-19 could delay the final phase of Brexit — the country's scheduled departure from the European Union (EU) at the end of the year. Following a 2016 referendum vote, Great Britain officially left the 27-member political and economic bloc on January 31. The two sides would have 11 months to negotiate new trade agreements. But some politicians urged that the talks be paused so officials could deal with the coronavirus.

Prime Minister Boris Johnson, an Oxford-educated Conservative whose extravagant personality and shock of bright blond hair invited comparisons to Trump, was confident that Britain was going to be okay. While wrestling fans were looking toward *WrestleMania 36*, Bojo was pledging to boost his country's economy by deepening the "special relationship" the UK enjoyed with the United States — its largest trading partner after the EU.

"Trading Scottish smoked salmon for Stetson hats, we will deliver lower prices and more choices for our shoppers," Johnson boasted.

As with Trump, a sizeable portion of the British public viewed their leader as, well, "a wanker" in the words of Zack Sabre Jr., who by early 2020 had held the Revolution Pro Wrestling promotion's British Heavyweight Championship on four separate occasions.

In 2019, Sabre — a technical marvel who'd built his international reputation by blending hard strikes and breathtaking flying maneuvers into his in-ring catalog — blamed a New Japan loss on the prime minister. "Boris Johnson, the sodding prime minister of a real country, not a joke country," Sabre ranted afterwards on social media, repeatedly smashing a chair against the ground.

Rolling onto the floor, Sabre — a Labour Party loyalist whose merch included a t-shirt reading, "I'll fight with my brain and an underlying hatred of the British Conservative Party" — continued, "I can't concentrate because I read the news all day."

New Japan cancelled all live events for a two-week period on February 26, following a recommendation from Prime Minister Shinzo Abe that sports and cultural events be postponed. Boxing, rugby, basketball, pro tennis and volleyball matches were called off, while Nippon Professional Baseball announced that 72 preseason competitions would be played in stadiums without spectators.

New Japan's president Harold Mejj insisted that, as the top promotion in Japan, it was the company's social responsibility to suspend all scheduled events during this state of emergency. "To do empty arena matches would reflect badly on ourselves and our industry," he said on YouTube. "We will not trade our reputation as a positive force for social good, even in the wake of harsh economic realities."

The company would not allow its wrestlers to step through the ropes again until June.

Although New Japan was certain to endure a financial hit, Mejj said that the company was strong enough to survive it, based largely on the revenue it generated over two days at *Wrestle Kingdom 14*.

While New Japan maintained fan interest by showing reruns of *Wrestle Kingdom 14* and other classic events on television, its sister company, the Stardom women's promotion, made the decision to do an empty arena card at Tokyo's Korakuen Hall on March 8. At this early stage, it was odd to see the performers playing to a nonexistent crowd. Before her main event, a lumberjack match against Saki Kashima, Mayu Iwatani addressed the awkwardness by throwing her wristbands into a collection of vacant chairs and shouting over the microphone, "Korakuen Hall . . . good evening!" When guest commentator Jushin "Thunder" Liger replied from the announce table, "Good evening," she answered, "Thank you, Liger-san."

In the U.S. the Undertaker appeared at a WWE meet and greet but made it clear that he did not intend to touch anyone. Sasha Banks signed autographs only after donning surgical gloves. Braun Strowman allowed nothing more intimate than a fist bump.

The Monster Among Men also posted a public service announcement on Twitter urging better hygiene. Playing off his catchphrase, "Get these hands," Strowman struck his large paws into the lens and growled, "Right now, I need everybody to *wash* these hands."

By March 11, the day WHO declared the outbreak a pandemic, more than 120,000 people had been infected in more than 100 countries. U.S. stocks recorded their worst day since the 1987 market crash. As the New York Knicks were en route to an uncharacteristic victory over the Atlanta Hawks, the National Basketball Association (NBA) announced that, following the game, the season would be halted until further notice. By the next day, Disneyland said it was closing, and Major League Baseball (MLB) the National Hockey League (NHL), Major League Soccer (MLS) and NCAA Division I Basketball suspended play. In the weeks to come, the Wimbledon tennis tournament was cancelled and the Olympics pushed back for a year. For the first time, all Catholic churches in Rome were shuttered, while the Church of Jesus Christ of Latter Day Saints — aka the Mormons — banned all public worship.

In Canada, Prime Minister Justin Trudeau conducted a special cabinet committee on COVID-19 and spoke to provincial premiers virtually — after the country's first lady, Sophie Grégoire Trudeau, tested positive.

More than 3,000 tickets had been sold for the *AEW Dynamite* held on March 11, but 500 fans chose to stay home. For "Murderhawk Monster" Lance Archer, it was both an exciting and unsettling night. Despite stints in both WWE and TNA, Archer believed that his career had fused in Japan, starting in 2011. Then, in December 2019, AEW opened negotiations.

"I was pitched on a short-term program," he told me. "But I was still committed to New Japan. And then, AEW offered me a multi-year contract."

After dropping the IWGP United States title to Jon Moxley at *Wrestle Kingdom 14*, Archer began envisioning a scenario in which both companies worked together on a regular basis — while he spent the bulk of his time in the United States. "I'd been going back and forth to Japan for several years, and this was an opportunity to come back home to a new adventure in the business."

After being presented with a variety of potential on-air managers, he was heartened about working alongside his eventual pick, Jake "The Snake" Roberts. "Jake was a natural fit," said the six-foot-eight-inch performer. "He's tall and can stand right next me and speak to my character in that smooth voice, cutting you with his silver tongue. They could have put me with anybody, but I felt like they let me decide. It's that freedom, that creativity that makes AEW as good as it is."

When he finally *did* appear on *Dynamite*, though, coming out with Roberts to scout Cody's match, the world was shutting down around them. Still, as with WWE, AEW would figure out a way to produce fresh television each week. On April 1, Archer had his first in-ring confrontation, destroying five-foot-two-inch Marko Stunt. "It did feel good to be with a company that wasn't cutting back, and was giving its talent a place to perform," Archer said. "But it was strange to be working while so many others were not."

Another AEW star, "The Bad Boy" Joey Janela, also appreciated his good fortune during a very uncertain time. "The highlight of the year for me," he said, "was getting a paycheck when a lot of indie wrestlers were selling t-shirts out of their garage."

After struggling on the indies since his teens, Janela saw irony in how his life had taken a positive turn during a period when much of the world was suffering. "I even met my new girlfriend because of the pandemic," he told me. With personal appearances limited, the pair became acquainted while The Bad Boy was doing a live Instagram chat. "She thought I was charming," he joked, "until she met me."

Like Janela, Hangman Page attempted to use humor to cope with the unprecedented challenges. While the world was closing down, he issued a press release that listed the safety precautions he intended to take. These included bringing his own beverages to arenas, rather than accepting beers from random fans, "exclusively drinking whiskey" in the hope that the higher alcohol content would protect him against infection, and no longer licking up and spitting back phlegm expectorated on him by fellow wrestlers.

He also advised his followers to continue to drink Corona beer. "Honestly, they have nothing to do with this."

On *Being the Elite*, the web series started by the Young Bucks when they were still on the indies — as a means to supplement and create new storylines for the Jackson brothers and their friends — Page was shown saying that he only packed essential items before leaving for the road — like his AEW World Tag Team Championship belt and libations.

Earlier in the year, Jeff Cobb had been introduced on *AEW Dynamite* as the special weapon Chris Jericho needed to weaken Jon Moxley. Although the former Olympian's surprise appearance excited fans, Cobb was clear about the fact that he was exploring different options in the wrestling business. "[AEW EVP] Cody was cool about me dropping in, then going other places too," he said.

Back in January, according to Cobb, WWE had tried to sign him. William Regal, the company's director of talent development and global recruiting, "is a great guy and a real wrestler," Cobb said. "He told me that I was going to get an offer. But I didn't want to jump into any contract. With WWE, it can be a real commitment, a five-or-six-day-a-week grind. I wasn't sure I was ready for that, and that's what I told them."

He was being advertised for ROH's *Supercard of Honor*, to be presented the night before *WrestleMania 36*, when he received an email informing him that the company was cancelling all live events at least through May. Suddenly, he was looking at the very real possibility of being inactive. "If you're a wrestler, you have a very small window before your body breaks down," he confided. "You miss a year, it's rough."

WWE's first empty arena telecast was a March 13 edition of *SmackDown* that had been scheduled for Detroit's Little Ceasars Arena and moved to the company's Performance Center in Orlando, where trainees and NXT athletes worked out, practiced promos and attended seminars on topics like acting and financial planning.

The broadcast began with an address from 14-time world champion Triple H. Back in 1999, The Cerebral Assassin was involved in a storyline in which he married Vince McMahon's daughter, Stephanie, under debatable circumstances. Stephanie appeared to be an unwilling participant, and a match was set between her husband and father at the *Armageddon* pay-per-view. The stipulation: if Vince could triumph, the marriage would be annulled. As the battle intensified, though, fans discovered that Stephanie actually *liked* being married to The Game. This became particularly clear when she helped her spouse blast Vince with a sledgehammer. As fate would have it, life imitated art, and Triple H and Stephanie married in real life.

It may have been the greatest investment the McMahon family ever made.

As the founder of NXT, Triple H was plugged into the indies, international promotions and fighting disciplines all over the world. There had never been a training facility like the WWE Performance Center, and Triple H's keen eye ensured that there was always a crop of top talent with their skills sharpened, ready to jump to *Raw* or *SmackDown* at a moment's notice.

Now, Triple H allowed viewers to get a small peek behind the curtain. There were clips of students learning the craft of professional wrestling at the Performance Center. He noted the many superstars who'd passed through the facility on the way up and emphasized that tonight, they'd return, not to train, but entertain.

This would be a night to forget about the problems in the real world, Triple H said, and — even in an empty arena — WWE was determined to help make this possible.

Like Mayu Iwatani at the Stardom show, The Miz parodied the fact that there was no audience to respond to his antics. Standing with fellow *SmackDown* Tag Team Champion John Morrison during a promo segment, Miz sneered over the mic that it was a relief not to hear booing or "you suck" chants. But even without fans in the building, he wanted to make one thing clear: Orlando was still a hellhole.

The one major glitch in the show occurred while Sasha Banks and Bayley were wrestling Alexa Bliss and Nikki Cross. When *SmackDown* went to a commercial in the United States, the international feed continued to broadcast what was occurring in the ring. Given the absence of a live crowd, the fighting stopped — even though all four women remained in character, pacing and pointing at their opponents in an accusatory way.

WWE Talent Relations would later send out an email mandating that performers "work through commercial breaks."

With *WrestleMania* drawing closer, WWE continued to hype its biggest event of the year. John Cena was interviewed by Michael Cole and recalled his encounter with Bray Wyatt at *WrestleMania 30*. Cena was victorious that day, the story went, and from the ashes of that defeat had come the newest incarnation of Wyatt's character, the evil Fiend.

Wyatt then joined the pair between the ropes. He agreed that his loss to Cena had been traumatic. But he had turned it into something positive by listening to the malevolent voices in his head. When the two had their rematch at *WrestleMania 36*, Wyatt pledged, John Cena was doomed.

The screen suddenly flashed with The Fiend's wicked face. As the picture went black, Wyatt's demonic laugh echoed over and over.

There had been scaled down broadcasts in the past — after 9/11 and the deaths of Owen Hart, Eddie Guerrero and Chris Benoit. Now, during the age of COVID-19, WWE had reached down, grasped for something new and managed to deliver. "The best thing about pro wrestling is it continued," Tommy Dreamer observed. "When everything else shut down, we still had wrestling."

Still, if this type of programming was going to become a regular thing, WWE had a great deal of work to do. From their quarantined living rooms, old time wrestlers ruminated over the empty arena telecast, predicting difficulties ahead for stars accustomed to using the audience to get themselves over.

"This is how it works," Tommy "Wildfire" Rich, best known for a four-day stint as NWA World Heavyweight Champion in 1981, told me with hands held apart. "If you have 50 people in the arena, you do this much." He spread his hands farther. "If you have 100 people, you do this much. But if you don't have anybody," he shook his head, "I don't know how these guys do it."

Ricky Morton, who, as a member of the Rock 'n' Roll Express with Robert Gibson, comprised one of the NWA's premier tag teams in the 1980s, was still active at 64. "Even at my age, I can take a big bump," he explained. "But it's hard to get the people going if you're performing in front of nobody."

In AEW, Sammy Guevara would stare out at the unoccupied chairs and imagine that time had gone in reverse. "It was almost like a rib," he told me in an interview for *Inside the Ropes Magazine*. "I got signed, and, less than a year later, it was like being back on an indie when no one would show up."

NXT headliner Candice LeRae would find it hardest to psyche herself up when her music hit. "I'm a cheerleader for myself when I go out for my entrance and the crowd and me are there together," she told *Newsweek*. "It's like you go to a sporting event and they announce the team, and they get that initial rush. Having nobody there and you're walking out, the weight is so heavy. 'Yup, there's the ring and I'm going to wrestle now.'"

Once WWE reverted to empty arenas, the business went into a different orbit. In Ireland, *Scrappermania 6*, a two-day Over The Top Wrestling (OTT) show slated for the weekend before St. Patrick's Day, was called off due to the pandemic. Like St. Louis and Houston in the days of the wrestling territories, OTT was one of the few places that fans could see wrestlers from groups that wouldn't normally work together. Along with some of the top representatives of WWE's British brand, NXT UK — including Trent Seven, Tyler Bate and Toni Storm — the event, scheduled for Dublin's National Stadium, was going to be highlighted by a non-title match between Moxley and OTT Champion David Starr, a Bernie Sanders supporter who'd been active in efforts to unionize wrestlers in the United Kingdom.

After drawing a nearly sold–out 4,300 fans to its TV tapings in Tijuana on the same night as *SmackDown*, MLW told fans that it was ceasing operations for at least 45 days. Founder Court Bauer was dubious about whether supporters would want to watch MLW televised from an empty arena and said that he had enough material to keep viewers entertained for several weeks.

MLW star Brian Pillman Jr. had returned from Mexico with flu-like symptoms and was planning to work for an outfit called Future Stars of Wrestling (FSW) in Las Vegas on March 15. Despite coronavirus fears, the show went on in front of a live audience. However, Pillman believed that he had no choice but to cancel. "I didn't have COVID," he told me. "But I didn't know it at the time, and I certainly didn't want to infect anyone."

He wouldn't wrestle on another indie card until July.

The same week as the FSW event, Sami Callihan, the former Heavyweight Champion for Impact — the company formerly known as TNA — announced his plans to stop competing until the scientific community could make better sense of COVID-19. "Fuck character, fuck storylines," he said on social media. "Our safety is the most important thing. Until this gets better, I'm not going to ANY wrestling shows."

Almost an hour later, he added, "My family . . . my animals . . . myself is more important than fake fighting in our underwear. I'm sorry. I'm not going to show until this is contained."

CHAPTER 5

THOSE WRESTLERS WHO made their living on the international circuit suddenly saw their options dry up. Even if a promoter was bold enough to attempt to put a show together, it was going to be very hard to get there. In mid-March, while deaths in Spain and Italy were soaring, the EU banned travelers from outside its bloc for 30 days. Meanwhile, the Canadian and American borders were sealed to everything but trade and essential services.

Australia imposed a mandatory self-quarantine for anyone — regardless of citizenship — entering the country. After drawing 1,500 people for a stadium show on March 14, the country's largest indie promotion, Professional Championship Wrestling (PCW) — a company that generally staged 90 events annually — shut down for eight months.

For the few wrestlers who managed to find work, even commuting was an eerie experience. "Walking through those empty airports reminds me of something out of *The Walking Dead*," said Tommy Dreamer. "Just total desolation."

Ray Lyn, an indie wrestler who'd worked for groups like Cleveland's Absolute Intense Wrestling (AIW), Championship Wrestling from Hollywood and ROH, had to find new ways to motivate herself to train. "Trying to stay on task when you don't have shows to go to, you ask yourself, 'Why am I working out?'"

When fans looked away from wrestling, they found few alternatives to occupy their attention. Ireland had closed its pubs, New York and Los Angeles their restaurants, bars, theaters and cinemas, Paris its cafés and landmarks like the Eiffel Tower. Even the U.S. Supreme Court delayed oral arguments, as justices began working from home.

Following his *Monday Night Raw* loss to Randy Orton, Matt Hardy continued talking with WWE about his future. Rumors circulated about him reappearing in NXT and working with the younger talent as both an in-ring competitor and backstage producer. "I don't want to be champion," he told *PWInsider*. "I don't want to be undefeated. I want to help people along the way . . . I think Hunter [Triple H] had a vision of making that happen . . . I appreciate Hunter because I think Triple H was really trying hard to keep me in the company."

Nonetheless, at midnight on March 2, Hardy took to his vlog and announced that he was now a free agent. For all his appreciation of WWE, he said, the company's creative perspective did not match with his. "The last three or four years I have as an in-ring competitor are really important to cementing my legacy."

On Twitter, Bray Wyatt posted a crying face emoji. "Don't go Matt," wrote Hardy's former Deleter of Worlds teammate.

Matt responded with a video clip of the two, writing, "I will always be near, my beloved compeer," utilizing a rarely used term for a person of equal rank or ability.

Two days later, on Matt's web series, the Young Bucks were seen pulling up at the Hardy Compound. "Bucks of Youth," the free agent greeted the pair in his Broken Matt voice, "I *knew* you'd come."

The next week, the exchange continued, with Matt ranting about his eternal desires and Nick and Matt Jackson questioning whether he wished to be booked badly.

"No, I've had more than my fair share of that done."

Instead, he asked to be buried and resurrected, prompting his Puerto Rican–born father-in-law — known to fans from earlier episodes as "Seen-yore Benjamin" — to appear. "We have to hurry," Matt urged. "Prepare the coffin for entombment."

As the Bucks helped carry the casket, Nick Jackson challenged, "Remind me why we're doing this."

"Just go with it," Matt Jackson replied.

Once they reached the desired location, Hardy instructed the Bucks to "kick out the zenith" possessing him — provoking a super-kick from each.

Speaking in a demonic tone, Hardy then referred to his guests — both executive vice presidents at AEW — as "executive vice pussies," inducing a second series of kicks that seemed to knock him out.

The installment ended with Matt placed in the coffin and buried, while the Bucks shoveled dirt on him. Benjamin was then shown plant-ing a cross on the grave, signaling that a resurrection was imminent.

On the March 18 edition of *AEW Dynamite*, in an arena empty but for a contingent of wrestlers spread out around ringside to compensate for the lack of fan reaction, Inner Circle members Sammy Guevara, Jake Hager and Proud-N-Powerful had just defeated the Elite — the Bucks, Hangman Page and Kenny Omega — when Chris Jericho grabbed the microphone. It didn't matter what was going on in the world, Le Champion — a name he continued using, even after losing the belt — declared. He was issuing a decree banning all fans from future AEW shows. The teams were scheduled to meet the next week at an event called *Blood and Guts* — a term Vince McMahon had used to disparage the AEW product during an investor's call — but Jericho gloated that the Elite were outnumbered. There were five members of the Inner Circle, and only four wrestlers in the Bucks' unit.

That's when Matt Jackson pointed to the rafters and introduced the Elite's newest ally, Matt Hardy.

The show ended with Broken Matt running his finger below his throat and repeatedly chanting, "Delete."

Earlier in the night, the Dark Order, a macabre sect of wrestlers whose numbers widened and narrowed, depending on the week, were set to finally reveal their leader, the Exalted One. They were interrupted by Frankie Kazarian and Christopher Daniels of SoCal Uncensored. Daniels demanded that the proceedings stop. There was *no* Exalted One, he said.

It was a cue for a video feed that showed a large man removing a black mask. It was hulking, bearded Brodie Lee — most recently known as Luke Harper in WWE. "You are not the first out-of-touch old man who didn't believe in me," he barked.

Although the insult was ostensibly directed at Daniels — who'd turn 50 later in the month — Lee was obviously talking about someone else.

In WWE, Luke Harper had been a glaring, backwoods presence in the Wyatt Family before he and fellow member Erick Rowan were taken off television and repackaged as the mallet-wielding Bludgeon Brothers. Although he'd won a number of championships — including the Intercontinental title and *SmackDown* Tag Team gold — he was unsatisfied with the direction of his career and had requested his release in December.

Interestingly, Lee was AEW's third choice to portray the Exalted One. The first had been "The Villain" Marty Scurll, who'd been a member of the Elite in Ring of Honor and New Japan. But when ROH offered him a lucrative contract, as well as the opportunity to help book upcoming storylines, Scurll opted to stay there. With his fantastic pronouncements, Matt Hardy appeared to be the next logical choice. The problem was that so many fans already *expected* this that the announcement would not be a surprise. Hoping to prove himself to spectators who hadn't had the opportunity to witness his varied in-ring repertoire, as well as his skills on the mic, Lee was anxious to step into the role.

The real-life Jon Huber had been slated to debut at a later *AEW Dynamite*, scheduled for his hometown of Rochester, New York — where fans, who'd been following him since his early days on the indies, would have exploded. "I got a call from Tony Khan saying, 'Hey, we are cancelling all these shows, but we still will be running in Jacksonville,'" he told *The Wrestling Inc. Daily* podcast. "'If you still want to debut, you're more than welcome to, but you're also more than welcome not to debut at that time.' And I chose to debut because I didn't know how long it was going to be, and I'd been sitting home for so long. I was dying to be a professional wrestler again."

After leaving much of his on-air persona in the hands of WWE's script writers since 2012, he now had to come up with his own material. His premier AEW broadcast "was pretty much the first time I've spoken on a live mic for over 10 seconds" in several years, he told Britain's talkSPORT radio station. "There's now pressure on me because there's nobody to blame. There's no writer to say, 'Hey, you wrote that. It wasn't good.' Now, I'm the writer. So if it's not good, it's on me. So there's another layer of pressure."

He seemed to transition with minimal exertion. It was fun to see Luke Harper, the near-silent swamp creature from WWE, wearing a suit and preaching the Dark Order doctrine. Later in March, Lee would manage to fire a few more volleys at his former boss. In one segment, he was seen dining with Dark Order members Alex Reynolds and John Silver. When Silver attempted to eat before Lee, the Exalted One kicked his follower out of the room. He then became annoyed when Reynolds sneezed. Although these moments meant nothing to most fans, business insiders had heard tales about McMahon becoming aggravated when underlings ate before he did or sneezed in his presence.

"It's just because he doesn't like anything he can't control," Stephanie McMahon, WWE's chief brand officer, had explained to *Barstool Sports*. "The fact he can't control the sneeze makes him upset."

With so much uncertainty, the *Blood and Guts* show, initially scheduled for Newark, New Jersey — a first for AEW in the New York City area — was postponed. Because the main event was supposed to feature the Inner Circle and Elite warring in two rings surrounded by a cage, the company chose to wait until a live crowd was around to pop for the planned spots. Instead, viewers saw an altercation between Jericho and Hardy. Liberated from the burden of having to broadcast everything live, the company attempted to record the segment the day before. But Jericho was unhappy with it, and a decision was made to reshoot the exchange the next day when the lighting in the amphitheater matched.

In the meantime, AEW tried to reschedule other live events. A Philadelphia show was pushed into July, a Houston card to November and New Orleans and Albuquerque broadcasts to December.

COVID prevented every one of these from taking place.

Nine days after a March 10 meeting with Prince Charles — at an event, coincidentally, for WaterAid, an organization encouraging handwashing and other hygienic measures in the third world — Albert II, Prince of Monaco announced that he'd contracted the virus. Within the week, Prince Charles would be diagnosed — with "mild symptoms" — as well.

On March 27, Prime Minister Boris Johnson reported that after developing a "temperature and a persistent cough," he, too, tested positive. Like the Prince of Wales, Johnson initially claimed to have a tepid illness. But after trying to fight off the virus for more than 10 days, he was moved into the intensive care unit at London's St. Thomas' Hospital. Only later would the public discover that he needed "liters and liters of oxygen," and doctors were actually preparing to announce his death.

In a scene that would have been difficult to imagine in North America or Europe, in April, representatives from New Japan and Stardom met with their counterparts from All Japan Pro Wrestling, as well as the NOAH, DDT, Diana and Tokyo Joshi promotions at Tokyo's Lower House Assembly Hall. Also in attendance was Hiroshi Hase, a former New Japan star who'd been appointed Minister of Education, Culture, Sports, Science and Technology by Prime Minister Shinzo Abe. The purpose of the gathering was ensuring that Japanese wrestlers received COVID-19 testing kits and were compensated for shows missed during the country's state of emergency.

A statement by eight-time IWGP Heavyweight Champion Hiroshi Tanahashi provided an insight into the way the "sport of kings" was regarded in Japanese society: "In the world of sports . . . I feel that professional wrestling should be the anchor. I think it should be acceptable for professional wrestling to be the last sport to return to full activity . . . When professional wrestling is back, then and only then, it means truly that Japanese entertainment has properly recovered."

CHAPTER 6

SEVERAL WEEKS BEFORE *WrestleMania 36*, Xavier Woods of WWE's New Day tag team was at home with an Achilles tendon injury, reading social media posts from fans. "So is like Mania happening?" he wrote. "Matter fact, is smackdown happening tomorrow? Y'all usually know before me."

At that stage, even people with the most peripheral involvement in the wrestling business seemed to occasionally have better information than the ones intimately associated with the industry. The truth was that, with the outbreak changing plans and rules, few really had any idea about what might occur.

The year before, according to WWE, fans from 50 states and 68 countries had converged on the New York metropolitan area for *WrestleMania 35* at New Jersey's MetLife Stadium. But now, President Donald Trump had announced sweeping restrictions on travelers from 26 European countries. Despite Trump's close relationship with the McMahon family, and the economic boon that *WrestleMania 36* would bring to the Tampa Bay vicinity, it was inconceivable that a fan from Norway or Latvia was going to be whisked through U.S. Customs because he wanted to see Rhea Ripley defend her NXT Women's Championship against Charlotte Flair.

If anyone possessed the sheer audaciousness to stage this type of event in the middle of a health emergency, it was Vincent Kennedy McMahon. For weeks, the company and local officials insisted that, despite the alarms being sounded, *WrestleMania 36* would take place, as scheduled, on April 5 at Raymond James Stadium. But once the WHO branded COVID-19 a pandemic, the pronouncements sounded a bit less resolute.

"Right now, *WrestleMania* is out about three weeks," Hillsborough County Commissioner Les Miller said the next day. "We came to the conclusion that at this point, we don't want to pull that plug. However, we wanted to give it at least a week to see what was going to happen."

On March 14, former WWE Champion CM Punk — known for his sometimes adversarial relationship with the company — was asked on social media if he intended to make a surprise appearance in Tampa. Punk replied that he was "busy in June."

At the time, Punk's supporters considered the answer hilarious. The coronavirus might delay *WrestleMania*, they reasoned. But the crisis would certainly be over by June.

Two days later, WWE announced that it was moving *WrestleMania 36* to the Performance Center. With the exception of the participants and essential personnel, no one would be allowed in the building — including fans. Wrestlers were to be sequestered at an Orlando hotel, then brought to the Performance Center in small groups to limit the number of people in the facility at any given time.

As disappointing as the news sounded, WWE insisted that it had little choice but to present the show. In fact, the company argued, with most other sports on hiatus, the organization was performing a public service. "We consider it a privilege and, in some regards, a responsibility to be able to provide this entertainment value for our fans," Stephanie McMahon told *Sports Illustrated*.

Shortly before the gates came crashing down, WWE Hall of Famer Bill Goldberg — remembered for, among other things, his 1997 and 1998 winning streak in WCW — made one of his periodic comebacks to defeat The Fiend for the WWE Universal title at *Super ShowDown* in Saudi Arabia. On the March 20 edition of *SmackDown*, he flipped the table during the contract signing for his *WrestleMania 36* battle with Roman Reigns, going eye-to-eye with the number one contender in the center of the ring.

Later that week, though, Reigns decided not to appear at *WrestleMania*. Just the year before, he'd returned to the ring after recovering from leukemia — a disease he'd previously beaten in college. Now, with his wife pregnant with the family's second set of twins, he concluded that entering a dressing room full of wrestlers who'd been practicing varying degrees of social distancing appeared too risky. Braun Stowman would replace him in the match.

"It's funny because for years now, for years, people have been like, 'Don't show up to *WrestleMania*. We don't want you in it,'" Reigns said on Instagram, describing those fans who showered him with scorn simply because WWE had opted to portray him as its top babyface. "There's a handful of dudes and haters that didn't want me there. But the moment I make a choice for me and my family, I'm a coward . . . For all my fans, you know I'm sorry I didn't get to . . . put on a show and entertain. But sometimes things are more important."

FITE TV was planning to broadcast 27 non-WWE events from the Tampa area during *WrestleMania 36* week, as well as host an in-studio program, analyzing the action. "There were some great shows fans wanted to see," the company's COO Mike Weber recounted at the time, "and a lot of those matches will probably never take place."

For top level independent wrestlers, the opportunity to perform — sometimes on as many as a dozen shows — in the course of the week meant making up for poor paydays, droughts or time recovering from injuries during other periods of the year.

New Jersey's Game Changer Wrestling (GCW) was arranging to have numerous promotions present a series of shows over several days in a single location. The Cuban Club, a landmark built in Tampa's Ybor City in 1917, contained four separate theaters and ballrooms. It was the ideal place to stage what GCW was calling "the Collective." "I saved every dollar to be put in the position where I could rent a space this size," GCW promoter Brett Lauderdale told me by phone while refunding purchases on his computer.

He mentioned a fan from Tennessee who'd bought tickets to eight separate events. "I'm just going through this and watching money disappear on the screen."

The highlight of the Collective, *Joey Janela's Spring Break* — the *WrestleMania* weekend event that built the company's international reputation before The Bad Boy was signed by AEW — had been projected to draw the largest indie crowd of 2020, with more than 4,000 fans paying to see a lineup that included British Heavyweight Champion Will Ospreay and Japanese legends Minoru Suzuki and the Great Muta.

"I've been working on this for more than a year — before *WrestleMania 35* was even held," Lauderdale said. "The loss is immeasurable. I can't even calculate the amount I've put into airline tickets for talent and crew. And no airline will give you a straight refund. They'll give you credit. Not GCW credit. Credit for the individual wrestler. But will that wrestler ever use the credit for GCW? I've spent close to $10,000 on equipment and rented porta-potties. And the situation is exactly like it is with the airlines. The vendors want to give me credit, not a refund. But if I'm not running a show in Tampa again, the credit's not worth anything."

Like many in the business, Lauderdale had never expected to be directly impacted by the coronavirus. "I was hoping we were good," he said, "until we weren't good."

Even when rumors circulated that *WrestleMania 36* would be cancelled, Lauderdale clung to the notion that the indie shows booked that week would go on as scheduled. "I didn't think the whole world would shut down."

Reality hit on March 12, the day after WHO's pandemic announcement. The group had an event scheduled at the Voltage Lounge in Philadelphia, and 40 percent of those who'd bought tickets chose to stay home. Throughout the afternoon, wrestlers arrived, talking quietly and monitoring their phones to track closures all over the world. "At around eight o'clock, we said, 'We're the last ones left,'" Lauderdale remembered.

Blake Christian, a high-flying Tennessean, had been planning to work two shows a day during *WrestleMania* week. As the talent sat around backstage in Philadelphia, wrestler after wrestler told him there was no point in going down to Florida. "I felt it [the lockdown] coming on right there," he said.

Just before bell time, the crew had a somber meeting. "All your other shows are cancelled," Lauderdale told them. "So let's go out and perform like it's the last show ever."

The wrestlers were motivated. After brawling all over the nightclub, Matthew Justice thrilled the crowd by laying his rival, Effy, across a door propped up on chairs, climbing to the balcony, sailing through the air and crashing onto his rival in the center of the ring. "Matthew Justice would dive into a pool of coronavirus if it meant having a good match," Lauderdale said. "He was determined to give his A-plus-plus game for the people who came out in the face of all the fear and all the hysteria."

The encounter was followed by a bar fight between Nick Gage and the normally technical Ophidian, a bloodbath between Shlak and former partner Jeff King, and a main event that saw Janela — his deal with AEW specified that on days when he wasn't needed, he could perform on the indies — deliver a brainbuster to Blake Christian on the bar. In the end, Janela lay down for his rival, happy to get a new star over. As Christian's arm was raised, the dressing room emptied, with wrestlers embracing one another and vowing to figure out a way to ride out the uncertainty.

In early 2020, Staten Islander Chris Dickinson was regularly referred to as the best indie wrestler not signed to a major company. "I haven't had another job in four years," he told Justin Barrasso at *Sports Illustrated*. "My job is wrestling."

At 32 years old, Dickinson was a headliner in GCW and had put in time with a number of other promotions that enjoyed cult followings, including Combat Zone Wrestling (CZW) and CHIKARA, as well as AAA in Mexico, Preston City Wrestling in the UK and Pro Wrestling Zero1 and Pro Wrestling Freedoms in Japan. In 2018, as a tag team co-titlist with Jaka in EVOLVE, an organization affiliated with WWE, he showcased his skills at *WrestleMania 34* Axxess — WWE's fan festival centered around the annual event.

He had nine matches planned for *WrestleMania 36* week, including a show for Germany's wXw, confrontations with New Japan's Shingo Takagi and Minoru Suzuki, and veteran Erick Stevens's retirement match. "This is unfortunately not only financially devastating, as it is the biggest week of the year, but it's extremely demoralizing," he told *Vice*. "I had a lot riding on some of these matches and a lot of eyes on me. This is a time where I could really break through to the next level and . . . some of these opportunities may never present themselves again."

After traveling to indie shows every weekend, he could not envision a scenario that involved simply sitting at home. "It's more than my career," he told Barrasso of his chosen profession. "It's my life. I'm a pro wrestler. I don't want to do anything else. This is what I love."

Since 2002, when he was 15 years old, Dickinson had been methodically smashing through each obstacle in the wrestling industry. COVID-19 was the one impediment he hadn't figured out a way to penetrate. "I'm here to fuckin' wrestle," he complained. "Now, I can't do it at all."

In an industry of august gimmicks, Danhausen had one of the more original ones. With a ghoulish grimace painted onto what he called his "88-year-old face," the performer added the suffix "hausen" to the ends of words and entered the ring carrying a jar of human teeth. While other wrestlers acted like they wanted to knock out their rivals' incisors, Danhausen tied them up and placed teeth in their mouths.

"As a kid, I used to like to draw comic book stuff," he told me. "And in some ways, I'm still drawing comics."

Trained at the House of Truth Wrestling School, run by former ROH manager Truth Martini outside Detroit, Donovan Danhausen had made his debut in 2013 with Metro Pro Wrestling (MPW) of Wyandotte, Michigan. Over the next four years, he started barnstorming for companies like Freelance Wrestling, Rockstar Pro, St. Louis Anarchy, Glory Pro and Black Label Pro in the Midwest and Inspire Pro in Austin,

Texas, as well as Ontario independents Destiny Pro, Superkick'D and Alpha-1.

As his confidence grew in the squared circle, he began crafting his character. In October 2017, he dressed up as a demon for Halloween, and something clicked. "I evolved [the gimmick] and twisted it until it was my own," he said. Although some believed Danhausen took his shtick from Jack Nicholson's Joker in the 1989 *Batman* movie, he'd been stimulated by a multitude of sources. His voice was an amalgamation of late-night television host Conan O'Brien, Skeletor from the *Masters of the Universe*, Cobra Commander and Dr. Doom from the Marvel series and the Monarch from the *Venture Bros* TV show on Adult Swim. His mannerisms were largely inspired by Mr. Burns on *The Simpsons*.

During his matches, when the song "Tequila" suddenly blared over the public address system and Danhausen launched into a ring apron dance, kicking a foe to the rhythm, he was channeling the biker bar scene in *Pee-wee's Big Adventure*.

It was in 2018, while Danhausen was a regular in Cleveland's AIW group, that his character truly took off. On Twitter, fans began adding "hausen" after their names while commenting on his matches. As his following grew, he boasted of having an "an Armyhausen of the Dead."

At home, Danhausen cut promos for fans online. "No one usually does promos without being asked. And I generally think that promos are boring. So I began making a spectacle out of my promos. My strategy was to create something visually appealing and say something within the first five seconds that would get people's attention."

The content was the pro wrestling equivalent of improv. "It was whatever came to my mind at the time. It was easier and less time-consuming than doing horror vignettes — although I would parody horror characters."

In another era, he realized, more mainstream fans might have been confused by his presentation. But there was always an undercurrent of followers who drifted toward pro wrestling because of its alternative nature, and they found it easy to relate and laugh along to the inside joke. "I was lucky to develop my following over the internet," he said, a place where he was safe from meddlesome promoters and others who might try to alter the gimmick.

In December 2019, while raising a family in Montreal, he was finally earning enough money from pro wrestling that he was able to quit his other job as a nursing assistant.

During *WrestleMania 36* weekend, he was planning to work for Freelance, Glory Pro and AIW, among others, and run his own show with fellow indie star Warhorse — his partner in a duo called Warhausen. Among the selling points of their "Wrestlevania" event: a "loser gets sacrificed to Satan" match.

The Florida State Athletic Commission rejected the pair's other proposal: an encounter in which the defeated party would be fed to wolves. "We can't legally feed people to wolves, but we can legally sacrifice them to Satan," he explained to *The Wrestling Inc. Daily* podcast. "That wasn't a problem [in] Florida, but the wolves were."

When we spoke after *WrestleMania 36* had come and gone, he noted that he and Warhorse had not given up on the concept of Wrestlevania. It would just have to take place when the world was safe from the coronavirus. "There was a lot to do, between wrestling and promoting, so it was a little bit of a relief," he said of the cancellation. "But I would have preferred a stressful four days to a yearlong pandemic."

Australian indie wrestler Shazza McKenzie had quit her data analyst job and spent $2,400 on a roundtrip plane ticket to the United States. She'd managed to book herself on 32 shows over the course of two months and was brimming with self-assurance — about the exposure she'd receive and the money she intended to earn to replenish her now-empty bank account. "It's an incredibly nervous feeling to leave your whole life behind for two months and couch surf in another country," she told *Sports Illustrated*. "But I just had to trust that things would work out."

And, under normal circumstances, her instincts would have been correct. But just hours after arriving, she learned that, one after another, her bookings were being cancelled. Fearful of being stranded in a country without cash or a support network, she returned to the airport and went home.

Fellow Australian Kellyanne had been training for 13 years when she was offered an opportunity to participate in the Ring of Honor Quest for Gold tournament. Not only was the contest cancelled before her departure, but Kellyanne soon found herself in a "Stage 4 lockdown," confined to her house for all but an hour a day and forbidden to travel more than five kilometers (or 3.1 miles).

"For me, when something good happens, I know something bad will happen," she told *The Wrestling Inc. Daily* podcast. "It's just how it is with my life."

Where her situation differed from McKenzie's was that ROH was part of the Sinclair Broadcast Group, one of the largest television companies in the United States, and had the money to pay wrestlers, officials and other staff after events were cancelled. As a gamer, Kellyanne was accustomed to spending long hours at home, and she used some of that time to create vignettes for ROH's platforms.

"The crowd can get to know me and see what I'm about," she said. "As much as it has been horrible to not be able to wrestle, it has given me a completely different outlet for my character."

Without *WrestleMania* week content, FITE TV's Mike Weber began looking elsewhere. Oriental Wrestling Entertainment (OWE), a China-based promotion previously affiliated with AEW, had shifted operations to Cambodia. As the rest of the world was under siege, Cambodia managed to survive 2020 without reporting a single COVID-19 death. So, starting on April 8, FITE began broadcasting shows from the Siem Reap Kun Khmer Arena.

In Belarus, President Aleksandr Lukashenko denied the seriousness of the pandemic. The authoritarian leader dismissed illness concerns as a "psychosis," recommending that citizens visit the sauna or drink vodka to poison the virus. In July, he cited an unsubstantiated statistic that 97 percent of those infected — including himself — were asymptomatic.

"Belarus isn't doing anything about the coronavirus," Weber told me. "So we're planning to do some boxing and MMA shows from there. I mean, Belarus and Cambodia, these are pretty closed countries, and they don't use a lot of outside talent. So who knows? Maybe they'll be safe."

In places where regulations were more stringent, promoters had to come up with innovative ways to funnel money to wrestlers who'd been sidelined by closures. An empty arena show held in London and broadcast on YouTube allowed fans to donate to a special fund. The card featured David Starr beating 17-year-old wunderkind Callum Newman and future IWGP World Heavyweight Champion Will Ospreay — the promoter of the event, along with *WrestleTalk* magazine — defeating his girlfriend, Bea Priestley.

In New Jersey, GCW owner Brett Lauderdale decided to stage a two-night event called Acid Cup 2 — named for Trent Acid, a speedster, high-flyer and hardcore brawler who succumbed to a drug overdose in 2010. "We weren't allowed to have fans," Lauderdale said, "but we could get a venue and a ring." Throughout the show, fans watching on the Independent Wrestling TV (IWTV) streaming service were directed to an Indiegogo site to raise money for talent.

Joey Janela, who wrestled as well as did commentary, told viewers this might be the last wrestling show they saw before "we're all locked in our houses."

The most memorable encounter was pro wrestling's first-ever social distancing match, pitting Janela against Jimmy Lloyd — a former child actor who was billed from Wuhan, China, for the night. Despite the close proximity every other competitor had had with his or her opponent, Janela and Lloyd were warned — by guest ring announcer Matthew Justice — that if they didn't remain six feet apart, the Centers for Disease Control (CDC) would shut everything down.

"I was sitting home one afternoon, processing refunds, and thinking about the Invisible Man," Lauderdale explained, describing a character occasionally featured as a special attraction on GCW shows. Both Janela and Lloyd had engaged in clashes with the Invisible Man — he also had a "brother" referred to as Invisible Stan — applying holds on the air in front of them and taking big bumps and selling during the unseen grappler's rallies. "I knew these guys could do this kind of thing," Lauderdale said, "so decided to make a social distancing match."

With a hint of sarcasm, announcers told the audience that this was what professional wrestling would become in the future.

The bell sounded, and Janela and Lloyd stood apart from each other, first exchanging pantomimed handshakes and going through the motions of locking up — without touching.

Those wrestlers who'd left the dressing room to watch the show were heard rhythmically clapping and chanting, "Six feet. Six feet."

In order to ensure that the combatants respected the rules, referee Kris Levin pulled out a tape measure.

Despite the expanse between them, Janela sold a number of faraway moves delivered by his opponent, including a Canadian destroyer and crossbody block. "In a wrestling match, you're usually trying to make the strikes look believable," Lloyd elucidated, "but in this case, we had to make everything look fake."

As the battle raged, a door was pulled into the ring. Janela paused to cleanse the surface with a disinfectant wipe before being tossed through the object.

Ultimately, Janela was victorious in the match — taking the microphone immediately afterwards to thank the others in the building and special guest John Cena, who appeared as a cardboard cutout.

To the shock of nobody, industry legend Jim Cornette, who spent as much time in 2020 bashing President Donald Trump as bad wrestling gimmicks, took to social media the moment he saw the match. Cornette had never been a fan of Janela's work, and the social distancing encounter did nothing to enhance that view.

To Cornette, the clash consisted of nothing more than "a skinny goof vs. a fat goof with no talent in front of no fans performing the sloppiest, worst attempt at playing pro rassler anyone has ever seen."

Lloyd had anticipated the former manager's response. "We knew that was going to happen. That was the goal."

Janela said as much in his social media reply to the Louisville Lip: "Without fail. Hook, line and sinker! Caught myself a big mouthed cuck bass."

Not content to let The Bad Boy have the last word, Cornette added one more comment: "So you WANT to be recognized as a complete buffoon and utter waste of flesh who excels at nothing and makes a pathetic attempt to emulate what real wrestlers do? You've actually succeeded at something!"

Before COVID-19, Michael Bochicchio had not only committed to organizing a WrestleCon around *WrestleMania 36*, but signed a contract to present the event in Los Angeles the week of *WrestleMania 37*.

The lawyer and native South Carolinian had been running the multi-day fan convention since 2013, while his company, Highspots, had been specializing in memorabilia and digital content for far longer. As wrestling fandom goes, his story was fairly typical: childhood devotion — in his case, he was watching 1980s legends like "Nature Boy" Ric Flair, Rick Steamboat, Rowdy Roddy Piper and Wahoo McDaniel in Jim Crockett Jr.'s Charlotte-based territory — followed by indifference as he matured through high school and acquired other interests. While attending Wake Forest University, he made friends with a fan of edgy 1990s promotions like Extreme Championship Wrestling (ECW) and Jim Cornette's Smoky Mountain Wrestling (SMW). The pair attended a few SMW shows, and Bochicchio left satisfied. It wasn't enough to return to the devoutness of his early years, but he realized that the taste was familiar, and felt a longing to indulge again.

On a trip to Mexico City during law school, he attended a show at the "Cathedral of Lucha Libre," Arena Mexico, and purchased a number of masks from vendors outside the building. Online commerce was a relatively recent development, but he decided to try it out and put the items up for sale on the internet. The masks sold out within a day.

His girlfriend was going to medical school in Mexico, so he had incentive to continue returning there. Each time, he'd pick up more merch and sell out just as quickly. "The internet was just exploding," he said. "The was no eBay or Amazon. I had no competition. It got to the point where I was traveling to Mexico every month, going into locker rooms and buying merchandise directly from the wrestlers."

By the time he graduated from law school, in the midst of WWE's "Attitude Era," "it was real easy to be a wholesaler for WWE products, so I signed up. It's tougher now. But you used to be able to buy the exact stuff you saw on TV and sell it to stores and flea markets and vendors at live [indie] shows."

Ultimately, he diversified, creating Highspotsnetwork.com to stream indie events online, as well as wrestling documentaries, often produced by cash-strapped but passionate fans.

In 2001, when *WrestleMania X-7* was held in Houston, local star Booker T organized a fan festival. Highspots arranged to have a table there to sell DVDs, videotapes and merchandise. To draw visitors, Bochicchio paid future WWE Hall of Famer and AEW manager Tully Blanchard to sign autographs and interact with fans.

"Even then, there was an international audience in town for *WrestleMania* week," Bochicchio noticed. "It wasn't just people from Texas who'd driven two or three hours. I'd been to a lot of wrestling shows, but this was different than anything I'd ever seen before."

The company hosted its first WrestleCon at the Meadowlands Expo Center in New Jersey the week of *WrestleMania 29.* Throughout the day, fans could gather in different parts of the building and watch live cards, featuring the best indie performers in the world. The names brought in to sign autographs were among the biggest in the business, including Bret "The Hit Man" Hart and the Ultimate Warrior. "It made WrestleCon a major event, right out of the gate."

With each passing year, WrestleCon had grown larger and more varied. By *WrestleMania 35*, the convention stretched close to four days. In Charlotte, Bochicchio's office had 15 employees.

Yet, his expectations for the week of *WrestleMania 36* were low. "I was disappointed [WWE] chose Tampa. I wanted someplace more accessible to international fans. The airport is small. There's no mass transit. And WWE had done a good job in tying up some of the better venues.

"I could see the year was going to be a little bit off. WWE had not sold out all of its ancillary events. But it was going to be good enough to do what we wanted to do."

Most notably, he felt fortunate to procure George M. Steinbrenner Field — located directly across Dale Mabry Highway from Raymond James Stadium — home of the New York Yankees Class A Advanced Florida State League affiliate and a public event space. "The timing was right for everybody. It was just after spring training but before it became uncomfortably hot."

Other events were scheduled for the Marriott Westshore.

Bochicchio was able to book Mike Tyson and Chris Jericho for autograph signings, along with 200 other wrestling personalities. "You're not going to meet that many stars in as short an amount of time anywhere else," he said. "We really got lucky."

Or so he thought. The rapid spread of COVID-19 took him completely by surprise.

"I didn't anticipate it would move so fast. I knew it would get here. But I was thinking, 'It probably won't be until mid-April when it really explodes in the U.S.' — a week or two after *WrestleMania*. But with each day, the news was getting worse.

"I knew that if WWE changed its plans, WrestleCon would have to be cancelled. The venues were downplaying the problem — they're in the business of selling space. And, contractually, I couldn't cancel first. That would be breaching a contract."

But once a ban was placed on travel from Europe, Bochicchio said that 25 percent of the WrestleCon guests scheduled to stay at the Marriott pulled out. "As part of our deal with the hotel, we had guaranteed that we'd sell a certain number of hotel rooms, and now we were below the threshold we promised."

He told the Marriott Westshore that, given the extraordinary circumstances, there would be no WrestleCon in 2020.

The news did not go over well. Bochicchio received a letter from Marriott International saying that Highspots had violated the chain's "cancellation and refund policy." "WrestleCon is a special event booked over heavy demand days," the communication read. "Since our hotel is prepared to perform as agreed, your . . . cancellation will cause damages to [Marriott]."

Those "liquidated damages" were estimated to be $144,202.

"Beaches were still open, and the hotels [in Florida] were pretending that it wasn't that bad," Bochicchio recalled. "Or at least, the franchisee had that attitude. I don't blame [parent company] Marriott International at all. It was the hotel itself that refused to refund."

His only recourse, he concluded, was posting the letter online and asking the wrestling community to assist. "We appreciate your help Twitter Army," he wrote. "But keep in mind the letter was written by the local Tampa Westshore Sales Director, not a national correspondence. I'm guessing once the parent company sees what is happening, they will step in and do the right thing."

Chris Jericho was among the first to leap to Bochicchio's defense. "Hey @wrestlecon, no court in the world would force you to pay this bill," he tweeted. "Shame on @Marriott for taking this stance in such an uncertain time! I have tons of fans who feel the same way."

Wrote Kevin Owens, "Before I made it to WWE, [Highspots] helped me provide for my family with events like @wrestlecon. Considering the circumstances and as a Titanium Elite member myself, I'm truly disgusted by what @Marriott is trying to do to those guys. Shameful!"

But Jericho was prepared to take it one extra step — contacting the WWE Hall of Famer who occupied the Oval Office: "Excuse me @realDonaldTrump-I think @Marriott doesn't understand your advice that NO gatherings over 10 ppl take place for the next few weeks & . . . its impossible & possibly illegal to move forward with @wrestlecon. So stop the threats #Marriott!"

Had Twitter existed in the 1960s, a message from Skull Murphy, Bull Curry or Mr. Moto would have had little impact on a large corporation's decisions. But in 2020, Vince McMahon's wife, Linda, had just stepped down as the head of the Small Business Administration — a cabinet position — and Tony Khan's father, Shahid, was considered the world's richest person of Pakistani origin. While the average citizen might not have been able to name Matt Hardy's drone, it was understood that wrestling fans followed the news and spent money. So was it really worth $144,202 to piss them all off?

"It was just so nice to see the support these WrestleCon guys got," Mike Weber noted. "You don't see that in every industry. I don't think you'd see it in MMA or boxing. But in wrestling — despite the carny aspects and the kayfabe — there's this feeling of everyone being in it together."

As the story gathered steam, the Marriott Westshore agreed to hold neither WrestleCon nor any of the fans accountable for the cancellations. "When Chris Jericho tweeted directly at President Trump, people thought it was pretty interesting," Bochicchio reflected. "I want to say that Jericho's campaign had nothing to do with what happened in the end. But things changed dramatically when he got involved."

CHAPTER 7

AS *WRESTLEMANIA 36* drew near, WWE was considering creative options to add to the fanfare. Rather than stage the exhaustive events of the recent past — in 2019, if you factored in the pre-show, *WrestleMania 35* stretched 7.5 hours — the Showcase of the Immortals would now air over two nights. Although the WWE Performance Center would be the linchpin of the proceedings, the company announced that certain confrontations would emanate from "multiple other locations" — stirring fan imaginings about special stipulations and exotic battle sites.

Unlike any previous *WrestleMania*, the spectacular would be taped in advance, along with future episodes of *Raw*, *SmackDown* and NXT. With the prospect of having to "shelter in place" in the very near future, WWE needed to quickly generate as much content as possible.

In those early days of the pandemic, when the world was trying to figure out exactly how to fight the virus, WWE boasted about a nightly "pandemic-level cleaning" method that involved fogging and ultraviolet light. "That could be overkill, quite frankly," Stephanie McMahon told *Sports Illustrated*, "but we really are trying to put in the best safety practices that we possibly can."

A company called Allied Bioscience — dedicated, according to its promotional material, to reducing "the global burden of infectious disease" — was brought in to coat the Performance Center, production trucks and WWE warehouses with a special spray. In an investors' call, Triple H described the glaze as a "sword that punctures the cell wall of the virus, or what causes the virus, and kills it on contact."

Seemingly convinced that it was imposing the most stringent standard in either sports or entertainment, WWE required all visitors to have their temperature taken before entering the building. A reading of anything above 100.4 meant expulsion. While the intent was certainly positive, doctors would later point out that this wouldn't prevent the spread of COVID-19, since carriers could be asymptomatic.

With an empty arena as a backdrop, the "go home" version of the *Monday Night Raw* leading into *WrestleMania 36* had its challenges. Despite his standing as the number one contender for Brock Lesnar's WWE Championship, Drew McIntyre was forced to do a remote interview. After traveling to the UK on a promotional tour, the challenger was now in quarantine. So was Sheamus, who'd accompanied Drew on the trip, as well as Bobby Lashley, who'd managed to get into the United States following an excursion to South Africa, and Kairi Sane, who'd recently married in her native Japan.

"If you've been out of the country or been . . . in contact with anybody who's been out of the country, you're not allowed in the facility," Stephanie told *Vanity Fair*. "We're taking every precaution we can. It's also why you don't see talent or anyone else in the audience. We really are adhering to all the guidelines that we can to maintain the health and safety of our performers."

The show drew a poor rating. Nonetheless, the major players who did appear on *Raw* kept fans engaged. The setting of the ring had been configured so viewers were not as aware of the rows and rows of empty seats. With a frenzied Lesnar standing beside him, Paul Heyman equated Drew McIntyre to other "special athletes" who'd previously fallen to the Beast Incarnate. "Next year, on the 'go home' segment on the 'go home' *Raw* before *WrestleMania*, do you know who is going to be standing here with the title over his shoulder?" Heyman asked, his voice vibrating off the walls of the Performance Center. "Brock Lesnar."

The gloom of the near-vacant building also worked particularly well for Edge when he accepted a last man standing match with Orton, vowing to drive the Viper so far down the hole from which his psychological deficits emanated that "you'll never get out."

In an interview with *Metro* news site in the UK, Edge explained that his job had always been helping fans forget the taxing circumstances of their lives. "This year, more than any year, we are all in the midst of something we have never experienced before. The world really needs outlets." By involving followers in the *WrestleMania 36* storylines, his goal was to help them "remember what it is to be human."

Unable to provide the commemorative folding chairs that ringside fans had long been allowed to take home from pay-per-views, WWE instead sold seats — for roughly $100 apiece — online with the slogan "I Wasn't There." The company also reprised its "In Your House" merchandise — named for a series of pay-per-views in the 1990s — and introduced a "Home 24/7" design depicting the 24/7 belt that titlists were required to defend at any hour of the day or night.

Despite having two days to present a range of matches, the seventh annual Andre the Giant Memorial Battle Royal, along with the third yearly *WrestleMania* Women's Battle Royal, were omitted from *WrestleMania 36*. Although each match provides a *WrestleMania*-caliber payday for titans otherwise excluded from the card, officials concluded that it just wasn't worth the risk to pack so many people together in a single ring.

Rather than have a celebrity guest begin the revelry by singing "America the Beautiful," WWE unrolled a moving montage of some of the greats from *WrestleMania*s past performing the song, including Aretha Franklin, Gladys Knight, Boys II Men, John Legend, Ashanti and Ray Charles. "When I saw that open, that history, it really brought a tear to my eye," said *Busted Open* co-host Dave LaGreca.

Because The Miz had taken ill shortly before the show — as it turned out, with a non-COVID sickness — the *SmackDown* Tag Team Championship match on night one, scheduled to showcase The Awesome One and John Morrison defending their titles in a Triple Threat Ladder contest, was altered. Instead of Miz and Morrison taking on the New

Day and the Usos, one member of each team was allowed to compete. The action ended with Morrison retaining after battling Kofi Kingston and Jimmy Uso on adjoining stairwells — then falling off, clutching the belts that had been dangling from the ceiling.

In another skirmish, WWE *Raw* Women's Champion Becky Lynch made history by besting Shayna Baszler, becoming the first female to win a title at one *WrestleMania*, then successfully defend it at the big event the following year.

And Braun Strowman — stepping in for Roman Reigns — survived four spears from Bill Goldberg to deliver four successive powerslams to capture the WWE Universal Championship.

"This year was so different," Triple H told host Corey Graves on WWE's *After the Bell* podcast. "I wasn't there for a lot of it because a lot of it was being taped and shot during the afternoon and stuff, and I went off to do a different shoot. And then, you get to *WrestleMania* itself and you're home and now, it's two days, but I'm sitting at home [watching the entire show] for the first time. I've never been home for *WrestleMania*. Even the one that I missed due to injury, I was there."

The one confrontation that commanded a disproportionate share of The Cerebral Assassin's attention was the Boneyard Match between the Undertaker and AJ Styles. For years, Vince McMahon had compared WWE to Hollywood, telling interviewers, "We make movies." But the Boneyard encounter literally *was* a movie, the first of several "cinematic matches" that would help fans of both WWE and AEW ignore the fact that there were no ticket buyers in sight.

The rules stipulated that the fight could only end when one man was buried in the ground. According to Triple H, though, no one was quite sure how the two would get there. As he conceptualized the details with McMahon, he asked exactly what the mogul imagined a Boneyard Match to be.

"He's like, 'I don't know. Like a graveyard. It's in a graveyard . . . They got this huge field and it turns into a graveyard in the middle of nowhere.' I go, 'So what do you want it to be?' And he's like, 'I don't know. Just make it good.'"

The day of the taping, Triple H got into a car with Michael "P.S."

Hayes — best remembered for his work as the most visible member of the Fabulous Freebirds tag team — the company's vice president of creative writing and booking. The pair drove about 35 minutes outside of Orlando to a one-acre lot behind a barn. Hayes was confused. The large field that Vince had described was nowhere to be found. But when he attempted to call the boss and urge him to stage the bout in another location, Triple H stopped him. "I said, 'Michael, this is it. This is the hand that we have.'"

Still, Triple H was troubled over the fact that there was only supposed to be one camera on site. As an alternative, he pitched McMahon on using the NXT digital team to surround the combatants and shoot the entire battle like a film.

"Well, I don't see we have much choice," Triple H recalled his father-in-law saying. "So that's what we're going to do.'"

The pair agreed to use seven cameras and several drones as the Undertaker and Styles fought after nightfall. A home situated nearby had the potential to cause complications for the production team, but the owners never turned on their lights. "There's actually one shot in there where there's a car that keeps going by," Triple H told Graves. "I'm like, 'If this guy drives by one more time, I'm going to run out there to like smash his car window or something to get him out of here.'"

To add to the drama, Metallica, which had been scheduled to play the Undertaker's entrance at Raymond James Stadium, agreed to help with the scoring.

The match began with a hearse arriving at the site while the Undertaker's theme played. Surprisingly, it wasn't the Deadman who emerged from the vehicle, but Styles. Suddenly, viewers heard the music the Undertaker used when he was known as the American Badass — a biker character he portrayed at the start of the 21st century — and the Man from the Dark Side blazed into the frame on his motorcycle.

Triple H had encouraged both competitors to talk trash as they waged combat, and Styles told the Undertaker that his grave had already been dug. The Phenom lunged at AJ, who moved out of the way while the Undertaker's arm crashed through the glass of the hearse.

As the two brawled, Styles fell into the hole. But he was quickly rescued by his close allies, Luke Gallows and Karl Anderson — whose association with the two-time WWE Champion went back to their days together in the Bullet Club in Japan. A group of druids — as the Undertaker's hooded confederates were once called — appeared. But as with the hearse, this was a swerve. Instead of attacking Styles, they went after the Reaper. The Undertaker fought them off, along with Gallows and Anderson, only slowing down when AJ managed to bash him with a cinder block.

A strike from a shovel sent the Undertaker hurtling into the grave.

With wrestling being what it is, Styles somehow found a bulldozer and managed to turn it on. Before he could fill up the hole with dirt, however, the Undertaker miraculously appeared behind the driver's seat to continue the war.

"AJ was flying around on the dirt on the hard ground with rocks," Triple H observed. "They were beating the tar out of each other."

The two repaired to the top of a shed, where the Undertaker hit his opponent with a blast of fire. After thumping Gallows and Anderson again, the legend caught Styles by the throat and chokeslammed him off the roof.

The Phenom climbed down to join him near the open grave. Humbled by the beating, AJ now apologized for his previous actions and begged not to be buried. Seemingly touched, the Undertaker hugged his enemy and praised him for his bravery. Then, he kicked Styles, face-first, into the ground, mounted the bulldozer and buried him alive.

The camera focused on a tombstone bearing AJ's name, and the Undertaker slipped back onto his motorcycle and rode off. Fans heard his traditional theme, then the "American Badass" song. As the segment ended, the American Badass symbol was projected onto the side of a building on the ranch.

It was a poignant moment. The Undertaker now had a *WrestleMania* record of 25–2. Although he'd symbolically left his hat, gloves and coat in the ring after losing to Roman Reigns at *WrestleMania 33* in 2017, the inclusion of the different themes left fans with the feeling that the end had finally come.

Not just the WWE faithful were moved. Despite the tensions generated by the Wednesday Night Wars, Chris Jericho tweeted, "Congrats to @undertaker & @AJStylesOrg for the tremendous performance and spectacle that was the #BoneyardMatch! I loved it!"

With arenas shuttered, there was no way for the Undertaker to embark on a retirement tour. Instead, WWE used its available resources to deliver the tribute he'd earned. On the WWE Network, the company presented a multi-part documentary series about Mark Calaway the man — and the character who'd added so much to his essence. In the final episode, he finally announced that he was stepping away from the squared circle.

It wasn't exactly what he wanted to do. But at 55 years old, he had little choice. "I just don't want to be that guy that goes out there, limps out to the ring, and the young guys are having to work around me only to get chokeslammed or dropped on their head," he admitted to the *New York Post*. "One, it's not fair to them. Two, it's not fair to the fans. I don't want to be the guy that uses the equity I've built up over all those years to make a payday or two. It doesn't feel right to me."

In what would have generally been a *WrestleMania* moment, the future Hall of Famer was given a retirement ceremony at the *Survivor Series* in November. He'd be officially inducted into the WWE Hall of Fame after fans returned in 2022.

"I realized I have taken every physical gift, tool that I have and used it up," he said in his *Post* interview. "There's no water left in the sponge."

Paul Heyman once told me that, somewhere in the middle of *WrestleMania*, the last wrestling season ends and the new one begins. Plotlines are resolved, and future intrigues start incubating. On night two, in a move probably choreographed to augment the importance of NXT during the Wednesday Night Wars, Charlotte Flair stepped into the ring with NXT Women's Champion Rhea Ripley.

Flair, the second-generation great who characterized herself as The Queen, had won the women's *Royal Rumble* in January. Given a choice of which title to pursue at *WrestleMania 36*, the top contender — for the first time ever — chose neither the *Raw* nor *SmackDown* crowns, but the NXT trophy. After a well-paced match, she trapped Ripley in a figure-four leglock. As the charismatic Aussie struggled to break free, Flair bridged her neck, turning the move into what she called the figure eight — reclaiming the title she first won as a relatively untested talent in 2014.

Elsewhere on the card, the unlikely romance between loveably rotund Otis and shapely blonde former fitness competitor Mandy Rose finally ignited — even after Dolph Ziggler and Sonya Deville conspired to derail it. But, on the Grandest Stage of them All, Otis and Mandy prevailed over the subterfuge, with Otis dispatching Ziggler in their match, while a meddling Sonya received a slap across the face from Mandy.

To be perfectly candid, it was a bit of a letdown when Otis and Mandy finally kissed — and there was nobody around to pop for it.

Indie competitor Ray Lyn watched the match at home. While she'd normally envy the *WrestleMania* participants, she admitted to feeling some sympathy this time. "You have to remember when *WrestleMania* took place," she said. "It was when everything was *really* locked down, and everybody was staying at home. So it was creepy. *Are we all going to die?* And I was sad for the wrestlers because this was their moment, and a pandemic took that moment away from them."

Impact wrestler Trey Miguel tried to imagine himself on the card. "I kept thinking about the wrestlers in their first *WrestleMania*," he told me. "They were still a part of history, but it couldn't have matched their imaginations."

When Drew McIntyre arrived at the Performance Center for the biggest bout of his life, he encountered a near-empty building. "It was the ultimate skeleton crew," he told Findlay Martin in an *Inside the Ropes* interview. "I was like, 'Man, this is *WrestleMania*? It doesn't feel like *WrestleMania*. I was worried that I wasn't going to quite get amped up for the match."

Still, he conducted himself as if he'd be challenging for the WWE Championship at Raymond James Stadium, going through the motions of preparing for the match. It wasn't until he turned the corner at the Gorilla position — the backstage spot just before the entrance ramp, named for the late Gorilla Monsoon, who'd situate himself at a small table there to deliver last-minute instructions — that he took in the weight of what was about to occur. "I looked over and I saw Brock pacing around and then it started becoming real."

Like Strowman's win over Goldberg the night before, this was a match between two powerful warriors. Virtually every maneuver was a big move, and the tempo moved quickly. McIntyre nailed Lesnar with a Claymore kick for a two-count. Lesnar dodged another Claymore and delivered a German suplex. Then another one — and another. Apparently irritated when McIntyre kicked out after this barrage, Lesnar executed his finisher, the F5, and covered the Scotsman for the pin. Once again, McIntyre kicked out.

When McIntyre managed to avoid yet another pinning combination, Paul Heyman shouted from ringside that the contender couldn't continue kicking out after every F5. Lesnar lurched forward, once again attempting to put away McIntyre with the finisher. Drew met him with a Claymore and then, in rapid succession, hit two more, covering the Beast Incarnate to become the WWE Champion.

The titlist was handed the belt but ended up stashing it in a room at home until *WrestleMania 36* aired. "Things are not official until they happen," he told ESPN. "Watching myself was very crazy, being on the couch — watching it like everyone else, wondering what was going to happen. I kind of pushed out of my mind what had happened. I was reacting to it like I was in the match. My wife had to move away from me because I was darting from side to side with every F5, with every Claymore. Finally, when I won the title . . . I went upstairs, I opened the door and I took the title out now that it was official."

He later had a Zoom call with his family, showing off the championship for them.

The last man standing match between Edge and Randy Orton was the one battle meant to be contested in an empty building. Few fans had really seen the various sections of the Performance Center and, as the pair fought all over the facility, viewers would receive a tour. Although The Rock and Mick Foley had engaged in an empty arena match during a broadcast shown at half-time during the 1999 Super Bowl, this type of clash had never taken place at *WrestleMania*. Edge described his task as filling an "entirely blank canvas" with a rich story fans would remember.

The match began with Orton disguised as a ringside cameraman shocking Edge with an RKO before the bell rang. As Orton stripped down to his ring gear, the referee told Edge that the match could only begin if he stood up. Eventually, he did — and was quickly felled by another RKO.

After the neck injury that led to his retirement, and the attack that followed the *Royal Rumble*, Edge seemed to be a beaten man. Naturally, fans knew that he was going to come back and receive a measure of revenge. But it was easy to invest in what viewers saw on the screen — Edge was old and battered, and may have been swimming in waters too fierce to navigate.

He'd counter this impression by staying in the match for some 40 minutes — a stupendous feat for someone who hadn't wrestled in nine years. "To me, it wasn't a last man standing match, it was a last man standing *fight*," he recalled on *After the Bell*. "The story was dirty. It was ugly. It was personal."

The duo continued into the Performance Center's gym, where Orton wrapped weightlifting equipment around his opponent's neck and tried to lynch him — a curious spot since anyone associated with WWE at the time remains profoundly disturbed by the way former WCW and WWE World Heavyweight Champion Chris Benoit committed suicide in 2007, hanging himself on a lat pulldown machine, after taking the lives of his wife and son.

Still, the last man standing match was too fast and too brutal for viewers to dwell on this point for long. Edge and Orton smashed each other on a platform festooned with LED boards bearing *WrestleMania 36* graphics, then ended up in an office, where Edge swung from the ceiling and dropped an elbow on his foe on top of a conference table.

Just as the Boneyard Match had concluded atop a shed, this fight climaxed on the roof of a production truck. There, Orton — joined by a referee — bashed Edge with a chair across the back. Looking Edge in the face, Orton sneered that he was going to send the former headliner back to his family, then placed a chair below the Rated-R Superstar's head. But when Orton raised a second chair to bring down on his former tag team partner, Edge leaped up and caught the Apex Predator in a standing arm triangle, rendering him unconscious.

There was no chance of Orton reviving. But Edge needed to close the circle begun in January. Sliding a chair below the Viper's skull, Edge executed a vicious con-chair-to, then stood — heaving with righteous rage — while the official counted to 10.

He later admitted to feeling exasperated by comments he'd read online about the match eating into time that would have been better spent on other confrontations. Labeling these pundits a "miniscule militia of malcontents who just want to complain about everything," he claimed to be shocked that, of all things, these people were grumbling "about the length of a wrestling match during a pandemic. Like really? Come on. But these are also the same people who are going to complain that [McIntyre] and Brock went for four minutes. I just think there's a segment of people that enjoy not enjoying things."

The second cinematic match of the weekend was a battle between "The Fiend" Bray Wyatt and John Cena — the Firefly Funhouse Match, named for the spooky children's show spoof Wyatt hosted on WWE programs. But, other than the use of the cinematic format, the two collisions had nothing in common. If the Boneyard Match was *True Grit*, the 1969 Western that Dusty Rhodes used as a model for many of his storylines, the Firefly Funhouse Match was *Eraserhead*, the experimental 1977 horror flick directed by David Lynch.

Where WWE deserves praise is that, despite its extensive inventory of regulations — announcers were required to say "medical center" instead of "hospital," and "rivalry" in place of "feud" — the Firefly Funhouse Match was peppered with parodies of the company, as one dreamlike scene bled into another. At one point, Vince McMahon was even depicted as an evil boss puppet, uttering terminology only insiders knew.

Cena was taken back in time to his 2002 *SmackDown* debut, when, as a WWE neophyte, he held his own with former Olympic gold medalist

Kurt Angle. The 16-time world champion was shown wearing his gear from that period and entering the scene by passing the giant fist that was part of the *SmackDown* set.

Chronologically, the match meandered, but that was part of its appeal. Flashes of the *WrestleMania 30* encounter between Wyatt and Cena were shown. This was the night, some of Wyatt's supporters have argued, that Cena could have established his opponent as a superstar by laying down for him at the Showcase of the Immortals. Instead, Cena went over yet again — to the detriment, critics said, of himself and the company.

Now, Bray tried putting away Cena with Sister Abigail — the neckbreaker variation that began with a kiss to the top of the head. Cena slipped out of the move and attempted to bash Wyatt with a chair. Bray disappeared — and soon, everyone was transported to yet another era.

In this case, Wyatt appeared decked out in the white-on-black attire representing the nWo — the faction that dominated WCW during its strongest years battling the World Wrestling Federation for TV ratings in the 1990s — introducing Cena, who strummed a spray-painted belt like a guitar. It was a gesture that was part of Hollywood Hulk Hogan's entrance during the period when he was the nWo's most compelling heel. Observers noted that this segment appeared to be ridiculing WWE for its longtime refusal to turn Cena — the company's number-one babyface — into a villain, even when a sizeable amount of the fan base was booing him.

By playing it safe, the logic went, Cena hurt himself, while the more daring Wyatt became stronger with each phase of his character development.

Unleashing his fury, Cena beat Wyatt down, but it soon became apparent that Bray was no longer his victim. Instead, Cena was pummeling Husky the Pig, a Firefly Funhouse character created as an homage to Wyatt's all-but-forgotten persona in his early days in WWE, Husky Harris.

That's when The Fiend materialized behind Cena, taking him to the mat with Sister Abigail and punishing the legend by executing the Mandible Claw — a finisher that involved jamming two fingers in a rival's mouth and pressing down on certain nerves. Laughter echoed as Wyatt appeared to count the pin — before standing proudly with arms extended.

On his Twitter feed, Glenn Gilbertti, better known as Disco Inferno during his WCW days, aptly asked, "How do you describe that to somebody??"

One explanation could have been that, in order to heal from his loss at *WrestleMania 30* and live up to his mission of becoming the Eater of Worlds, Wyatt needed to destroy Cena.

Former WCW president Eric Bischoff — who was himself lampooned during the nWo section — effusively praised McMahon for taking the risk. "It was an inside shoot, but it was done in such a creative and effective way," he said on his *83 Weeks* podcast. "I think the Firefly Funhouse and Boneyard Match are probably the catalyst for the next evolution of storytelling in wrestling."

When Dave LaGreca and I spoke the day after *WrestleMania 36*, we didn't moan about missed spots, contrived finishes or the lack of atmosphere. Instead, we felt a sense of gratitude to the men and women who'd masked up, strapped themselves into airplanes and exchanged hip tosses and upper cuts at close quarters. "Well, we had *WrestleMania*," LaGreca reflected. "It's not the *WrestleMania* anyone wanted or expected but, for a few hours, we were able to escape. It was nice to see something trending besides the coronavirus.

"Ten or 20 years from now, people are going to remember what was going on in the world at the time, and how *WrestleMania* and WWE delivered."

CHAPTER 8

WHETHER *WRESTLEMANIA 36* was a factor or not, NXT on the following Wednesday managed to eke out an uncharacteristic win over AEW, powered by a cinematic-style match that featured Johnny Gargano and Tommaso Ciampa brawling all over the Performance Center. After Candice LeRae helped her husband, Gargano, score the victory, the two were seen fleeing in a car — before the camera panned over to another vehicle to reveal a debuting Karrion Kross — a future NXT Champion who'd been known as Killer Kross in Impact — and his real-life partner, Scarlett, watching.

The next week, NXT would score another win, this time behind a main event that saw Pete Dunne and Timothy Thatcher upend Roderick Strong and Bobby Fish. Once again, the margin of victory for WWE's third brand was small. But some wondered whether NXT was beginning to reverse the supremacy AEW had largely enjoyed since *Dynamite* premiered in October 2019. Could these back-to-back conquests be part of the same pattern that saw the World Wrestling Federation overtake WCW in the ratings in 1998?

It was not to be. Despite an outstanding roster of male and female talent, NXT would not enjoy another Wednesday Night Wars triumph until late June. Regardless, the fans who pledged allegiance to NXT had little to complain about, while WWE could take solace in the fact that its ingenuity had enshrined the cinematic match as an everlasting part of the industry.

Rather than hosting the signature event of its next pay-per-view, *Money in the Bank*, in the Performance Center, the company flew a sizeable number of performers to the corporate offices in Stamford, Connecticut. While generally the *Money in the Bank* match involves a battle up a ladder in the center of the ring toward a briefcase containing a contract for a title shot, in this instance the wrestlers had to run a gauntlet through the building until they reached the roof. It was only then that the prize could be claimed.

The taping took place several weeks before the pay-per-view aired on the WWE Network, starting in the morning and continuing until nearly midnight. At times, multiple scenes were shot simultaneously in different sections of the building. Like on a Hollywood set, there were also long stretches during which certain wrestlers were reportedly waiting around to be summoned into this unusual match.

Both the men and women started their contests simultaneously on the ground floor, and special guests periodically popped in to add to the diversion. Brother Love — the red-faced televangelist character who first graced World Wrestling Federation programming in 1988 — was seen alighting a bathroom stall and running into Rey Mysterio. Doink the Clown — well, someone dressed as Doink the Clown, since Matt Borne, the wrestler who first popularized the gimmick, died in 2013 — greeted Daniel Bryan and Otis. Paul Heyman ended up in the middle of a food fight in the cafeteria. Dana Brooke was shown entering a conference room, from which a *Money in the Bank* briefcase dangled. But when she grabbed it, Stephanie McMahon was there to point out that the object was a prop. Bryan and AJ Styles brawled into Vince McMahon's office, prompting the boss to order them out. They did as asked — but returned to carefully reorganize the fastidious boss's chairs.

Known for his acute aversion to germs, McMahon then applied hand sanitizer and continued his work.

The most bizarre moment occurred on the roof, as Mysterio and Aleister Black fought on the ladder below the suspended briefcase. First, Styles tipped over the object — standard fare in a ladder match. But what occurred next was something I never expected.

Rather than simply beating down Mysterio and Black, Baron "King" Corbin tossed them off the side of the building.

A loud thud was heard as each competitor seemingly hit the ground.

Even after the battle ended — Asuka won the women's competition, and Otis managed to be in the right place at the right time, catching the cherished briefcase while Styles and Corbin were tussling over it on the ladder — fans were in a state of confusion.

Were Black and Mysterio dead? I mean, we knew Corbin was a heel. But a *murderer*?

Black fueled the speculation by tweeting a photo of a ghost.

Wrote Styles, "No one has heard from @WWEAleister or @reymysterio, @BaronCorbinWWE is running from the law. @WWEDanielBryan is still rearranging furniture in the office, and I was CHEATED out of my #MITB by @otiswwe! A travesty!"

The next day, the company admonished us not to make more of it than it was. Mysterio and Black only fell six feet to another section of the roof, WWE stated, sustained minor injuries and were cleared to compete.

You can all calm down. It was only a work.

And, once again, for a couple of hours at least, no one who'd seen the show was talking about COVID.

Even those viewers who had COVID themselves.

The next month, at the *Backlash* pay-per-view, Edge and Orton reprised their feud in what was billed ahead of time as the "Greatest Match Ever." The fracas was aided by sound effects, multiple takes and recorded crowd reactions and, according to online pundits, lived up to its billing. Both men relied on their extensive wrestling proficiency to tell this story in a meaningful way; Edge reportedly discussed the fine parts beforehand with WWE Hall of Famer Bret "The Hit Man" Hart, whose moniker, the Excellence of Execution, was based on his meticulous style. The match unfolded slowly, with every major move carried out to add to the drama, rather than simply dazzle. After nearly 45 minutes, Orton apparently concluded that Edge was the better man, so rather than trying to beat him with skill, reverted to the antisocial tendencies that had gotten him here in the first place — stealing a win following a low blow and punt to the head.

At this stage, the so-called "WWE Universe" had completely bought into this ongoing rivalry, and the company could have continued to book them on top without any fear of burning out the fans. Each combatant had logged a win, and spectators would have welcomed a rubber match — perhaps at *SummerSlam*. But the two would not collide again for eight months, due to a triceps tear sustained by Edge during the Greatest Match Ever.

"I took an RKO and I felt a little nauseous and I got a cold sweat, not a hot sweat," he reflected to *Sports Illustrated*. "That's generally when you know you've popped something. It wasn't all that painful in comparison to my neck pain over the years or compared to tearing both pecs or tearing my Achilles. I just thought, 'I might have torn it a little bit.' And then, I found out I tore it completely off the bone."

WWE's *Extreme Rules* pay-per-view altered its name to emphasize the fact that fans would be seeing a cinematic match. Dubbed "The Horror Show at *Extreme Rules*," the card was centered on a "Wyatt Swamp Fight," featuring Bray Wyatt and WWE Universal Champion Braun Strowman in a non-title encounter in the Florida marshlands.

In the promos leading up to the match, Wyatt pointed out that Strowman had started out as a member of Bray's perverse "family." Fans were shown videos of the two together. It had been Wyatt who'd created the man who now wore the gold, declared the Eater of Worlds, and it was Wyatt who possessed the power to "bring back the dead" — in this case, the character Strowman portrayed before his singles push. As a warning about what might transpire in the Swamp Fight, Bray urged viewers to look skyward and "follow the buzzards" — an End of Days cry he'd uttered during an earlier phase of his WWE tenure.

Behind the scenes, many of the ideas for the conflict sprung from the mind of Bray Wyatt — much as the Hardy Compound struggles were largely conceptualized by Matt Hardy. Several days before the pay-per-view, the combatants and a production team drove to a secluded bog some two hours from Orlando to bring Bray's notions to life. For the equivalent of a traditional workday, the crew shot the battle from a variety of angles.

The match began with the head of the Wyatt clan swaying in his rocking chair, as Strowman drove toward him. Suddenly, the screen went dark. When light returned, Wyatt was gone. A baffled Strowman embarked on a search. Imagery of animals flashed before his eyes — before Wyatt returned out of nowhere and attacked.

As Strowman lay on wet ground, we saw what was churning in his mind: a view of himself as a member of the Wyatt Family, menacingly swinging a weapon.

Then, once again, the screen went black.

Cut to Strowman chained to a chair. Wyatt stood before him, denigrating the human race and urging Braun to return to the dark side. If they only merged their energies, they could rule as gods.

Strowman now had to contend with a series of nightmare scenarios. A guy appeared, holding a serpent — not Jake "The Snake" Roberts because he was on the AEW payroll — which promptly dug its fangs into the Monster Among Men. Some aggressors in black entered the scene, forcing Strowman to fend them off. A woman's voice was heard, beckoning Strowman to come home.

It was Alexa Bliss, the eye-catching blonde who'd patterned her gimmick after the Joker's accomplice in the Batman series, Harley Quinn, and had held the women's championship on both *Raw* and *SmackDown*. Bliss would later play a larger role in the Fiend's storylines, but the Wyatt Swamp Fight was the first time she came out as a disciple.

As the match wore down, Strowman and Wyatt were fighting on a pier. His stupefaction about the environs notwithstanding, Braun actually did okay in this part of the confrontation. At least for a while. Bray ended up in the water, and Strowman declared that that the contest was over — which, of course, it wasn't. Again, Wyatt emerged out of nowhere, this time trapping his opponent in the Mandible Claw. As the pay-per-view ended, Strowman sunk into the water, and Wyatt rose from the depths as The Fiend.

Wait — had Stowman drowned?

As with Mysterio and Black at *Money in the Bank*, the Monster Among Men wasn't dead — or even waterlogged. He'd return to WWE TV, and continue the plot by dropping the Universal Championship to The Fiend at *SummerSlam*.

The Eye for an Eye Match between Seth Rollins and Rey Mysterio could never have taken place during my youth. With audiences packed with true believers, promoters tried to avoid inciting spectators to the point of riot. When Stan Stasiak defeated Pedro Morales for the World Wide Wrestling Federation (WWWF) — WWE's original moniker — Heavyweight Championship in 1973, for example, ring announcer Buddy Wagner avoided informing the crowd at the Philadelphia Arena about the title switch, assuming that this bit of news would result in untold property damage. So just imagine what might have occurred if the beloved Rey Mysterio had lost a contest whose purpose was the extraction of one's eye?

In 2020, however, fans were clued in to the fact that, despite the stipulation, Mysterio's vision would probably remain intact. After all, even after King Corbin tossed Rey and Aleister off the roof of an office tower, not one observer, as far as I know, deemed it necessary to call the police — something my late grandmother, Ida, and her sister, Yetta, threatened to do on those sporadic occasions when "Living Legend" Bruno Sammartino happened to find himself Pearl Harbored.

In the age of COVID-19, the cinematic took precedence over the factual.

"At the end of the day, was it ideal?" Rollins said of his confrontation with Mysterio during an interview with TalkSPORT. "No. Did it catch people's attention? Sure. It ended up on TMZ."

Because the Eye for an Eye Match shared billing with the Swamp Fight at the "Horror Show at *Extreme Rules*," the burden was on the talent to leave fans with something to talk about. Not that anyone wanted to upstage Wyatt and Strowman, but there's no doubt that Rollins and Mysterio hoped to keep pace with them. The action started with each man going after the other's orbital socket. In this kind of encounter, you really couldn't be judged for fighting dirty, but Rollins heeled it up by utilizing a foreign object — a kendo stick — on his rival's eye and introducing rope in an effort to tie the masked hero to the bottom ring strand. For his part, Rey didn't prescribe to Greco-Roman standards, either, breaking the kendo stick and jabbing the weapon into Rollins's face, then thrusting his eye into the corner of the ring steps.

Following a superkick and curb stomp, Seth turned the tide, holding Mysterio by his mask and jamming his face into the side of the stairway. In a sequence that never aired, prosthetic makeup was said to have been used to create the illusion that Rey was blinded. But McMahon reportedly was unsatisfied, prompting WWE to appeal to viewers' imaginations, having the cameras focus on Rollins as he appeared to retch at the sight of his opponent's dislodged orb.

We need some help from the back.

Fans were told that Mysterio had been rushed to a nearby clinic to be treated for his injury. As with *Money in the Bank* and the Strowman submersion, it turned out that things were not as bad as they seemed. Doctors were apparently able to save Rey's vision, and he later returned to action with both eyes still in his skull.

Over at AEW, Chris Jericho and Tony Khan had a good laugh at WWE's expense, but not for the reasons you'd think. On social media, they pointed out that, earlier in the year, after the Inner Circle had pitched a spike into Moxley's eye, the number two promotion labeled a fight between The Loose Cannon and Santana an "Eye for an Eye."

"Eye for an Eye Match?" Jericho taunted. "You're welcome."

That self-satisfaction could only stretch so far. Within weeks of the Boneyard and Firefly Funhouse Matches at *WrestleMania 36*, AEW was integrating cinematic devices into its own programming.

In late April, Jericho presented what he called a "Manitoba Melee" featuring an array of people striking the camera as if going after an individual. The person who was supposed to be hit would then be seen selling the move, before hitting the camera again, as the segment moved on to the next personality. The wrestlers featured included Sammy Guevara, Jake Hager, Santana and Ortiz, Jungle Boy, Peter Avalon, Luther and Sonny Kiss. There were also former WWE legends like Soul Train Jones, known as "Million Dollar Man" Ted DiBiase's manservant, Virgil, in the World

Wrestling Federation; Swoggle, the diminutive entertainer formerly billed as Hornswoggle; and Vicky Guerrero. There was also a variety of non-wrestling notables featured, among them, Lou "The Incredible Hulk" Ferrigno — who wielded a taser, by the way — Jay and Silent Bob, Guns N' Roses' Duff McKagan, comedians Gabriel Iglesias and Ryan Niemiller, Slipknot's Corey Taylor, James Garretson — the strip club owner from the *Tiger King* documentary series — and Jericho's father, Ted Irvine, a onetime member of the New York Rangers, Boston Bruins, L.A. Kings and St. Louis Blues who whacked the lens with a hockey stick.

A confrontation between real-life dentist Dr. Britt Baker and Big Swole was called a Tooth and Nail Match and held in the former's office. After smashing her foe with a framed diploma, Baker tried pulling Swole's tooth. But Swole fought back and the row spilled outside, where Baker's assistant, Reba, insinuated herself into the proceedings. Swole chucked the intruder into a dumpster, then returned to the office, where Baker attempted to use a drill and a syringe of Novocain. Somehow, Swole took possession of the needle and injected it into Baker's leg. As she tried to rouse her lethargic limb, Baker was pummeled and shoved into the dentist's chair, where a mask was strapped to her face. The referee awarded the match to Big Swole after the dentist was put to sleep by a burst of laughing gas.

What fans didn't know was that the company had little choice but to stage this type of contest. During a match earlier in the year, Baker sustained tears to the tendon and LCL, as well as an interior tibia fracture. Although she'd hoped to recover by the time of this match, she hadn't fully healed. Hence, AEW went to the cinematic well instead of cancelling the confrontation.

In terms of work rate, the Tooth and Nail Match bore little resemblance to Ricky "The Dragon" Steamboat vs. Randy "Macho Man" Savage at *WrestleMania III*. But now that the cinematic match had been become an authentic genre in sports-entertainment, Baker and Swole served their purpose, adding garnish to a card that featured more competitive matchups.

AEW's Stadium Stampede — the high point of May's *Double or Nothing* pay-per-view — was on par with any of WWE's cinematic offerings. The collision — held at the home of the Jacksonville Jaguars, TIAA Bank Field — pitted the Inner Circle (Jericho, Guevara, Hager, Santana and Ortiz) against the Elite (Omega, Hangman Page and the Young Bucks) with Matt Hardy. While many fittingly described the confrontation as "ridiculous," the level of absurdity was so exhilarating that others considered it the match of the year.

"There's comedy wrestling, there's hardcore wrestling and, now, there's cinematic wrestling," Sammy Guevara told me.

Taped the night before the pay-per-view with 18 separate cameras, the Stadium Stampede was AEW's statement about what you could present if you dipped into the bountiful minds of the talent rather than script writers who'd never taken a bump. As face-masked cheerleaders urged on the participants and four referees spread over the length of the field, the teams charged each other, swinging a variety of weapons. True to his nickname The Cleaner, Omega wielded a broom. Page, whose cowboy gimmick included drinking in saloons, galloped across the stadium on a white horse, chasing Guevera off the gridiron.

While this was very much a brawl, and the maneuvers had the potential to jeopardize careers, the performers were playing for laughs, and accomplished their objective. When Page ran over Jericho with a line marker, for instance, no one feared that the champion would be crushed to death. Instead, viewers were amused when Le Champion came out of the altercation painted white. Likewise, after Nick Jackson kicked out of a near-fall, Jericho issued a challenge to the official's count. After repairing into a review tent, referee Aubrey Edwards declared that "the call stands."

Incensed, Jericho countered, "You're a shitty referee!"

The thrills continued. As Guevara, Jericho and Nick Jackson were tangling by the goal post, Matt Jackson borrowed a ladder, climbed onto the crossbar and executed a moonsault onto the combatants.

He later noted that, although the NFL had a rule about outsiders touching the goal post, Tony Khan was able to get clearance. Sometimes that happens when your family owns a football team. With nothing firm on which to balance, Jackson compared standing on the object to attempting to steady himself on a rolling log in the ocean.

Matt Hardy's highlights included taping Ortiz into a wheelchair and propelling Santana into an ice machine, then locking it shut with a broom.

"Cold as ice," announcer Jim Ross said, paraphrasing the 1977 Foreigner song. "He's willing to sacrifice."

During another segment, Proud and Powerful managed to throw Hardy into the stadium's pool. Despite the fact that the water was no higher than the wrestlers' waists, Ortiz refused to jump in, complaining that he couldn't swim. With an underground camera capturing everything, Hardy was seen smiling while Santana dunked him, changing into different versions of Broken Matt each time his head rose above the surface.

In the course of searching for Guevara around the stadium's corridors, Page seemed to give up at one point, park his horse and enter one of the venue's bars. Noticing the animal, Hager followed Hangman into the establishment and sidled up next to him.

"You came here to fight, or you came here to drink?" Page asked before taking the first swing.

In the dust-up that ensued, Page was slid across the bar, crashing into every object in front of him. But Omega turned up to shatter a champagne bottle over Hager's head. The Cleaner hit a V-Trigger on a wobbly Hager, and Hangman leaped off his partner's back with a buckshot lariat. Then, Page and Omega each returned to the bar, where Hangman poured his cohort a glass of milk before helping himself to a whiskey.

While hostilities raged elsewhere, the cameras periodically picked up Matt Jackson suplexing Guevera across the field. When they wound up in the end zone — and the announcers heralded what they claimed to be "100 yards of suplexes" — Matt spiked his rival's head into the grass and launched into a victory dance.

Referee Rick Knox flagged him for excessive celebration.

The match ended with a worn Guevara running for his life as Hardy and Omega pursued him in a golf cart. "The theme of the match was 'Sammy can't catch a break,'" Sammy told me. "I got hit with sprinklers, chased by a horse, run over by a golf cart."

Guevara scampered into the empty stands, but Omega and Hardy ran after him. Hurling chairs at his tormentors, Guevara turned and tried to choke out Hardy. The appearance of Broken Matt's new drone, dubbed Neo 1, provided distraction enough for Omega to catch the Spanish God and deliver a One-Winged Angel 15 feet down to the field.

"I wanted to go off something really high," Guevara said. "But it had poured rain just before, and it was really slippery. I had to put my trust in Kenny Omega. When I looked him in the eye and he said, 'I'll take care of you,' I knew I could believe him."

Omega scored the pinfall and, like winning NFL coaches everywhere, received a Gatorade bath.

The fireworks display that lit up the sky above TIAA Bank Field did nothing to impress Jim Cornette. "I will never watch this fuckin' shit again," he raved on his podcast *Cornette's Drive-Thru*. "Fuck all you people. I'm ashamed of Matt Hardy. I'm ashamed of [AEW announcer] Tony Schiavone. I'm ashamed of Jim Ross for not walking out on this. I'm ashamed of everybody involved in it . . . I don't want to see them personally again . . . I don't want to see them professionally again . . . If that is what wrestling is now, it needs to die."

As with GCW's social distancing match, Cornette's indignation heartened the organizers into believing that they'd done something right. When Tony Khan was questioned about the bout, he told reporters that, even when the coronavirus was no longer scaring people away from venues, he hoped to make the Stadium Stampede an annual event.

By the time this book was completed, another had taken place at *Double or Nothing* in 2021 — starting in an empty stadium and culminating in front of the rapturous audience packed into Daily's Place. Remaining true to the cinematic concept, this match would be shot over a four-day period and include a stunt coordinator whose goal was to make the scenes feel like part of an action movie.

CHAPTER 9

ALTHOUGH THERE WERE fewer and fewer fans who remembered the glory days of the National Wrestling Alliance, the NWA Worlds Heavyweight Championship still transcended time to a certain degree. Regardless of the fact that the title was now primarily defended at smaller arenas, it never went away, and, for the past several years, its importance had risen. Fans who appreciated the roles of classic NWA kingpins like Lou Thesz, Dory and Terry Funk, Gene Kiniski, Jack Brisco, Harley Race and Ric Flair wanted to see the organization achieve greater prominence, and the Crockett Cup — a revived tag team tournament originally staged to honor the late Charlotte promoter Jim Crockett Sr. — had the potential to build on recent gains and help with this goal.

In September 2019, the month before the first AEW *Dynamite* broadcast, the storied organization debuted a new weekly show, *NWA Power*, on YouTube. Shot in front of a live audience at GPB Studios in Atlanta, *NWA Power* was a throwback to the intimate studio wrestling programs of the territory days. This was the latest phase of a mission begun in 2017 by owner Billy Corgan and the league's creative visionary, Vice President Dave Laguna, to complement the NWA's rich history with contemporary athleticism and a modern pro wrestling mindset.

"When AEW came along, they took a lot of oxygen," said Nick Aldis, whose reign as NWA World Heavyweight champion added credibility to a title that had primarily been defended on the indies since 2007, when the group's relationship with TNA ended. "And then, we debuted *NWA Power*, and there was a lot of interest. There were a lot of important eyeballs on that show."

Aldis told me that, despite Corgan's fame in the alternative rock universe, the NWA knew it was facing a herculean task. "We weren't getting any rights fees for that show. We were using it to sell tickets and merchandise and pay-per-views. We were exploring advertising through YouTube. Because it's not just WWE and AEW that are well-funded. Ring of Honor and Impact were owned by billion-dollar companies and had massive safety nets. But that's why I think we did a better show. There was an incentive. If we don't get people to buy our pay-per-views, we go out of business."

From its founding in the years after World War II, the purpose of the NWA had been to unite various regional territories under one banner — with a single world champion. At its height, participating promotions included groups as far away as Japan, Australia and New Zealand. Although that number had shrunk significantly by the time the Crockett Cup was first staged in 1986, the surviving NWA territories sent tag teams to participate. The final version of the tournament was presented in 1988 — the same year Jim Crockett Jr., who'd named the event for his father, sold his promotion to media mogul Ted Turner — until Corgan opted to resuscitate it in 2019.

That show, which also included wrestlers from ROH, was highlighted by Crockett Cup winners Brody King and PCO also claiming the NWA World Tag Team Championship. Excitement was high for the follow-up Crockett Cup, booked for April 19, 2020, at the new Gateway Arena, outside Atlanta, the focal point of the NWA during the final years of the territory era.

The main event was to feature Aldis defending his title against his "former best friend," Marty Scurll. "The wheels were in motion," Aldis said. "It was two weeks after *WrestleMania*, and the Gateway Arena had just opened up. This was our first show at a big arena since Billy Corgan bought the company."

By March, half of the tickets for the 5,000-seat venue had sold. Lagana was quoted as saying that the company planned to generate a half-million dollars that day. There were also talks with the global entertainment company Live Nation about partnering on events. But once the pandemic occurred, the NWA was forced to postpone the show, bringing the group's energy to a disappointing halt.

Meanwhile, WWE and AEW continued to churn out weekly content, even as some wondered whether wrestling should be presented at all. Tony Khan emphasized that his company had a network contract and wasn't going to jeopardize the livelihoods of the talent by breaching it. In the early phase of the pandemic, when the Daily's Place parking lot was converted into a coronavirus testing center, AEW shifted tapings to the Nightmare Factory in Norcross, Georgia, the wrestling school co-owned by Cody Rhodes, QT Marshall and former WCW performer Ray "Glacier" Lloyd. After Georgia imposed a stay-at-home order, the facility was visited by a code enforcement officer, who checked permits and other paperwork, then allowed the tapings to proceed. While the stopover was described as routine, some fans speculated that officials had been alerted by WWE.

Stooging to authorities about possible violations was a tactic employed by rival promoters since the carny days, and would indicate that WWE truly viewed AEW as a threat. As titillating as this possibility seemed, though, there wasn't a hint of evidence that it was true.

Shortly after *WrestleMania 36*, WWE was named an "essential business" in Florida, allowing some live broadcasts to resume, even if much of the rest of the state was under shelter-in-place restrictions. According to the revised directive, "essential services" applied to "employees at a professional sports and media production with a national audience." Despite *Raw*, *SmackDown* and NXT remaining closed to the general public, a spokesperson for Governor Ron DeSantis's office told ESPN that the broadcasts were "critical to Florida's economy."

The designation invited questions over whether DeSantis, a Republican who'd linked himself closely to the Trump agenda, might have been persuaded by the fact that America First Action, a Super PAC (Political Action Committee) promoting the president's re-election, was headed by the administration's former Small Business Administration head Linda McMahon.

Perhaps not so coincidentally, America First Action had reportedly committed to spending $18.5 million in the Sunshine State.

To be fair, WWE wasn't the only wrestling enterprise whose owner was known to support the 45th president. ROH's parent company, the

Sinclair Broadcast Group, was famously conservative, and had run a series of promotional segments on its 193 television affiliates decrying "fake news." Tony Khan's father, Shahid, was one of four NFL team owners who'd donated $1 million to Trump's 2017 inauguration. The elder Khan would later say that, despite benefitting from the president's economic policies, he was personally offended by Trump's decision to ban travel to the United States from five majority-Muslim nations. He also expressed a "different viewpoint" on social issues.

Still, the warmth between the McMahons and Trump seemed to transcend both politics and business. When Linda McMahon was sworn in to her cabinet post, the entire clan posed for a photo with the world's most successful WWE Hall of Famer — with one of Triple H and Stephanie's daughters proudly holding a still of the president shaving her grandfather's head at *WrestleMania 23*. A presidential press conference with sports commissioners, held on day one of *WrestleMania 36*, included the WWE chairman. The same month, at a briefing about restarting the sports economy, Trump singled out "the great Vince McMahon." On the day an edition of *SmackDown* commemorated Triple H's 25th anniversary in the industry, the president tweeted, "@TripleH is a total winner!"

But since its fan base was as divided as the rest of the population, WWE — like the other major promotions — made a concerted effort never to mention the president's name on television. The company's mission, it repeatedly said, was "putting smiles on people's faces" — not provoking them into unfriending each other over political squabbles on Facebook.

Still, if the presumed leader of the free world wanted to invoke the accomplishments of The Cerebral Assassin, there wasn't much even Vince McMahon could do about it.

In some ways, both major American political parties were facing the same quandaries as the wrestling business. With the general election slated for November, how were supporters going to safely gather for their respective conventions and nominate their candidates? In April, the

Democratic National Committee announced that it was postponing its conclave from July to August in the hope that the perils associated with the virus would fade. But Biden conceded that social distancing concerns might force a "virtual" event.

"We may not be able to put 10,000, 20,000, 30,000 people in one place, and that's very possible," he told ABC News.

At that point, there were no plans to move the Republican National Convention in Charlotte. "We have no contingency plan," Trump said. "We're having the convention at the end of August, and we think by the end of August, we're going to be in great shape."

In Trump's vision, 50,000 partisans would congregate indoors without social distancing or mask wearing. He wanted nearby hotels, restaurants and bars to operate at full capacity. The scenario was unacceptable to North Carolina governor Roy Cooper, a Democrat, who said in a letter to the Republican National Committee that they needed to plan for a more cautious, scaled-down event.

In June, the president declared that he was no longer interested in making his acceptance speech in the city where Jim Crockett Jr. once ran his promotion out of 421 Briarbend Drive. (Trump didn't actually mention the Crocketts, but I wouldn't have put it past him.) Instead, Jacksonville — in Ron DeSantis's Florida — would host the GOP convention. North Carolina was going to lose "hundreds of millions of dollars and jobs," Trump tweeted, and it was Governor Cooper's fault.

There was really no need to panic, Trump regularly assured the public, since he had a few ideas about ending the pandemic sooner than the experts predicted. "If I ran as a liberal Democrat," he'd once said, "they would say I am one of the smartest people anywhere in the world." At an April 23 press conference, he provided his own interpretation about using sunlight, humidity and disinfectant to kill the presence of COVID-19 on surfaces. "Supposing we hit the body with a tremendous, uh, whether it's ultra-violet or just very powerful light . . . Supposing you brought the light inside the body, which you can do either through the skin or in some other way . . . I see disinfectant, where it knocks it out in a minute — one minute — and is there a way we can do something like that by injection inside, or almost a cleaning?"

On the podium, Dr. Deborah Birx, the administration's coronavirus coordinator, stared ahead uncomfortably, while Trump's enemies amused themselves by trying to guess the thoughts running through her mind.

The president later claimed he was only being "sarcastic" and blamed "fake news" outlets for trying to make him look stupid. "What is the purpose of having White House News Conferences," he tweeted, "when the Lamestream Media asks nothing but hostile questions & then refuses to report the truth or facts accurately . . . Not worth the time and effort."

The controversy compelled the manufacturer of Lysol to issue a statement that its disinfectant products should never be administered into the human body.

In pro wrestling, former ROH World Champion PCO — whose gimmick involved rising from the dead with the assistance of jumper cables — posted a video of himself receiving what appeared to be a Lysol injection, along with a message of thanks to the American president.

"Perfect Vaccine for Perfect Creation One!" he wrote. "Monster PCO is definitely NOT HUMAN!!"

Weary of the hollow sound that came from wrestlers hitting the mat in a vacant venue, AEW was the first of the large promotions to assemble an audience. Early on in the pandemic, Tony Khan had been watching *The Tonight Show* on NBC and was impressed with how host Jimmy Fallon encouraged his band to react to his routines. "They had an atmosphere and it was more intimate," Khan told *Busted Open*. "It still conveyed a lot of excitement, and it was better than having dead air out there."

On AEW shows — *Dynamite*, as well as the company's YouTube program, *AEW Dark*, and pay-per-views — non-participating wrestlers and production staff were stationed at ringside to cheer and heckle. The mood felt spontaneous, like the off-duty performers were enjoying themselves as fans. On television, the energy resembled *NWA Power*'s studio wrestling show, a setting that allowed viewers to sometimes hear spectators' specific comments.

"It's very organic," Brian Pillman Jr. explained to me. "We're wrestlers, but we believe in the product. We're fans of Kenny and Cody and the

Bucks. They're the ones who inspired the revolution that wrestling is going through now."

Even though Daily's Place was an open-air facility, Khan stressed that everyone at ringside had been tested. "It lets you keep the energy without the risk of having people so close to the ring where the people are exposed to people yelling and screaming at them who haven't been tested for corona," he told the *New York Post*.

As the weeks went on, employees of the Jacksonville Jaguars were also invited to fill out the crowd. "There are basically 50 people in the audience," AEW announcer Excalibur told *The Sports Bubble with Jensen Karp* podcast. "They're all spaced out. The way it works is if you are coming backstage . . . whether you are a wrestler, a lighting guy, a pyro guy, a rigger, or catering or security, you get a blood test and temperature check."

While the arrangement was better than what preceded it, Jeff Cobb argued that both television viewers and combatants benefitted from shows in which the audience had no ties to the promotion. "We're trained to react to the crowd, not employees," he said. "The paying fan always ups the game. They're investing their money, and they're the ones with the real emotions."

Reportedly, Vince McMahon was hesitant to create a cheering section at ringside because he did not want to convey the impression that WWE was being irresponsible in the middle of a health emergency. But something was clearly lacking, and, by May, developmental wrestlers who were already training at the Performance Center were told that they were needed to create an environment for the company's broadcasts. The trainees were forbidden to drive to the Performance Center themselves. Instead, they reported to a medical facility for a screening. Once staff determined that there were no signs of the virus, the aspiring wrestlers were transported to the events by bus.

Even though these observers were permitted to sit between matches, they were required to stand — and be loud — once the bell rang. When one factored in the various WWE broadcasts — even when shows like *Raw* and *SmackDown* aired live, other programs were taped for the WWE Network and a number of international partners — the group was sometimes on its feet for more than six hours, losing their voices while reacting to the players between the ropes.

In June, WWE allowed a small number of fans into the Performance Center, primarily friends of the talent, as well as local diehards. They were required to have their temperatures taken and fill out a questionnaire, along with a waiver that is said to have indemnified WWE if they were to contract the virus. But the experiment was discontinued after a trainee tested positive for COVID-19. Reportedly, others associated with the company tested positive as well. Former NWA World Heavyweight champion Adam Pearce — an on-screen authority figure on *Raw* and *SmackDown* — backstage producer Jamie Noble and interviewer Kayla Braxton were among those who said they came down with the coronavirus.

It was Braxton's second bout with the illness. "YOU CAN GET COVID-19 MORE THAN ONCE!" she tweeted. "I had it back in early March and then thought I was invincible after I recovered. Not true. Don't be dumb like me."

Fears over contagion forced WWE to air a version of *SmackDown* with a limited roster on June 26. To make up for time, the company showed the Boneyard Match from *WrestleMania 36*, along with clips of talent commenting on the Undertaker's career.

The outbreak led to a number of policy changes within the company. The day before every taping, wrestlers were now obliged to report to the parking garage for a nasal swab. Only when they tested negative were they given their plans for the following day's show.

The eruption triggered a strong reaction in Kevin Owens. His wife had recently lost her grandfather to the disease, and she was uncomfortable with her husband possibly jeopardizing the family's health. Owens took a sabbatical from WWE. Upon returning, he expressed his concerns to Vince McMahon.

Most notably, the former WWE Universal champion believed that the company was not enforcing mask-wearing. Owens recalled once being fined for cursing on television, and never repeating the mistake. If McMahon told the wrestlers that they had to do something, Owens said, the talent would listen.

Almost immediately, McMahon issued an edict. Masks had to be worn whenever a performer was off-camera. A $500 fine would be issued to anyone ignoring the decree. For a second violation, the fee went up to $1,000.

The decision left Owens confident that the company was willing to evolve with the changing landscape. And this didn't just apply to safety measures. As it became obvious that the coronavirus wasn't going to fade within the next few months, WWE began incorporating ascending rows of virtual fans live streamed on video walls.

For NXT, the Performance Center was remodeled and rebranded the Capitol Wrestling Center — a tribute to the forerunner of the World Wide Wrestling Federation, the Capitol Wrestling Corporation, founded by Jess McMahon and Toots Mondt prior to its first card in 1953. By October, when the refurbished venue debuted, the company was able to supplement the virtual fans with 100 masked attendees, all of whom passed a COVID test the day before.

On *SummerSlam* weekend, WWE began what it called an "extended residency" at Orlando's Amway Center, the home of the NBA's Orlando Magic, for *Raw*, *SmackDown* and pay-per-view events. Although other sports leagues had performed in front of limited audiences or cutouts of fans, the WWE ThunderDome set the tone for COVID-era shows — the way the World Wrestling Federation popularized pay-per-view in the 1980s.

WWE emphasized that the virtual fans at the ThunderDome — named for the 1985 movie *Mad Max Beyond Thunderdome* — would not be seen on flat boards. Instead, their faces appeared on close to 1,000 LED screens in an effort to replicate the arena experience. The project was coordinated with The Famous Group (TFG), which had previously provided virtual audiences for the NFL.

"We can now do things production-wise that we could never otherwise do," WWE's executive producer Kevin Dunn told *Sports Illustrated*. "We're flying drones in the arena. We are putting a roof inside the Amway Center and we'll be able to project content onto the roof. So when a big star like Drew McIntyre comes down to the ring, the whole arena will turn into his content with lasers, pyro, smoke, projections on the top of the building and on the floor." Dunn described the entrance as even "better than *WrestleMania*."

While the coronavirus might have allowed the company to cut back on the rigors of touring, the ThunderDome presented different challenges. Along with the 21 production trucks required to transport a typical touring set, eight more loads of rigging and truss were needed, along with seven of video gear, five of lighting equipment, and one for special effects paraphernalia and more than 6,100 pieces of pyrotechnics. Six tractor trailers were used to ship the 32 projectors lining the arena floor and a fabric ceiling that was 100 feet in diameter.

"It's an expensive venture but I think the dividend is well worth it because we're helping move to some type of normalcy," WWE's senior vice president of event technical operations, Duncan Leslie, told *The Wrap*.

Fans were able to register for their virtual seats at a ThunderDome website, as well as WWE's pages on Facebook, Twitter and Instagram. While no one told the spectators specifically to cheer the babyfaces and boo the heels, event coordinators encouraged the audience to be animated in front of the cameras. Hence, the glut of thumbs down gestures when something villainous occurred. The most energetic fans were rotated into the first row throughout the broadcasts.

Signs and t-shirts were permitted so long as they pertained to the product.

From time to time, the production team would supplement whatever noise observers were making with canned effects. Initially, some pundits noted that the audio didn't always correspond with what was transpiring in the ring. The issue was obviously not lost on WWE. As I said during a podcast to promote *Too Sweet: Inside the Indie Wrestling Revolution*, "If *we're* talking about it, *they're* talking about it." Each week, the sound was tweaked a bit more — to the point that the piped-in noise could be mistaken for authentic heat.

To add to the ambiance, virtual fans from *Raw* and *SmackDown* were inserted into the WWE's other programs.

As always, WWE tried to leave little to chance. Obscene gestures were banned. But so were the flags of Hong Kong, Taiwan and Tibet, an effort, most likely, to appease China, the United States' third-largest trading partner and a place where the company once sent a Mandarin-speaking John Cena to promote the brand.

Insubordinate fans were dealt with harshly. During *SummerSlam*, a spectator managed to display a photo of Chris Benoit, whose murder-suicide case continued to be a painful subject behind the scenes. On a *Raw* broadcast, another watcher showed off an image from a Ku Klux Klan rally. Both offenders were booted from the live stream and, according to the company, banished from future events.

In a more innocent gesture, a fan tried tweaking the organization by exhibiting a photo of Kenny Omega. Few were as amused as Omega himself. "I was just trying to have a good time," he joked on Twitter. "I honestly didn't think anyone would notice."

Still, these were minor incidents. The ThunderDome met WWE's objective of achieving a big sports vibe. There were detractors, obviously. In an interview with F4WOnline.com, Jon Moxley called the innovation "dystopian," claiming he was "tripped out" by what he compared to a "Zoom call with all the faces on the wall."

But, as with AEW's Stadium Stampede, there was the suggestion that the ThunderDome would remain a fixture in the wrestling business even after the risk from COVID was addressed — further evidence that, in a crisis, necessity could truly be the mother of invention.

"The technology will still be available to us," Duncan Leslie said in *The Wrap*. "We developed it, we planned for it, we executed it and now, it's up to creative to decide how they want to implement it in the long-term."

CHAPTER 10

DESPITE THE GENERAL enthusiasm for COVID-era improvisations, the feeling at WWE was that no one there was in position to take a victory lap. The world had changed, the future was ambiguous, and the company knew that it could not continue the way it had. Construction of WWE's new corporate headquarters was halted, at least for the time being, and on April 15, Vince McMahon convened employees for a conference call to warn that cutbacks were coming.

"Given the uncertainty of the situation, the company also identified headcount reductions and made the decision to furlough a portion of its workforce, effective immediately," WWE said in a statement to investors. "The decision to furlough versus permanent [terminations] reflects that the company believes the furlough will be temporary in nature."

According to WWE, the actions would save the organization an estimated $4 million monthly.

Even before the pandemic, kayfabe info leaked from the WWE dressing room like the geysers in Yellowstone National Park. Despite proclamations about the evil emanating from wrestling's fourth estate — the dreaded dirt sheets — there were certain insiders who couldn't get a good night's sleep without a post-midnight call to *Wrestling Observer* founder Dave Meltzer. So while Vince was still addressing his employees, fans were practically following along in real time.

Telephone. Telegraph. Tell a wrestler.

When the decision was finally made, the names came in a flurry. In NXT and the Performance Center, 20 people were either cut or furloughed, including Deonna Purrazzo, a veteran of promotions like

Impact and Ring of Honor who'd reached the quarterfinals of the Mae Young Classic women's tournament and appeared on *Raw*; Kassius Ohno, who, under the name Chris Hero, had been a star on the indies; and Serena Deeb, a training facility coach who still sparkled between the ropes. Listed among the producers — formerly known backstage as "agents" — who helped the wrestlers lay out their matches, were WWE Hall of Famer Kurt Angle, David "Fit" Finlay, Sarah "Sarita" Stock, Shane "Hurricane" Helms, Scott Armstrong and Mike "Irwin R. Schyster" Rotunda — father of "The Fiend" Bray Wyatt. TV director Kerwin Silfies, a popular figure backstage whose tenure with the company dated to 1985, was also furloughed.

On the main roster, Rusev, Luke Gallows, Karl Anderson, Curt Hawkins, Heath Slater, Eric Young, EC3, Lio Rush, Erick Rowan, Sarah Logan, Mike and Maria Kanellis, Drake Maverick and Zack Ryder were shelved.

"Sometimes you fall out of favor and it's nothing that you did or didn't do," Young told *Busted Open* of the WWE power structure. He described an environment in which there was "no creativity. They want everyone to do things the same and be the same and bump the same and sell the same. And there's millions of rules, the secret rules. Those change daily, and it's really hard to understand what's going on and why it's going on. The system is flawed and . . . I would say that to Vince himself."

Levis Valenzuela Jr., who portrayed No Way Jose, a merry character who came to the ring on a conga line, had just wrestled Bobby Lashley two days earlier. When the initial cuts were announced, he was texting friends in WWE, assuming that no other names were in peril. "We're talking about how bummed out we are that those people were released," he told *Inside the Ropes*. "And then minutes later, two or three more names get added. And we're like, 'Oh shit.' Then, 15 minutes later, two more names get added. And we're like, 'Ohhh.' They just keep going. It's continuous."

He was preparing for his workout when he received a call from the company's head of talent relations, Mark Carano.

"You calling me because you love me, brother?" the wrestler joked.

In a serious tone, Carano responded, "You know why I'm calling."

Noted Valenzuela, "You could tell it was tough for him to make those calls. At least it appeared to be."

But it was even tougher for the man who'd been performing as No Way Jose. "Didn't even see it coming . . . Blindsided the hell out of me. I was there Monday and gone Wednesday morning, man. Wow."

Another casualty was the company's longest-serving referee, Mike Chioda, who'd joined WWE in 1989. On his *Monday Mailbag with Mike Chioda* podcast, he maintained that, for more than 30 years, he'd enjoyed the "loyalty" of the McMahon family. "I don't know where the loyalty went at this point, but it is very disappointing . . . It breaks my heart a little bit." He said that, if asked, he would have been willing to retire from the ring and done whatever the company requested, whether it was training other referees or "mopping floors."

Having had so many pleasant exchanges with Vince McMahon over the years, Chioda found it difficult to imagine that the order came from him.

By the end of the month, there were more cutbacks: Cain Velasquez, a two-time UFC Heavyweight champion who'd won his first MMA title by beating Brock Lesnar but seemed to falter in WWE after a knee injury, and third generation wrestler Curtis Axel, son of the late Curt "Mr. Perfect" Hennig.

In November, during another round of releases, Tony Chimel, who'd been a ring announcer on *SmackDown* and oversaw the ring crew, and Derek Casselman, who directed merchandise sales at the various arenas, were also let go. Each was known for adding to the levity backstage; the crew-cutted, round-faced Casselman was renowned for contorting his features like a jack-o'-lantern in photos taken in front of international landmarks — and had been with WWE for more than a quarter century.

"It's all in the name of 'we're a publicly traded company,'" AEW announcer Jim Ross, WWE's former executive vice president of talent relations, said on his *Grilling JR* podcast. "Just because you're a publicly traded company doesn't mean you can treat people like shit . . . You still have to be a people company. They were loyal. They did their jobs very well."

Some theorized that, in the pandemic, WWE had no choice but to cut its payroll after stacking the company with names it didn't want to see in AEW. "If they had done something with me, then that would have been fine," Purrazzo told the *Wrestling Inc. Daily* podcast. "But I feel that in the last year . . . with AEW, [WWE] tended to be hoarding. Talent wasn't being released, but so much talent was being brought in." Her creative suggestions, she said, "fell on deaf ears because the attention wasn't for me to be a superstar. It was just to maybe take me off the table."

Gallows and Anderson were not even eight months into a five-year deal, and, after the roles they'd played in the Boneyard Match, each assumed he was secure. Because of his genuine friendship with the pair, AJ Styles would later express regret about not being able to telegraph and prevent their firing. But less than a week after their dismissal, the team appeared to have moved on, focusing on the expiration of the 90-day non-compete clause in their contracts.

Tweeted Anderson, "85 Days 15 Hours 18 Minutes . . ."

Slater seemed to leave WWE under the best of terms, even appearing on an episode of *Raw* after his release, getting squashed by old tag team partner Drew McIntyre, then embracing him in the ring. Like Gallows and Anderson, though, he'd begun looking beyond WWE.

"I was burnt the hell out," he told the *Chasing Glory* podcast. "I knew it. My family knew it. My co-workers knew it . . . It's one of those things where you're putting everyone over [losing] for 10 years, and it can take a toll on somebody. You know, confidence, your drive, all of that."

Now, he dared to visualize himself in an environment where his job description didn't include getting regularly buried on television. "I've never been to any other federation . . . There are so many cool things out there that you can do. That's what excites me . . . This is like a new journey for me."

Ultimately, he became one of the first released WWE names to land in Impact.

Although TNA's original purpose had been competing with WWE in the years after the corporation absorbed both WCW and ECW, the promotion struggled creatively and financially and regularly appeared to be on the brink of going under. In 2017, Anthem Sports & Entertainment, a Toronto-based broadcasting and production company, purchased a majority stake and rebranded the promotion Impact Wrestling. By 2019, much of the old regime was gone. Anthem now had controlling interest of Impact and began airing the group's show on its AXS television network every Tuesday night.

CEO Leonard Asper grew up watching the American Wrestling Association (AWA) in his native Winnipeg before the World Wrestling Federation swiped its top talent — including Hulk Hogan, Jesse "The Body" Ventura, announcer "Mean" Gene Okerlund and "Dr. D" David Schultz, who subsequently got into a bit of trouble for slapping a TV reporter on-air for using the term "fake" and challenging Mr. T to a shoot amidst the excitement leading up to the premier *WrestleMania*. "You have a company run by a big wrestling fan who also happens to own his own network," said Tommy Dreamer, who became a member of the Impact creative team in 2019. "And Impact Wrestling is the most watched show on that network."

Using a baseball analogy, he compared the promotion to the Tampa Bay Rays — whose home stadium would later host the ThunderDome — and WWE to the Yankees. "We have a hard-working roster. We have history. We have credibility. We're not going to have *WrestleMania*, but we can blow away WWE sometimes, just like Tampa Bay can beat the Yankees."

In fact, a few months after our conversation, the Tampa Bay Rays would end the COVID-shortened season as the American League Champions, losing the 2020 World Series four games to two to the Los Angeles Dodgers.

In April, the pandemic forced Impact to postpone its *Rebellion* pay-per-view in New York City and reschedule the event as two separate broadcasts taped later in the month on a closed set at Skyway Studios in Nashville. Nine weeks of television would also be recorded during that period.

With the airlines still figuring out how to transport passengers in a tightly packed, sealed space, Dreamer opted to drive 15 hours from New York to the tapings. "Fifteen hours is a long-ass haul. You'd pull over at a gas station, and no one's there. It was like paying your dues in the business all over again."

Not every member of the roster could make it. Some were on the West Coast and unwilling to make the drive. One performer was in Mexico and apparently unsure of the border restrictions. But the show had to go on. "We made some phone calls to fill the holes," Dreamer recalled. As a result, performers like Kimber Lee, Crazzy Steve and Tasha Steelz all ended up with Impact contracts.

Lee told me that her final bout before the shutdown was on February 27 in Pomona, California, for Joey Ryan's Bar Wrestling promotion. She'd had a satisfying match, losing to accomplished Taya Valkyrie, a former Impact Knockouts — or women's — titlist, who went into 2020 as the AAA Reina de Reinas (Queens of Queens) champion. "Then, the carpet got pulled," Lee remembered.

At the same time that wrestling shows were being cancelled, restaurants were also shut down. That meant that Lee no longer had the bartender's gig she was using to support herself between bookings. "Not only did I lose my wrestling, I lost my real life."

Trying to take advantage of the down time, she registered for an online class to become a veterinary technician.

Then she received the call from Impact.

From her home in Dayton, she drove to Nashville, making it to the tapings in just under five hours. "I did what they asked," she said. "If they wanted me to lose, I didn't care. That's not wrestling to me. It's the story, the emotion — how we get you there."

When she was invited to the next set of tapings, she suspected that she might become a regular. "I told myself, 'Let me ride this as long as I can.'" By the summer, she was an official member of the roster.

Trey Miguel had crossed paths with Kimber Lee often. He'd been on the same Bar Wrestling show in February. In 2018, he started at Impact, initially as enhancement talent — losing to the more established personalities. But opportunities abounded. Soon, he was a contender for the X Division Championship — the promotion's cruiserweight title — and member of a high-flying trio called The Rascalz with Dezmond Xavier and Zachary Wentz. Just before the pandemic, he saw a future that involved finally winning the X Division belt and defending it on indie cards on the weekends.

After the shutdowns began, he found himself locked in his home, rewatching his old matches and analyzing what he could have done better. "I began retraining myself," he told me.

When he finally was invited back to Impact, he tried finding inspiration in the empty arena. "The only way to do that was thinking about the fans at home, what they wanted to see. It was almost like a new sport without the bells and whistles. In the locker room, we'd give each other pep talks, talking about feeding to the camera like you'd feed to the crowd. At every taping, you'd think, 'What's going to happen next in this world? Are we ever all going to be together again?' So when you were at the arena, you treated the time sweetly, letting wrestling be your therapy and escape from all the things that bother you in the real world."

Yet, he periodically asked himself whether he'd ever perform in front of a capacity crowd again. "That's sad because fan interaction is what saves you on a bad night. But we knew the fans were out there, and we couldn't forget that. They were watching us, just in a different way."

One by one, more former WWE performers were joining him in Impact. Deonna Purrazzo arrived in May, branding herself The Virtuosa. Gallows and Anderson — now referred to as The Good Brothers — signed a deal that would reportedly allow them to appear in New Japan after restrictions were lifted. In early July, they posted a video with their former Bullet Club partners, the Young Bucks, suggesting that The Good Brothers' arrangement would also allow them to wrestle in AEW.

Outside activities notwithstanding, Impact heavily invested in the tandem. In November, at the *Turning Point* pay-per-view, The Good Brothers defeated The North ("All Ego" Ethan Page and Josh Alexander) for the Impact World Tag Team Championship.

The time when the company was seen as a viable adversary to WWE had long receded. Nonetheless, with a surplus of former WWE athletes suddenly available, a message was being sent that, while Impact could never compete with WWE in terms of marketability or reach, it might be a place where certain talent might capture the fulfillment that evaded them in Stamford.

"When you're getting pushed, WWE is the happiest place to be in the world," Dreamer explained. "When you're not, it's the worst."

July's *Slammiversary* pay-per-view featured the former Heath Slater — now simply going by his legal first name, Heath — and The Good Brothers, along with Eric Young and EC3 — both of whom had held the TNA World Heavyweight Championship before migrating to what they thought were the greener pastures of NXT. Purrazzo challenged Jordynne Grace for the Knockouts title and captured it with a double armbar.

As Dreamer watched the show, he found himself relating to the talent. "When I left WWE in 2009, I left a large contract on the table," he said. "I did it because I was no longer happy, and I went to Impact because I thought I had something to prove. Well, all these people you saw on *Slammiversary* had something to prove. And, that night, 'Slammiversary' was trending right in the middle of the pandemic."

On the next Impact broadcast, the WWE refugees were joined by Brian Myers, who'd been Curt Hawkins in WWE during two stints totaling 12 years. On Twitter, he referenced the *WrestleMania 24* moment in which Shawn Michaels expressed his admiration for Ric Flair before retiring him from WWE with a foot to the jaw: "@VinceMcMahon I'm sorry, I love you. *superkick."

Despite the dearth of spectators in the building, Impact was embarking on a period of high morale. In September, Eric Young defeated Eddie Edwards to win a third World Championship with the promotion — more evidence, he believed, that Vince McMahon had miscalculated his abilities.

"I'm definitely not the first person that he's made a mistake on, and I won't be the last that he's made a mistake on," he said in his *Busted Open* interview. "Unfortunately, for a lot of people there, a lot of creative people and a lot of really talented people, they're never going to be able to fully do what they can do because of the way the system is organized. It's sad . . . But now, I can say I can smile because I don't have to deal with that anymore."

In Jacksonville, Tony Khan was also keeping track of available talent. In addition to filling out cards — particularly *AEW Dark* on YouTube — with indie performers who needed the income, Khan was perusing the names released by WWE and analyzing which could be brought in to generate a buzz.

Zack Ryder had been one of the first wrestlers to launch a YouTube series. In 2011, he declared himself "WWE Internet Champion" — showcasing a children's replica belt adorned with stickers — and developed a cult following. Although his career ebbed and flowed in WWE, he managed to procure the company's Intercontinental, United States and *Raw* Tag Team Championships. Even when the man who'd proclaimed himself "Long Island Iced Z" saw his television time shrinking, he always received on ovation from those fans who appreciated his originality.

Behind the scenes, he'd developed a close friendship with Cody Rhodes over their shared love of theme parks.

So it made perfect sense that when Cody was being manhandled by the Dark Order after a television victory that Ryder — now using his real name, Matt Cardona — rushed to the rescue. The two would then join Scorpio Sky in a six-man tag team match against the Dark Order at September's *All Out* pay-per-view.

That same month, Rusev — now billing himself as Miro (the Bulgarian Brute's birth name was Miroslav Barnyashev) — arrived on *Dynamite* as Kip Sabian's backup. Miro — whose push in WWE dithered even after partner Aiden English drew intrigue to the character by singing a tune about an eternal holiday called "Rusev Day" — then took the mic and ranted about the "brass ring" WWE performers were expected to grab to secure a top position.

"You can take that brass ring and shove it up your ass," he spat. He ended the promo by asserting, "My name is Miro, and I'm All Elite."

In a YouTube video released a few hours later, he disclosed, "I absolutely meant every word of that promo. For 10 years, I was constantly told about an imaginary brass ring that I already told you what to do with. This was not a promo, but my actual feelings."

AJ Styles was among the WWE stars openly praising Miro's move to the upstart promotion. "Listen, this is a business we're all in," Styles said on his Twitch stream. "As a wrestler, you have to go where the business takes you . . . It doesn't matter what promotion in the world. There is no good or bad thing here."

When Styles's son, who also appeared in the video, questioned why Miro's wife, Lana — also known as CJ Perry — chose to remain with WWE, AJ answered, "Because it's a job. Why can't two married people work in separate places? Your husband works at Pepsi and you work at Coke. It is what it is. It's not the first time that this has happened, and it won't be the last."

In WWE, Lana was enduring her own challenges. For much of the fall, she would be involved in a plot that had Nia Jax putting her through a table every week. In June 2021, she was deep-sixed as the cost-cutting bacchanalia continued.

Even referee Mike Chioda ended up in AEW, exciting the fans at home when he appeared in August to officiate Cody Rhodes's TNT Championship — a secondary AEW title, named for the cable network that carried *Dynamite* — defense against Scorpio Sky.

About a week after WWE announced its first round of layoffs in April, fans learned that 73-year-old Gerald Brisco had also been let go.

Brisco's fingerprints were all over the pro wrestling landscape. The Hall of Famer had been with the company since 1984, when he and his brother, former NWA World Heavyweight champion Jack Brisco, sold their shares in the Georgia territory to Vince McMahon as he expanded around the United States. Brisco was also credited with discovering a young Hulk Hogan while he was playing bass in Tampa barrooms and directing him to Florida promoter Eddie Graham and trainer Hiro Matsuda. In WWE, after his in-ring career ended, Brisco, a former amateur standout at Oklahoma State University, became one of the company's most prolific scouts, recruiting Kurt Angle and Brock Lesnar, among others.

He and Pat Patterson had portrayed themselves as McMahon's "stooges" in some of the more comical skits of the Attitude Era.

At first, observers wondered if Brisco would be brought back when the coronavirus passed, and he was free to travel to college tournaments again. As the months went on, the company found positions for producers like Fit Finlay — who'd coached many of the female performers — and Hurricane Helms. But in September, McMahon phoned his longtime employee and respectfully informed him that, while his contributions to the growth of WWE would not be forgotten, he no longer had a job.

I admit to feeling some sadness about the situation. During the more than two decades I wrote for WWE's publications, Brisco was a fount of insider information — not about the company itself, but the carny traits that promoters exhibited when he was barnstorming in the territory days. While I was co-authoring Ric Flair's autobiography and including quotes from associates who could add richness to the story, it was Brisco who put me in touch with Jim Barnett.

Few people knew more about the inner machinations of the business, and had more secrets, than Barnett. An effeminate gay man in a macho, homophobic business, Barnett used his cunning to manipulate and punish enemies, as well as friends. He'd been in the industry since the advent of television, working with promoter Fred Kohler on his Chicago-based *Wrestling from Marigold* program — seen nationally on the DuMont Television Network — starting in 1949. In 1964, he and Johnny Doyle were responsible for the 10-year pro-wrestling boom in Australia, where he named his group World Championship Wrestling (WCW) — later importing the acronym back to the U.S., where it gained a great deal more infamy. Although his homosexuality dissuaded his fellow promoters from electing him NWA president, Barnett controlled the bookings of the NWA Worlds Heavyweight Championship, a very important job at the time, since it significantly raised the proceeds for whoever was featuring the champ on top. But he was a master at working both sides of the street. When the Briscos sold their Georgia shares to McMahon, Barnett was right there with them, trading his portion as well. He worked with Vince through the first three *WrestleMania*s, then returned to the NWA as Jim Crockett was selling out to Ted Turner. After WWE won the battle with WCW, Barnett survived yet again, taking a job with the McMahons as a consultant.

He was also apparently involved in a sex scandal that included Rock Hudson and the University of Kentucky football team.

I couldn't wait to talk to Barnett — on the record and off — and learn things that were so kayfabe, I probably wouldn't even repeat them to myself.

But when I phoned, he treated me like a mark who wanted to know if Baron Mikel Scicluna really *was* from the Isle of Malta — despite my repeated reminders that I was Ric Flair's co-author and Gerald Brisco had asked me to call.

"Well, you know, Jim," Brisco later said laughingly in his Oklahoma drawl, "he's old school."

To this day, I still hypothesize about the unseemly things Barnett might have revealed.

"Mah boy . . ."

There did appear to be one happy ending to the WWE cutbacks story. Even after his release, Drake Maverick continued to appear on NXT, cutting emotional promos, pledging to work so hard that, in the end, WWE would have no choice but to keep him. He made it through the NXT Cruiserweight Championship tournament until losing the final to El Hijo del Fantasma. But it didn't seem to matter because, as soon as the match was over, Triple H presented Maverick with a new contract.

Whether the whole thing was a work, designed to play off popular disillusionment over the layoffs, or an authentic example of a performer grabbing the brass ring is a question I don't have the knowledge to answer. All I know is that it felt pretty good to watch the show sign off with Maverick proudly holding up the contract.

Unless you were Lio Rush, who hinted at retiring from the squared circle after WWE clipped him. On Twitter, he called the storyline a "slap in the face" to everyone who lost their jobs, and he expressed a desire to time travel back to his childhood "just staring at the bright lights on the TV screen being a fan. Instead of being so self-aware of corporate."

He made it clear that he did not blame Spud — the character Maverick played in TNA. The scorn, he said, was entirely reserved for WWE and an angle he perceived as nothing less than "disgusting."

Maverick's good fortune with WWE lasted all the way to November 2021, when he was seemingly sacked for good.

CHAPTER 11

DURING THE FIRST weekend of May, I was asked to participate in an unprecedented event.

Since I never uncovered any evidence to the contrary, I'm going to say that it was the first virtual wrestling convention. Even though "Wrestling Bookmarks Covid-Con" had a nice complement of grappling names — including Sid Justice, Fred "Typhoon" Ottman, the Blue Meanie, Sabu, Koko B. Ware, "The Genius" Lanny Poffo, Hornswoggle, Dutch Mantel, Al Snow, Bushwacker Luke and Diamond Dallas Page — the primary focus was on wrestling authors. Pat Laprade and Bertrand Hébert, who'd recently completed their comprehensive Andre the Giant biography, were among the 60 guests, as well as Bill Apter, the iconic wrestling magazine columnist and photographer; Greg Oliver, the man responsible for profiling every great Canadian wrestler in a single book; Memphis territory historian Mark James; Dick the Bruiser biographer Richard Vicek; and Gernot Freiberger, who plied us with tales about the old Catch Wrestling Association (CWA) in his native Austria.

"The idea was a show for wrestling fans who were marks for books," said Kenny Casanova, co-author of the Kamala, Sabu, Vader, Tito Santana and Brutus Beefcake autobiographies, who organized Covid-Con with John Cosper, whose works include *Eat Sleep Wrestle*. "That's why it was called 'Book*marks*. It was like a *Royal Rumble*, except every 30 minutes, someone new came in."

The weekend started with a dress rehearsal on Friday night to make sure all the technology worked. "In addition to social media, we were also on FITE TV," Casanova explained. "So we couldn't be too indie." There were guests who were only available that night, but others — including myself — stopped by for what Casanova called "run-ins."

While my official segment was over by 10 the next morning, I hung around, taking in the remainder of Covid-Con until late Sunday night.

"I thought people would watch for a little while and leave," Casanova told me. "I didn't think they'd stay with us all weekend. I guess we touched on a concept that really needed to be out there."

The son of a Salvation Army minister, Casanova grew up in Haverhill, Massachusetts, schooled on the concept that the better you are on the stick, the bigger the house. Some of his early memories included watching Chief Jay Strongbow, Baron Mikel Scicluna, Mr. Fuji and a young babyface named Ted DiBiase warring at New England house shows. "I don't really remember there being any kind of security. There was a string tied between two poles to hold the fans back, not even a barrier."

At age 14, he attended a taping of the NBC special *Saturday Night's Main Event* in Providence, Rhode Island, and ended up tussling with a group of fans trying to grab a shred of Hulk Hogan's discarded t-shirt. "I still have it, so I became a huge Hogan mark after that."

He was living in Binghamton, New York, two years later when he heard about "Captain" Lou Albano appearing at a charity card with some former names from the World Wrestling Federation and AWA. Casanova volunteered to assist, selling tickets and carrying the combatants' robes back to the dressing room. As a reward, he ended up at a table with the Manager of Champions later that night, eating chicken wings.

Once you get that close to the business, you always need a little more.

As an English literature major at the State University of New York (SUNY) in Albany, Casanova would turn up at the Knickerbocker Arena, devising various ways to shift the limelight to himself. The most successful method was creating signs that heaped praise on peripheral personalities like ring announcer Bill Dunn and referee Tim White. The routine worked — both guys enjoyed looking out into the audience and seeing their names — and Casanova got in a little closer. Soon, he was training at a wrestling school in Elmira, New York, and working as a manager at small indies, playing off his other job as a wedding deejay by singing bad karaoke. When the babyfaces went after him, "I was told my bumps were too crisp. So I started bumping sloppy like Bobby Heenan."

But Kenny also knew how to write. And after his books started getting published, he figured out other ways to ingratiate himself to talent, arranging podcast appearances and designing websites. He respected the business, and past and present wrestlers tended to be happy to hear from him. So when John Cosper was first conceptualizing Covid-Con, he knew the guy to approach.

In early April, while cruise ships with critically ill passengers were stranded off the coast of Florida and health officials despaired over the shortage of medical-grade masks for hospital workers, Cosper sent Casanova a link to a virtual college fair on Zoom. "You think we could do something like this, but with wrestling?" he asked.

Casanova decided to pattern Covid-Con after a live streaming event previously presented by Suicide Girls, a nude pin-up site. "Each girl would be on for a limited amount of time, and their fans would wait around all day to talk to them live," he said.

Generally, the wrestling authors began an appearance by going one-on-one with a host via split screen. But there would also be panel discussions for guests to catch up with each other — Greg Oliver and I reminisced about a flight I once missed after talking wrestling and drinking bourbon on his porch — and answer questions from fans.

Although the event was free, everyone was invited to hawk his or her merchandise.

Naturally, there were glitches. Some of the guests were confused about the time they were supposed to appear. Broadband issues affected transmission from time to time. At one stage, Kamala the Ugandan Giant popped up, but fans were unable to hear him. But "The Wild Eyed Southern Boy" Tracy Smothers's spot went smoothly.

On the indies — performing as a heel in an anachronistic outfit bearing the emblem of the Confederate flag — Smothers would threaten to commit "ultra mega mass homicide" if anyone in the crowd dared to shout, "Tracy sucks."

He'd also characterize himself as a thug: "T is for terrible. H is for hell. U is for ugly. And G is for jail — because a thug can't spell."

Now, despite several recent rounds of chemotherapy, he reported feeling much better.

Viewers were grateful for the opportunity to exchange a few words with him, hear his wrestling philosophy and listen to his stories. He still had his smile and his spark. Smothers was fading, but he wasn't going to tap that easily.

He hung around for another six months. In October, I was signing copies of *Too Sweet: Inside the Indie Wrestling Revolution* in a socially distanced setting — readers were lined up in the street and admitted one or two at a time — at the Wrestling Universe store in Queens. Smothers was supposed to be there, too, but cancelled because he felt too sick.

He lost his battle with lymphoma in November.

Kamala had passed three months earlier from COVID-19.

On the May 11 edition of *Monday Night Raw*, a tearful Becky Lynch relinquished her WWE *Raw* Women's Championship to recent *Money in the Bank* winner Asuka. Throughout her time in WWE, Lynch had fallen in love with Seth Rollins — as a shoot, not a work. Now, she and the Monday Night Messiah were engaged and expecting a baby. "You go be a warrior," she told Asuka, "cause I'm going to be a mother."

She was one of two top female stars about to step away from WWE. At *NXT TakeOver: In Your House* in June, Charlotte Flair's 63-day NXT women's title reign came to an end when Io Shirai emerged with the gold following a Triple Threat match that also included Rhea Ripley. Following the loss, Flair disclosed that she was taking time off to undergo surgery.

In the past, female competitors had been cautious about admitting that they'd had breast implants. But as the daughter of "Nature Boy" Ric Flair, Charlotte viewed herself as an entertainer as much as an athlete, and cosmetic enhancements — like a beautiful ring robe — were part of the presentation. Like her father, who could be his own worst critic, Flair believed in being open with her fans about both her strengths and her challenges.

After *WrestleMania 34*, Flair needed medical attention after falling ill, and learned that she was experiencing silicone poisoning. "My implant had been leaking for quite some time," she wrote on Twitter. "It was one of the worst cases the doctor had seen."

She underwent surgery and believed that the matter was resolved until 2020. "Something felt off," she said, "so I went back to the doctor. Same issue again." She agreed to another procedure "even though the recovery period is a little longer than I would like."

She was written off television with an arm injury said to be sustained in an altercation with Nia Jax.

Fortunately, the level of women's talent in WWE — a roster that included Bayley, Sasha Banks, Alexa Bliss, Tegan Nox, Dakota Kai, Shayna Baszler, Candice LeRae and Shotzi Blackheart, among many others — ran so deep that the company could sustain the absences.

In San Diego, wrestler and promoter Mikey Gordon took a subversive approach to drawing eyes to his product, using social media and an FM radio transmitter to stage clandestine shows in parking lots and industrial parks. Although he deliberately avoided running his safety protocols past local authorities — too many rules hinder creativity, he reasoned — he didn't want to be responsible for anyone catching the coronavirus. As a result, he required most attendees to remain in or around their cars.

When the occasional police cruiser happened by these drive-in shows, Gordon invited the officers to stick around and have a look for themselves. They generally moved on, convinced that, aside from the coarse language, thumbtacks and blood, Mikey was running a pretty innocent scene.

Much of the intrigue in his FIST Combat promotion centered around Gordon's alter-ego, "Dirty" Ron McDonald, who came to the ring in white pancake makeup and a painted smile, and was said to be the illegitimate son of the fast-food chain mascot with a similar name. According to Gordon, Dirty Ron was training to take his father's place, but found the clown shoes just too big to fill. In lieu of entertaining young consumers, Dirty Ron favored drugging and whoring and random acts of violence. After brutalizing a restaurant manager who tried forcing him to adhere to family tradition, the younger McDonald was cut off.

With his life plan in tatters, he gravitated to professional wrestling.

For the person behind the character, that career choice was all but an inevitability.

Gordon's mother was in the business, wrestling under a mask while attending St. Louis University. As Sue Savage, a short, stocky heel, she worked Midwestern indies before taking a more domestic route. "My father was jealous of my mother being around the wrestlers," Gordon explained. "So she decided to play it safe and leave the business."

Still, he grew up being regaled by anecdotes about the Kiel Auditorium and *Wrestling at the Chase*. Every year, the family had a *WrestleMania* party at the house. "I learned a lot about life through wrestling," Gordon said. "Everything we see is a manipulation of emotions. Life is full of getting heat, comebacks, turning heel, turning babyface."

Gordon began training in 2000, when he was still a teenager. "Matt Sydal and myself were the only two 17-year-olds who had wrestling licenses in the state of Missouri." While listening to a wrestling radio show one day, he discovered an indie group called Gateway Championship Wrestling and started appearing on cards with future NWA World Women's Champion MsChif, as well as Daizee Haze and Delirious, who'd eventually become the head booker in ROH.

After a while, he developed a routine: watching *Raw* on Monday, training on Tuesday and Thursday, working for Coliseum Championship Wrestling (CCW) in Evansville, Indiana, on Wednesday, and wrestling for anyone who'd book him on the weekend.

He started FIST — for "Finest Independent Stars Today" — in St. Louis in 2007.

He also worked as a tour manager for Afroman, the rapper best known for his songs "Crazy Rap" and "Because I Got High." The two were at a show in Chico, California, in 2013 when "three different people told me, 'I can get you 50 pounds of weed.' And I thought, 'I think I'm going to stay here.'"

After wrestling for Oakland's Hoodslam promotion — which deliberately melded the mat wars with performance art — he revived FIST in

2015, presenting "21 and up" shows that were heavy on adult content. In 2017, he shifted operations to San Diego, where he began moonlighting as a stand-up comic and shuttling up to L.A. for acting gigs.

His promotional strategy involved finding venues that he didn't have to rent. "In fact, they sometimes give me a percentage of the bar." Prior to the pandemic, FIST appeared at the Pure Platinum strip club, with the dancers performing between matches, the first Friday of every month. Every 30 days or so, the group also set up a ring on the spacious patio at Jammyland, a cocktail bar and Jamaican restaurant in Las Vegas.

Talent included Fruit of the Doom, a Road Warriors rip-off consisting of members Hawkamelon and Bananimal. Among the duo's tactics: smashing watermelons over rivals' heads and encouraging fans to slip on the banana peels tossed onto the floor. The Trash Panda frequently attacked his opponents with various forms of garbage. Congo Crush was listed at more than 500 pounds. "He has bigger boobs than Pam Anderson," Gordon said.

Three days after WHO declared a pandemic, the promotion held its final indoor card: a birthday party. Gordon was meeting an obligation and knew he couldn't push the boundaries for much longer. By the next day, all of FIST's venues were shut down. "As someone who either wrestles or does comedy, there was nothing to do.

"At first, no one wanted to go out. Then, they said they would if there was social distancing. Wrestlers wanted to wrestle, and people wanted to see shows. So I started asking on social media about who was interested in coming to a drive-in wrestling show."

As he promoted his upcoming card, he compared it to classic events like the first *Starcade* and *WrestleMania*, as well as ECW's premier pay-per-view *Barely Legal*: "Greensboro, North Carolina, November 1983. Madison Square Garden, March 1985. Philadelphia, April 1997. May 2020. An undisclosed location, San Diego. Where were you when FISTory was made?"

Fans who expressed interest were sent private messages. It was impressed upon them that this was kayfabe; no one wanted the event closed down before it was even held. Gordon had 25 parking spots available — $80 for the front row, $60 for everywhere else.

On May 16, he used a burner phone to text attendees a secret location to gather for further instructions. Using a friend's FM transmitter, he then told the fans to drive to another parking lot, where a ring was set up.

"You had to be within a mile radius to pick up the signal. I had all the license plate numbers and the make of every car. There was no way a narc was going to get in."

The show started a little late — "lucha time," according to Gordon — and featured six matches. Face coverings with the FIST Combat logo were sold to fans in their cars. Wrestlers, including Curt Stallion, Lucha Daddy, Ryan Kidd and Jheri Gigolo, had their temperatures taken by a nurse. "Some of the guys were scared of the coronavirus. Other wrestlers didn't know if they were going to get arrested."

It took the talent a while to get accustomed to spectators watching them from the other side of a windshield. "You're not going to get the feedback you're used to," Gordon said. "Nobody was in ring shape. But the world could hear us."

More than 10,000 fans watched on live stream.

The group staged four more shows over the next five weeks. "We're not making a political statement," Gordon told me in early June. "We're not protesting against 'stay at home' orders. We're moving forward, trying to get back to life.

"Hopefully, this is the beginning of that."

In late May, a tag team debuted in AEW that instantly altered the tone of its tag team division.

Cash Wheeler and Dax Harwood had been Dash Wilder and Scott Dawson respectively in WWE, where they'd wrestled as The Revival. This was not a name that had been simply stamped on them. As students of classic tag team wrestling, they planned to "revive" the celebrated styles of the past, particularly the repertoire exhibited by their heroes, the Brain Busters, Tully Blanchard and Arn Anderson, a believable tandem who'd held the gold in both the NWA and WWF in the 1980s.

Like Blanchard and Anderson, Wheeler and Harwood took a mat-based approach between the ropes, rather than bedazzling with aerial maneuvers. The point was sending the message that, in a shoot, the pair would prevail. Their motto? "No flips, just fists."

In WWE, the two held the tag team titles on *Raw*, *SmackDown* and NXT. Yet, they'd been seeking to leave the company for some time, citing creative challenges. Their experience, they said, was similar to that of Matt Hardy, who told *PWInsider*, "If you're kind of in Vince's mind in a certain role, that's where he's going to keep you and you can't get out of it."

The relationship had been disintegrating for some time. Although the company was said to be offering a generous raise for the Revival to sign a five-year deal, the partners appeared uninterested. They resented seeing script writers in first class while the wrestlers flew coach. McMahon, they said, was surrounded by a coterie of subordinates who feared his mercurial reactions too much to pass along ideas suggested by talent.

On February 18, they attempted to trademark the "No flips, just fists" slogan. Less than a week later, WWE contacted the United States Patent and Trademark Office to do the very same. On March 8, the duo was pulled from a six-team Elimination Chamber match ultimately won by *SmackDown* tag team champions The Miz and John Morrison.

Finally, on April 10, WWE issued a statement that the Revival "agreed to their immediate release." True to form, the company added, "We wish them all the best in their future endeavors."

Before their departure, McMahon personally apologized to the pair, Harwood told *Inside the Ropes*, "because we had been sending all these pitches in and he had never seen them because the writers were too afraid to approach him."

After the tandem made their AEW debut — by doing a run-in to save then face down the Young Bucks — fans were informed that the unit had adopted the name FTR. The initials stood for a number of refrains, including "Fear the Revolt," "Fear the Revelation" and "Fuck the Rest."

Management seemed to take a personal interest in their latest arrivals. "We get texts from the guys in charge or Tony Khan saying, 'What are you guys thinking for this week?'" Harwood said. "They want the input 'cause they know the talent knows better than anybody else."

Unquestionably, Wheeler and Harwood were being fast-tracked. At *All Out* on September 5, they dethroned Kenny Omega and "Hangman" Adam Page to distinguish themselves as the first tag team to hold championships in both WWE and AEW — a historical homage, some would argue, to their heroes the Brain Busters.

CHAPTER 12

STARTING WITH THE passing of David Von Erich in 1984, there was a new, tragic element to wrestling fandom. Sooner or later, it seemed, someone you admired would die early. Much of this had to do with the cocktail of performance enhancing and recreational drugs wrestlers abused — and a lifestyle that encouraged talent to ignore concussions and other injuries while pushing themselves in ways that defied the human condition. In recent years, starting with the implementation of WWE's wellness policy in 2006, the trend reversed. Still, wrestlers remained public figures, with all the pressures that status entailed, and there was neither a study nor a program that could fully insulate the industry from misfortune.

On May 17, Shad Gaspard and his 10-year-old son, Aryeh, were swimming near Venice Beach in Los Angeles. Gaspard, 39, and partner JTG had been part of WWE's Cryme Tyme tag team between 2006 and 2008. Even after the duo split, he remained with the company for another two years, and maintained friendships with members of the mat fraternity. Away from wrestling, he worked as a stunt man and actor, appearing in the 2015 comedy, *Get Hard* with Will Ferrell and Kevin Hart, and the television show *Key & Peele*.

In the ocean, Gaspard and his son were among a group of swimmers caught in a strong rip current. When a lifeguard reached them, the native New Yorker told the rescuer to bring the boy to shore first. According to a witness, a wave then crashed over Gaspard, sweeping him farther out to sea.

He didn't resurface. As the U.S. Coast Guard looked for him, JTG, along with fellow wrestlers Chris Masters and John Morrison, joined the searches. Three days after he disappeared, Gaspard's lifeless body washed onto the beach, close to where he was last seen.

Former governor, bodybuilder and action star Arnold Schwarzenegger posted a photo of himself at a memorial to the fallen wrestler. "He was a hero in bodybuilding," Schwarzenegger wrote, "a hero in wrestling, and the moment he told lifeguards to save his son first, the ultimate hero."

In the early morning hours of May 23, the same week that Gaspard drowned, retired Japanese wrestler and MMA competitor Kyoko Kimura entered her daughter's Tokyo apartment. Inside, 22-year-old Hana Kimura, a multiple titleholder in the Stardom promotion and a reality show star, was dead from an apparent suicide.

Her death came following a bombardment of negative online comments about her performance on the television series *Terrace House: Tokyo*.

Her fame and success notwithstanding, Hana had been bullied for much of her life, due to the fact that her biological father was Indonesian and, according to the inflexible rules of traditional Japanese society, her mixed ethnicity was worthy of scorn.

In 2019, she debuted on the Terrace House series, a franchise begun on Fuji Television in 2012, and streamed overseas on Netlfix with subtitles. The program's promotional material described the arrangement as three women and three men "looking for love while living under the same roof."

Kyoko Kimura said the show incorporated storylines no different than wrestling angles. In one scene, Hana became enraged when her housemate Kai Kobayashi, a professional racewalker, shrunk one of her ring outfits in the washing machine. Had this been a shoot, her anger would have been understandable; the outfit had been worn at *Wrestle Kingdom 14*, in the first women's match in the Tokyo Dome since 2002. But Kyoko said that her daughter told her that the producers had encouraged her to exaggerate her wrath and slap Kobayashi in the face. While Hana wasn't willing to do that, she allegedly agreed to knock the hat off his head.

The backlash from viewers was astonishing. "Nearly 100 frank opinions every day," she wrote in her final tweet. "I couldn't deny they hurt me. 'Die.' 'You are disgusting.' 'You should disappear.'" Along with being characterized as a "gorilla" because of her weightlifting were ethnic slurs due to her half-Indonesian ancestry.

"I believed these things about myself more than they did," she wrote. "My whole life I wanted to be loved."

After a recent rerun of the show, Hana had attempted to slit her wrists. On the day she died, she visited the Stardom office and took photos with her kitten. Then she returned home and ended her life.

In her last Instagram post, she told fans, "Goodbye. I love you, have fun and live a long time. I'm sorry."

Her mother found her on the bed with a plastic bag over her head. A container holding a mixture of toxic chemicals was nearby, along with several suicide notes.

"We are very sorrowful [about] Hana's passing," Stardom said in a statement, "and only wish for her to rest in eternal peace."

The company asked fans to respectfully stay away from Hana's family, as well as Stardom performers, the promotion's offices and the dojo during this period. Reporters were told that any request to interview the group's wrestlers would be denied.

The coronavirus had delayed the *Terrace House* shooting schedule. But after the suicide of Hana Kimura, few were interested in seeing the show continue.

The series was cancelled.

Tokyo police also opened an investigation, sifting through 1,200 disparaging posts directed at Hana from 600 separate accounts, arresting an Osaka man who — under an assumed name — had wished her death. He later apologized to Hana's family and was required to pay a small fine.

Both the ruling Liberal Democratic Party and its main opposition, the Constitutional Democratic Party of Japan, began exploring the possibility of imposing harsher punishments on those convicted of cyberbullying. "It is important for the legislature to play a role to make a society where such incidents do not happen," Hiroshi Moriyama, the Liberal Democratic Party's chief of affairs for the country's Diet — or parliament — told the *Kyodo News*.

Long Island's own Maxwell Jacob Friedman (MJF) used the COVID era to distinguish himself as pro wrestling's most compelling villain since "Rowdy" Roddy Piper.

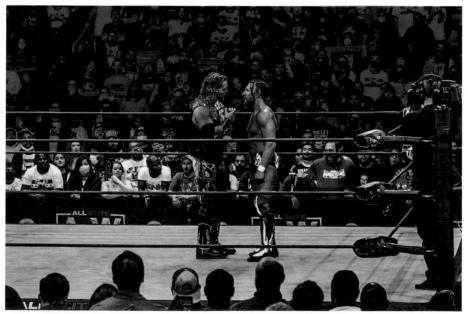

Five months after competing in the main event of *WrestleMania 37*, Bryan Danielson rocked the industry by jumping to All Elite Wrestling (AEW). He soon emerged as the top contender for "Hangman" Adam Page's AEW World Championship.

As COVID restrictions declined, AEW's first traveling show feartured the debut of Malakai Black, who'd dip into his dark past and form a faction called the House of Black.

After a lifetime and career peppered with disappointments, Eddie Kingston (seen here on an AAW Pro show) let his personality guide him to superstardom in AEW.

"I'll cough on you. I came from Florida." During a COVID surge in the Sunshine State, manager Frank the Clown (with protégé Robert "Ego" Anthony) heels it up for the Warrior Wrestling crowd in Chicago Heights.

KC Navarro surveys the outdoor Warrior Wrestling audience, spread into socially distanced pods on the Marian Catholic High School football field.

Lifetime wrestling fan and AEW founder Tony Khan led the assault on WWE by luring away talent, and "opening the forbidden door" to working with other promotions.

After quitting his day job as a nursing assistant, "very nice very evil" Danhausen supported his family through the lockdown by working his gimmick, selling online merch and creating horror/comedy vignettes on Patreon.

As part of Tony Khan's "forbidden door" policy, NWA Women's Champion Thunder Rosa (seen here wrestling Kylie Rae in Warrior Wrestling) began appearing in AEW. She eventually went full-time, winning the AEW Women's World title in 2022.

When the Sinclair Broadcast Group's ownership of Ring of Honor ended, the ROH World Championship was in the proud possession of Jonathan Gresham (seen here stretching Trey Miguel).

Getting the rub. WCW legend and WWE Hall of Famer Sting's 2021 affiliation with Darby Allin in AEW elevated the 27-year-old sensation.

AEW's 2021 signing of CM Punk, after a seven-year hiatus from mat competition, had an explosive impact on the company's war with WWE, culminating in "The Voice of the Voiceless" winning the promotion's championship in May 2022.

Yet another example of the "forbidden door" being breached: Christian Cage was recognized as Impact World Champion while regularly appearing in AEW.

Kenny Omega (left) clings to his AEW World Championship while his confederates in "The Elite" back him up. From left: Don Callis, Nick Jackson, Adam Cole, Matt Jackson.

Referee Kris Levin uses a tape measure to ensure that Jimmy Lloyd (left) and Joey Janela are the requisite six feet from each other at the start of their "social distancing match."

Janela sells a sidekick from six feet away. "In a wrestling match, you're usually trying to make the strikes look believable, but in this case, we had to make everything look fake," noted Lloyd.

Keeping it safe. Masked and enveloped by the sea air, the Game Changer Wrestling (GCW) faithful go wild at a July 2020 card on the Atlantic City boardwalk.

"Bad Boy" Joey Janela shows the wrestling public what it's been missing by launching himself off the roof in Atlantic City onto Lio Rush.

Joey's head comes down hard on the boardwalk planks. "I had to do it," he later enthused. "I needed to get it out of my system."

Sonny Kiss (standing) and Cassandro in a battle of LGBTQ icons at Effy's Big Gay Brunch.
The event, staged in front of a masked, socially distanced crowd in 2020, was part of GCW's
Collective, a combination of indie promotions held over several days at a single location.

Following his victory, Cassandro gratefully
drapes his body around Kiss, as fellow LGBTQ
wrestlers surround the ring and cheer the
performance. Kiss later said it was an honor to
lose to the "exotico," a male Mexican wrestler
with deliberately feminine traits.

The self-professed "sober, queer, punk
rock pro wrestler of your dreams," Effy.

Blake Christian (left) spent part of the COVID era in NXT, where he was rebranded Trey Baxter. Released in late 2021, he blazed back into the indies. Here, he wars with Chris Dickinson.

Jon Moxley pounds former UFC Heavyweight Champion Josh Barnett in the main event of Josh Barnett's Bloodsport, an event patterned after MMA fighting and held at GCW's Collecitve.

EARL GARDNER

"Woo, woo, woo. You know it!" A long way from his days as good-time suburban bro Zack Ryder in WWE, a blood-drenched Matt Cardona (bottom) is about to take a light tube from Nick Gage, en route to winning the GCW World Championship.

EARL GARDNER

EARL GARDNER

Following a bout with COVID-19, Alex Zayne was signed by WWE and repackaged as Ari Sterling in NXT. Upon his release, he returned to his old indie haunts and NJPW Strong, captivating fans.

Ageless Japanese legend Minoru Suzuki ventured to the U.S. during the pandemic, creating memories for fans who'd never seen him.

FTR's Cash Wheeler endures a flurry of blows from Jon Moxley as the action spills outside the ropes.

Flanked by her consort Rebel, real-life dentist Dr. Britt Baker luxuriates in the glow of her AEW Women's World Championship reign in early 2022.

"Keith Lee is All Elite." In his AEW debut, the former NXT Champion chucks Isaiah Kassidy across the ring.

FIST COMBAT

A bloody "Dirty" Ron McDonald and opponent Guy Cool lay on the asphalt outside the ring at a clandestine FIST Combat drive-in show held in the midst of the lockdown. Fans could only find the location via a special FM transmitter.

FIST COMBAT

"Dirty" Ron looks into a police car dispatched to the drive-in card. After observing the proceedings, officers decided to let the show go on.

MARKO SIMONEN

As the rest of Europe closed up, SLAM! Wrestling Finland continued its expansion into Estonia. Here, Baltic fans toast Nordic Champion Stark Adder.

MARKO SIMONEN

Only 50 fans were admitted into a Finnish oil silo to see Polar Pekko flipping off the top turnbuckle onto StarBuck at a June 2020 show dubbed "Quarantine Combat."

Erik Sabel of Denmark's Easy Loverz tag team makes his ring entrance in a protective face covering.

PETER TROEST

Spain's Carlos Zamora strikes a pose for a masked camerawoman at a scaled-down event for Denmark's BODYSLAM! Wrestling.

"Follow the buzzards" was one of the many ominous phrases uttered by Windham Rotunda's WWE character, Bray Wyatt. In one Twitter post, he elaborated, "Underneath the buzzards, you will find death, decay, survival, absolution." If any figure represented the age of COVID-19, it was Wyatt's gruesome alter-ego, The Fiend. His WWE release in the summer of 2021 was almost as baffling as some of the early prognostications about the virus.

Five days before the World Health Organization (WHO) declares an international pandemic, Braun Strowman hurls a small table at Sami Zayn (unseen) during an episode of *SmackDown*. Strowman would be called upon to substitute for Roman Reigns at *WrestleMania 36*, winning the WWE Universal title from Goldberg. Just prior to his June 2021 release, the real-life Adam Scherr was a top contender for the WWE Championship.

After recently recovering from his second bout with leukemia — and with a pregnant wife at home — Roman Reigns opted to sit out *WrestleMania 36*. When he returned, he seemed to lean into his true personality, becoming the villainous "Tribal Chief" of his Samoan wrestling family and turning into one of the most spellbinding characters WWE ever presented.

Business relationships aside, WWE head Vince McMahon and President Donald Trump appeared to share a genuine affection for one another. Under Trump, Vince's wife, Linda, was appointed administrator of the Small Business Administration. Yet, during the entire Trump era, WWE never once invoked the president's name, apparently not wishing to alienate those fans who viewed the WWE Hall of Famer's time in the White House as a historical aberration.

After becoming the first woman to win a championship at *WrestleMania* and successfully defend it at the following one, Becky Lynch (seen here punching it out with Sasha Banks) took time off to become a mother. She'd return from maternity leave and promptly win the gold again, proving that her boast about being "The Man" in WWE was 100 percent true.

Another disaster was averted on August 16 when an alleged stalker was arrested at the Florida home of WWE star Sonya Deville.

According to the Hillsborough County Sheriff's Office, Phillip A. Thomas II, a 24-year-old worker at a South Carolina's Applebee's, began plotting to kidnap Deville eight months earlier. Although she was at war with Mandy Rose — her former partner in a unit called Fire and Desire — in TV storylines, the two remained close friends, and were in the house together when it is alleged that Thomas parked at a nearby church, walked to Deville's sub-division and cut a hole in her patio screen. Police said that he remained on the patio for hours, watching and listening through the windows as the pair watched a UFC pay-per-view.

At about 2:45 a.m., after the two had gone to sleep in separate bedrooms, police said that Thomas entered the house with a knife, plastic duct tape, zip ties and mace, among other items, tripping a burglar alarm.

Alerted by the noise, Deville left her room to check a sliding glass door. As she reached down to ensure that it was locked, she spotted Thomas. "Who are you?" she asked. "What do you want?"

Rather than answer, he purposefully walked toward her. "That's when I realized this person was not here to rob me," she said in a legal petition, "he was here to hurt me."

Rushing to the room where Rose was sleeping, Deville told her guest they were in danger. In the meantime, Thomas purportedly lost track of Deville and went onto another floor.

Deville and Rose quickly fled, calling 911 from the car.

Perhaps it was Thomas's good fortunate that Deville, 26, a former mixed martial artist, never got close to him.

Believing that the two women were hiding, Thomas allegedly continued wandering the house. When deputies arrived and confronted him, they said that he disclosed that he intended to abduct the raven-haired wrestling personality. After first disabling Deville with pepper spray, authorities said, Thomas's plan involved binding her wrists with the zip ties and arms with the duct tape.

He was charged with aggravated stalking, armed burglary of a dwelling, attempted armed kidnapping and criminal mischief. If convicted of all charges, he stood to spend the remainder of his life incarcerated.

"Our deputies are unveiling the suspect's disturbing obsession with this homeowner who he had never met, but stalked on social media for years," Sheriff Chad Chronister said in a news release.

Because Deville had such a large social media following, she hadn't bothered reading his private messages.

But anyone who'd seen his Twitter page would have realized that he was fascinated by Deville. On July 30, for instance, he praised the openly gay performer — referring to her real name Daria Berenato — for participating in an event for GLAAD, a non-profit that monitors the portrayal of LGBTQ people in the media and entertainment. "I'm so proud of you Daria you're a inspiration to me."

According to her petition, "The nature of the messages . . . were obsessive, suicidal, idolizing, saying, 'You are the only person I'll ever love.'"

On August 8 — six days before he made the drive to Deville's home — he replied to a psychiatrist who posted that every human was perfect. "But what if I'm not and I have no self confidence or self worth? I'm asking for your advice because I need a second opinion on something that could determine what happens next in my life."

Through social media, Thomas had allegedly attempted to inform Deville that he'd found her home address. By now he was accustomed to being ignored and went through with his plan anyway. Shortly after arriving at the house, he wrote her, "Look outside, baby, I'm by your pool. I'm here. I'm gonna kill that little bitch you have inside with you."

Only after the arrest, when Deville read through the various messages, did she grasp the amount of danger that she had been facing. Police said that Thomas had vowed to harm her, along with several of her family members. In one post, he allegedly wrote about going to *SummerSlam* as her date.

The fixation apparently continued after Thomas was in custody and listed Deville's address as his own. Although the jail corrected this, months after the incident, his legal documents were still being mailed to her home.

Ultimately, Thomas was found mentally incompetent to stand trial.

The story had a perverse effect on a small segment of people following the case. Deville was terrorized by individuals who sent her menacing messages anonymously. According to court documents, one threatened to "finish the job that Phillip started." In another communication, she was told, "My knife is sharper than Phillip's."

As the New Year dawned, Alexa Bliss and her fiancé, singer Ryan Cabrera, would find themselves victimized by another stalker, this one who maintained that he already had a relationship with Bray Wyatt's on-air disciple. In this instance, Bliss attempted to confront the man directly, writing him back, "Sir, once again, for the one millionth time, you do not know me. I do not know you. We have never spoken, and we have never met. Stop making multiple accounts every time I block you and stop harassing my fiancé."

The man was not discouraged. In February, he wrote to fellow Bliss followers that he was "dead serious about getting rid of that piece of shit Ryan Cabrera so stop calling me a fucking troll. I'm a lover of Alexa Bliss. I will be at her house in Orlando, FL to pay her a little visit."

He ended his post with a hashtag used to promote Bliss's plotlines with The Fiend: #LetMeIn.

CHAPTER 13

ON THE NIGHT of May 25, in the Powderhorn Park section of Minneapolis, an employee at the Cup Foods convenience store examined the cash he'd received for a pack of cigarettes and concluded that he'd been handed a counterfeit 20-dollar bill. After some hesitation, workers left the store and approached the SUV where the customer was sitting and asked that he return the cigarettes.

George Floyd said no.

The 46-year-old old Floyd was six-foot-four and 223 pounds, and the employees had no desire to get physical with him. Instead, the manager had a worker call the police, reporting that Floyd was passing fake money and was "awfully drunk" and "not in control of himself."

Officers arrived and removed Floyd from the SUV. He was handcuffed and seated on the sidewalk in front of a restaurant. After placing the suspect under arrest, police walked him toward their cruiser. Before he could enter the vehicle, he fell to the ground. Police yanked him up and stood him against the door.

Floyd — a former college athlete who later struggled with substance abuse issues and compiled a criminal record that included drug charges and aggravated robbery — was not acting as compliant as the officers would have liked. But he told them not to get the wrong idea; he wasn't resisting arrest. He was recovering from COVID-19, he said, had claustrophobia and anxiety, and did not want to sit in the car. As more officers arrived, a brief struggle ensued. Floyd was placed in the car, then removed. Once again, he fell to the pavement.

Even before Officer Derek Chauvin used his knee to pin down Floyd's neck, the suspect had complained that he couldn't breathe. Bystanders pulled out their phones, capturing Chauvin — who worked security at the same club as Floyd, but may not have known him — on top of Floyd.

"You got him down," one witness complained. "Let him breathe."

"I'm about to die," Floyd said.

Chuavin told him to relax.

"I can't breathe," Floyd said again. "Please, the knee in my neck. I can't breathe."

On the video, he could also be heard calling for his late mother.

One of the officers radioed for an ambulance. A medical examiner would later determine that Floyd's heart stopped while he was being restrained.

Sadly, the circumstances surrounding the death of George Floyd had become all too familiar.

But when video of his final moments circulated, it touched a nerve. Perhaps observers could no longer abide by yet another image of a white police officer holding down an unarmed black man — in this instance, prosecutors would say, for nine minutes and 29 seconds — resulting in the loss of life. Or maybe, after being locked down through the winter, some people needed to take to the streets and vent.

Very quickly, protests spread from Minneapolis to more than 140 cities all over the United States. In St. Louis and Las Vegas, police were shot and wounded. In New York City and Buffalo, officers were struck by cars. As protestors gathered outside the White House, President Trump was rushed underground to a bunker previously used during terrorist attacks. He later claimed that he simply went there for an "inspection."

The National Guard was activated in more than 20 states, as well as the nation's capital, where units backed police storming into a peaceful protest. Both activists and journalists covering the event were wondering why the streets were suddenly being cleared. What they hadn't bothered to think about was that, nearby, in the White House Rose Garden, the president was making a speech about law and order and threatening to deploy the military. When he was finished, he left the podium and passed through the White House gate. The demonstrators — so loud before he began speaking — were gone.

As staffers trailed him, Trump crossed through Lafayette Square and H Street NW, marching to St. John's Episcopal Church, which had sustained mild fire damage during an earlier demonstration.

Holding a Bible aloft, the president posed for pictures in front of the sanctuary sometimes labeled the "Church of the Presidents."

Biden would later mock Trump for holding the Bible upside down. Trump defended himself, insisting that that part of the story was a work. News outlets examined the photo op frame by frame. And this time, it was the Democrat who was telling tall tales.

"Black Lives Matter" became the cry of an international movement denouncing systemic racism. There were protests in Britain, France, South Korea and Japan. In Australia, Aboriginal people performed a traditional smoking ceremony — burning plants in the hope that the herbal fumes would ward off bad spirits — before a Sydney demonstration. Some 15,000 gathered in Berlin, while elsewhere in Germany, marches were held in Dusseldorf and Munich.

The Bundesliga had just resumed its season on May 16, and Bayern Munich players entered the field on June 7 in Black Lives Matter shirts. As the Premier League prepared for its own restart on June 17, Liverpool FC players took a knee in solidarity with protestors during a training session.

George Floyd's brother would address the UN, as well as the Democratic National Convention, invoking not just his sibling's name, but those of other African Americans who died after encounters with police, including Eric Garner, Breonna Taylor, Atatiana Jefferson, Sandra Bland and Stephon Clark. After another fatal police shooting, this one claiming the life of Jacob Blake in Wisconsin on August 23, MLB, NBA, MLS and Women's National Basketball Association (WNBA) games were postponed.

"I could not play this game I love so much tonight knowing the hurt and anguish my people continue to feel," tweeted Colorado Rockies outfielder Matt Kemp.

With racial sensitivity at the forefront of international consciousness, the NFL's Washington Redskins finally acquiesced to calls from Native American groups and supporters to change its name.

Once again, the grimness of the real world intruded on the fantasy of pro wrestling.

In AEW, the entire roster and crew had a Zoom call to discuss the Black Lives Matter movement and the history that led to it.

WWE created an email address specifically for wrestlers or employees who wished to bring up diversity concerns, along with links to training courses on the subject. Before the *NXT TakeOver: In Your House* pay-per-view in June, Triple H spoke to talent, mentioned Black Lives Matter and offered to have an open conversation about any issue involving race. During his match with Johnny Gargano at the show, Keith Lee performed in an outfit with "Black Lives Matter" sewn on the back.

On *SmackDown*, Kofi Kingston and Big E each took a knee and wore black arm bands that included the names of African Americans who died in confrontations with law enforcement. Big E also became involved in an animated series called "Our Heroes Rock," specifically to highlight African American historical figures to children.

WWE Hall of Famer Mark Henry had grown up respecting law enforcement. At one point, he'd even contemplated a career in blue. At the same time, he understood the rage that pulsed through the Black community since, as a large, African American male, he'd been targeted by the police himself. "I've been put on the ground at gunpoint in dress clothes going to church," he said on journalist Chris Van Vliet's YouTube channel.

It was after hearing accounts like these — from African Americans he'd befriended in WWE — that Randy Orton embraced the Black Lives Matter cause. "My only regret is that it took me a bit longer and some soul searching to see it," he told CBS Sports.

Mustafa Ali understood the controversy from a variety of perspectives. Ali was a former police officer, but as the Illinois-raised son of a Pakistani father and Indian mother, he related to the people of color he saw marching on TV. Black Lives Matter, he told *Sports Illustrated*, "isn't something that happened overnight. It's not something over one black man being murdered. This is 400 years of being shoved and hit and kicked and spit on and murdered and raped . . . There's going to be a permanent scar there, and the only way to really repair that relationship is massive change. And yes, it starts with police."

For his part, inaugural WWE Universal Champion Finn Balor, who'd begun the opening match at *WrestleMania 34* with members of New Orleans's LGBTQ community surrounding him on the entrance ramp, included a Black Lives Matter t-shirt in his apparel line, pledging to donate all proceeds to the NAACP.

"Until there is equality for everyone," said the multiple NXT kingpin, "there is equality for no one."

Likewise, NXT UK stars Pete Dunne, Tyler Bate and Trent Seven printed up their own Black Lives Matter gear, selling out in less than 24 hours and funneling the money to a civil rights organization.

As a crossover celebrity with Hollywood credentials, John Cena did not feel the need to sell merchandise to raise funds. Upon learning that K-pop band BTS and its record label, Big Hit Entertainment, contributed $1-million to Black Lives Matter, the Doctor of Thuganomics matched the donation.

In a phone conversation with author Bob Woodward, the president acknowledged the existence of racism, qualifying his comment by adding that it was "less here than most places or less here than many places." When asked during another call whether Caucasians needed to work harder to understand Black anger over white privilege, Trump snapped, "No. You really drank the Kool-Aid, didn't you? Just listen to you. Wow. No, I don't feel that at all."

In a speech at the White House, Trump put the experiences of George Floyd in the context of the administration's achievements. While some pundits predicted a rise in the jobless rate, the president pointed out that the number fell to 13.3 percent in May after reaching a staggering 14.7 percent the month before. "Hopefully, George is looking down and saying this is a great thing that's happening for our country. [It's] a great day for him. It's a great day for everybody. This is a great, great day in terms of equality."

Mayor Glenn "Kane" Jacobs, a Republican, admitted that he sometimes wished that the commander-in-chief would watch his mouth. "A lot of the stuff he says, I say, 'Dude, you're right, but say it a little differently,'" the future WWE Hall of Famer said during an interview with *TPA Talks*, a speaker series promoting breast cancer awareness.

In WWE, a trio called the Forgotten Sons had recently been called up to the main roster. The three — Jaxson Ryker, Wesley Blake and Steve Cutler — were portrayed as military vets who'd been overlooked by the government and the elites. They were mad, intense and — since pro wrestling involves hitting people — violent. Some wondered if the routine was a bit too familiar to the country's newly emboldened alt-right extremists. While Blake and Cutler appeared to be playing characters, Ryker — a former U.S. Marine who'd referred to Black Lives Matter as "garbage" in 2019 and would later encourage airline travelers to "raise those masks" in flight — seemed to believe at least some of what he said. As civil rights protestors directed anger at the president, Ryker tweeted, "Thankful for the @POTUS we have! God bless America. Built of freedom! Forgotten no more."

The message moved Donald Trump Jr. to reply with an admiring post: "My father will always stand up for our country and everyone in it. Thank you for your service in the Marines!"

Reportedly, the Forgotten Sons had been scheduled to clash with the New Day on *SmackDown*. While the logic behind the feud might have been inserting an unsettling racial undercurrent to a ring rivalry, Ryker's position in the wake of George Floyd's death added "bad heat" to the gimmick. Both Blake and Cutler went out of their way to distance themselves from their teammate's politics. And several WWE performers, including Sami Zayn, Kevin Owens and Ricochet, voiced public disapproval.

Wrote Mustafa Ali, "I'm thankful you posted this because I'm now aware what you stand for. When black brothers and sisters are crying, you praise someone that refuses to acknowledge their hurt."

From AEW, Joey Janela chimed in, "Someone is gonna take a nice shit in your gear bag," a common wrestling rib in the days before a WWE Wellness Policy and Board of Directors.

In an instant, it seemed, the Forgotten Sons were . . . well, forgotten. The unit's name ceased to be mentioned on TV. Cutler and Blake were used to back up King Corbin. But the act didn't get traction, and Cutler was released in February 2021. Blake was one of the names cut in the immediate aftermath of *WrestleMania 37*.

Ryker would remain until his own dismissal the following November, in the diminished capacity as a protector for *Raw* brand troubadour, Elias (the relationship would later combust, with Ryker playing the role of an apolitical babyface). To those who tuned in and noticed him in the early days of the Biden presidency, the long-bearded Ryker was a surly, tattooed presence, but more because he was playing the part of the obnoxious guitarists' muscle than the fact that he seemed like the kind of guy who might be spotted on security cam footage, raiding the U.S. Capitol.

"We will plant our flag on the desk of Nancy Pelosi."

More about *that* particular incident later . . .

CHAPTER 14

IN JUNE, A wave of sexual harassment allegations swept through the wrestling business via social media. Few promotions appeared exempt, as the accusations built day after day. Some of the women were labeled "crazy" and accused of trying to capitalize on the hysteria. But several male wrestlers either resigned or were terminated from various companies because of the movement that became known as #SpeakingOut.

"Women in wrestling have always been afraid of men who had power over their spots," said Kenzie Paige, a Tennessee-based performer who wrestled in AEW hours after she graduated high school. "But, nowadays, at least, if you have a problem, people my age know they can go to somebody, and there are men in the business who will back you up."

This is a difficult chapter to write since, as of the spring of 2022, not one of these cases had been adjudicated in court. So many names were mentioned that it feels irresponsible to place all of them in print for posterity, particularly if the charges are later retracted. Some of the men initially mentioned have resumed their wrestling careers with little backlash, and I'd prefer not playing a role in their ostracism until more details are known.

What's also confusing is the degree to which people committed misdeeds. There is a big difference between making an ignorant joke and physically assaulting somebody. On one occasion, I saw an online chart listing supposed sex criminals in the wrestling industry. People who'd never been accused of harming a child were labeled pedophiles. The term "rapist" was thrown around.

"Are people guilty? Sometimes it's not cut and dry," said referee Kris Levin, who — as you'll read shortly — maintained that he lost his job at Impact for supporting one of the women who'd been harassed. "It's called a nuanced conversation. And if you ask for a nuanced conversation, you're called an enabler and an apologist. Twitter doesn't allow for a nuanced conversation."

Gail Kim, remembered for winning the WWE Women's Championship in her first match in the company in 2002 and the inaugural TNA Knockouts title in 2007, told me that she hoped most of the accusers were speaking honestly. "Otherwise, the people who are telling the truth will suffer. As it is, when you speak up as a female, you're looked at as tearing down the business."

Traditionally, pro wrestling was a pretty misogynistic place. Women who engaged in relationships with wrestlers were derided as "ring rats," with both stars and preliminary grapplers feeling entitled to ply them with alcohol and drugs and take liberties. At each level of the industry, female performers, every bit as athletic as their male peers, were objectified and harassed — backstage, in cars and airplanes, in bars and hotel rooms. Even the most skeptical of us knows that they weren't all "making it up."

"I don't know a single female who hasn't been affected," Brittany Blake, whose credits include GCW, Combat Zone Wrestling (CZW) and Chicago's AAW (formerly All American Wrestling), told me. "I've always been a weird outcast, so when I got into wrestling and people were being nice, it took me a while to figure out who was doing it because he was an amazing person, and who was doing it because he was a scumbag with other motives. There have been a number of times when saying no wasn't enough, and I had to get a male friend in the business involved."

Allie Katch, an indie star known for, among other things, her believable hardcore matches against men, compared the wrestling business to the general entertainment field. "People want to make money, and if the bad people are making you money, you keep them around. But maybe not anymore. I don't want to have to grin and bear it or I won't get booked again."

Just like Black Lives Matter, #SpeakingOut was a long time coming. With women main-eventing in major promotions and enjoying positions of corporate authority, medieval thinking and sexual impropriety were no longer going to be overlooked. And it wasn't just physical altercations that were the issue. It was the overall perception of the women who chose to make professional wrestling their lives. As Session Moth Martina, who did a drunk comedy routine in her native Ireland before signing with ROH, said in a tweet: "When we gonna talk about boys in the back slut shaming?! Boys will be boys but if a girl does it she is DIRT."

Although I've chosen not to name every alleged perpetrator in this book, I feel justified in writing about a few of the more high-profile cases involving men who either defended themselves, publicly apologized or both. But I have drawn the line at mentioning any of the accusers by name, including those who'd been outspoken. As a crime reporter as well as a wrestling writer, I know that special victims detectives do not identify the sufferers; those who are legitimately traumatized cannot heal if people can find them and say they're lying. Regardless of how the various cases shake out, I stand by treating the women involved in #SpeakingOut with caution and respect.

Among people in wrestling, the early stages of #SpeakingOut was an uncomfortable time, when women feared the repercussions of telling their stories, and men began agonizing over every uncertain exchange they'd had on the road, wondering whether theirs would be the next name cancelled. But maybe restraint in certain types of situations is wise. Regardless, what #SpeakingOut did was create a dialogue, and hopefully, this chapter will add to a conversation that's going to continue for a very long time.

On June 17, a former girlfriend of David Starr's accused him of sexual assault. "Unfortunately, I'm not the only one with terrible stories," she said on social media. "I'm just the only one ready to post right now. This is so much harder to do than people think."

Starr had wrestled all over the world, viewing the sport of kings as both a vehicle to showcase his skills and spread his message of social activism. Referring to himself as "the Bernie Sanders of professional wrestling," he railed against the U.S. health care system, advocating for universal coverage. In addition to blasting the way undocumented immigrants were treated at the American border, The Jewish Cannon was harsh in his assessment of Israeli government policy regarding Palestinians. In a skirmish with Jay Lethal on a kibbutz, or collective farm, in Israel, Starr wore tights ornamented with both the Israeli and Palestinian flags. He claimed that prior to the indie show, Ring of Honor deliberately had Lethal lose its championship in order to spoil the narrative of an American Jewish kid fighting for the belt in the Holy Land.

In a tweet, he referred to ROH's corporate owner, Sinclair Broadcasting, as a "far right wing extremist corporate propaganda machine."

Although he'd had a respectable career in the U.S. — defeating Orange Cassidy, Darby Allin and Jeff Cobb in the opening rounds of PWG's prestigious Battle of Los Angeles tournament in 2019 — Starr had been spending much of his time in Europe. In the UK, he worked with Equity, the British union for "creative practitioners," to organize talent, and even discussed the issue with members of the country's parliament.

But once the sexual assault allegations became public, Starr — whose union advocacy may have led to his previous departure from WWE-affiliated promotions PROGRESS in England and wXw (Westside Xtreme Wrestling) in Germany — was stripped of his titles in Revolution Pro Wrestling, Ultimate Pro Wrestling and TNT Extreme Wrestling in the UK and OTT in Ireland.

Although Starr denied that he was a sexual predator, he wrote, "With nearly every partner I've had, I have lied, cheated, lied about the cheating, then repeated that cycle. When it comes to relationships with my partners, I am emotionally immature to say the least. This comes from a lack of self-value. That lack of self-value stems from a lifetime of parental issues amongst numerous other surrounding circumstances. This is no excuse . . . but rather just to say that I've recognized where I've done wrong."

He said that he was now in therapy but would not make an effort to defend himself since "no matter what I say, I'm the bad guy. No pity party. It is what it is."

Before deactivating his social media accounts, he tweeted, "If this is the end of wrestling for me, that's ok."

Starr's departure was disappointing to some UK talent who'd hoped to see a wrestling union. But the fight continued without him. When

Revolution Pro began promoting again after the coronavirus shutdown, the organization announced that the cards would be attended by Equity representatives.

No one was indispensable. Not even the Bernie Sanders of professional wrestling.

Ah, Joey Ryan. Where do we even begin with that?

To someone who didn't follow indie wrestling, it would be tough to explain how Ryan became so popular. But I'll give it a shot. The guy could wrestle, had a sense of humor, and was self-depreciating enough to build an entire gimmick around his dick. Sporting a bushy mustache, not unlike cinematic heartthrob Burt Reynolds at the time of his 1972 *Cosmopolitan* nude centerfold, Ryan wiggled and thrust his hips, coated himself with baby oil, and seemed to have a bionic penis. When an adversary grabbed his crotch, Ryan used his purported pelvic strength to flip his opponent to the mat.

"I've been wrestling a long time and tried stuff that worked and tried stuff that didn't work," he told me for *Too Sweet: Inside the Indie Wrestling Revolution*. "It's the evolution of me as a wrestler and as an artist."

I'm being objective when I say that the routine was immensely entertaining. With the exception of Jim Cornette — who characterized Ryan as "Dick Boy" — virtually everybody found something to enjoy about The King of Dong Style. He nicknamed his moves the Mustache Ride and YouPorn-plex, after the online porn company. At *All In*, the 2018 indie card that led to the birth of AEW, he marched to the ring with an army of walking penises — a spoof on the Undertaker's druids in WWE — to dick flip "Hangman" Adam Page while fans chanted "Rest in penis." During the 2019 WrestleCon, he hosted something called "Joey Ryan's Penis Party," for which enthusiasts lined up and paid $30 to pose for photos of themselves grabbing Ryan's crotch.

But was Joey guilty of — to use the carny term — being a mark for his own gimmick? Once the Starr allegations came out, attention shifted to Ryan — with 17 separate women accusing him of unwanted sexual advances and assault, among other acts. Like Starr, Ryan admitted to emotional shortcomings, while conceding that he might have misread nonverbal cues and invaded personal space. But in no way, he emphasized, was he a sex criminal.

Many of those who'd been applauding Ryan's hyper-sexual routine were now picking it apart. Given the sheer volume of the allegations, there was no way that he was going to win. He disabled his Twitter account, as well as the one for his company, Bar Wrestling.

Impact terminated its contract with Ryan. An episode of the company's weekly show almost didn't make air, as producers and editors scrambled to excise a pretaped Ryan match. According to *PWInsider*, had the procedure taken an additional 30 minutes, AXS TV would have had to show something else.

Footage of Ryan was scrubbed from the Young Bucks' YouTube series, *Being the Elite*. "Out of respect to the victims," said a message that accompanied an episode that followed the allegations, "we have begun the process of taking down *BTE* videos which featured an accused sexual abuser. Our biggest regret is providing a platform unknowingly for such a despicable person."

Given the friendly way Ryan would be portrayed in the Bucks' autobiography, *Killing the Business*, the description indicated that even his close wrestling associates were turning against him.

In July, a clean-shaven Ryan briefly returned to YouTube to mount a long and vigorous defense. "I have never had sex with a woman without her consent," he said, "and I have never acted criminally towards a woman with sex." One by one, he went through a series of allegations in an effort to explain the circumstances. One person assented to perform a sex act on him at a wedding, he said. Another accuser boasted of engaging in a consensual threesome, he continued. He was particularly bitter about Impact firing him via email, he emphasized, since not one of the alleged incidents occurred while he was working for the company.

He told fans that he was working with a therapist, connecting with God and considering the legal routes he could take.

He later deleted the video.

He'd eventually file lawsuits against several accusers, as well as those who repeated claims made against him, and Impact's parent company,

Anthem, citing both the loss of his reputation and more than $15-million in revenue.

With the exception of the breach of contract suit against Impact, he opted to discontinue this battle. "This got me thinking," he wrote in a statement to the SoCalUncensored website, "that if I 'win' these cases, what do I win? Would it be a vindication or just validation? And if it's a validation, then for whom? Even if I 'win,' I've still been a womanizer, been unfaithful, been selfish and self-seeking in my broken life. That doesn't make me feel like a winner. But none of these things are criminal acts, and those are the things I can and am working on. . . . I can't fully give my resentments to God and expect to move forward and past them if I'm bound to these cases."

In the meantime, he said, he continued to attend online and in-person meetings with a 12-step group called Sex and Love Addicts Anonymous.

It almost sounded like a storyline for Joey Ryan's character. Was the guy really finished with the wrestling business?

In March 2021, a Knoxville fundraising event was cancelled after Ryan's image appeared on the poster and Bar Wrestling was listed as the promoter. All proceeds from the wrestling card were supposed to go to an organization associated with Project GRL, a charity run by Joyce Meyer Ministries for "every girl who has been mistreated, marginalized or feels insecure or hopeless." As soon as Tony Khan became aware of Ryan's involvement, he refused to allow any AEW talent to participate.

In his SoCalUncensored statement, Ryan said that the Bar Wrestling ticket account was being used to help the sales process go smoother — and his only goal had been achieving some closure by assisting an organization that he believed was empowering women. "I'm not trying to 'come back to wrestling,'" he said. "I know that wrestling is full of carnies who think that wrestling is full of carnies, but I assure you there was nothing more to it."

As more #SpeakingOut stories were appearing on social media, a woman in the UK posted a passage describing a sexual encounter she had with "The Villain" Marty Scurll five years earlier when she was 16 and "incredibly drunk."

Scurll had been a member of the Bullet Club's Elite faction, a gifted athlete and bona fide personality who would have been a star if he'd signed with AEW and had the potential to achieve the same status in WWE. But as previously mentioned, before the pandemic, the British-born grappler instead agreed to continue as a key talent, as well as a co-booker, in ROH, which was affiliated with New Japan, CMLL in Mexico and Revolution Pro in the UK. His clash with NWA World Heavyweight champion Nick Aldis, which had been scheduled at the ill-fated Crockett Cup, was seen as an effort by ROH to use Scurll's fame to extend its reach to other organizations.

Now, the presence of Scurll on the roster was problematic. Although the female met the age of consent in her country at the time of the encounter, fans were uncomfortable with the notion of Scurll having sex with a girl who would have been a junior in high school in the United States. "It was quickly circulating that I was a slut," she wrote, "but not the part where he sexually assaulted a drunk child."

Publicly at least, Scurll attempted to take the high road. "I am aware that a young woman has bravely come forward with her account of sexual abuse . . . five years ago," he wrote online. "Although I truly believe that our encounter that evening was consensual, and the fact that our encounter was legal, is almost not the point. I understand that she now views our encounter as part of a bigger problem within the wrestling community."

Certain observers were quick to point out the similarity between Scurll's wording and that of a statement by late basketball great Kobe Bryant after a woman at a Colorado lodge accused him of sexual assault in 2003: "Although I truly believe this encounter between us was consensual, I recognize now that she did not and does not view this incident the same way I did."

Scurll would later elaborate about the circumstances in another post: "In 2015, after a wrestling event in the UK, I had a brief consensual sexual encounter with a woman. In that moment, at a bar, in those circumstances, I had no cause to question her age. I don't . . . seek absolution for my ignorance. Although I did not become aware of her age until after the encounter, the reality of the age disparity is not lost on me. I understand that although our encounter was technically legal in the UK, my lack of good judgment that evening has disappointed many fans."

He added that the industry had "failed" the young woman and that he "could not begin to understand the difficulties she must experience." He urged fans to respect her privacy.

"My immediate priority is to seek forgiveness for unknowingly contributing to a culture that for too long has promulgated ego over humanity and hurt many along the way," he continued. "For those of us with a voice that can reach beyond our own doorsteps, it is our shared responsibility to do better and to do more."

Despite this act of contrition, no higher power reached down to pardon him. When Ring of Honor resumed television production after its COVID hiatus, Scurll's name was not included in the plans. In October, he was removed from the company's website. In January 2021, The Villain and the organization officially parted ways.

It would be eight months before he appeared on another wrestling show.

"It was a difficult period," referee Kris Levin told me, as we went over some of the #SpeakingOut allegations. "Every day, you'd wake up and you wouldn't know if one of your friends was going to be called out for being a monster. Or if another friend was going to reveal that horrible things had happened to her and you never knew about it."

When he did hear about a familiar name being accused of something egregious, his emotions swung from revulsion to wondering if the stories were accurate. "I can't hit a button and say, 'I no longer care about this person.' It was confusing, frustrating."

By that point, he felt that he'd already paid a price for his knowledge about sexual harassment in professional wrestling.

It started, he said, toward the end of 2019 when two friends — members of a wrestling couple — were trying to part ways with Impact but were encountering roadblocks regarding their contracts. He recalled that the female told him that she was being harassed, while the male maintained that he was being "starved out," or not booked as much as he needed to be. According to Levin, the charges were serious enough for Impact to bring in an outside investigator. "She asked me what I heard, and I told her. I didn't want retaliation, and she told me that our conversation would be confidential. No one would know that the information came from me. So I told her what I knew. But when it was time for me to renew my contract, they ghosted me. I didn't hear back from anyone for weeks."

Convinced that his time with the company was ending, he said that he texted several friends in the office, informing them that he was moving on. "About 20 minutes later, I received a call, saying I was fired. I can only suspect that the confidential conversation was shared."

In an interview with the *Wrestling Inc. Daily* podcast, he elaborated, "I've worked 13 years, my entire adult life, to try to make a living in pro wrestling and I'm very aware that there's this standard that referees shouldn't say anything. You should just shut your mouth and you shouldn't bring attention to yourself. . . . But I decided that if there's any company that would [punish] me for speaking the truth against predators and abusers, then I wouldn't [want to] work there."

Because of his dismissal, he now considered Impact one of those companies.

When *Wrestling Inc.* contacted Anthem Sports & Entertainment for a reaction, the website received the following statement: "We are aware of what Kris Levin has posted on social media and have no comment other than to deny the allegations he has made."

The referee asserted that he had no motive other than reiterating what his friends had told him. "I read comments on Twitter about me, saying that I said these things because I was bitter at Impact. But why would I do that? It's not like I spoke out to help my career. Because you know what people are saying about me now? 'We can't trust him. He's not professional. He can't kayfabe.'"

Some Impact employees insisted that, even before #SpeakingOut, the promotion had become one of the most progressive in the business, with Gail Kim and another former Knockouts titlist, Madison Rayne, working as backstage producers. The additions spawned a form of backstage communication — for both male and female athletes — that the company's defenders said hadn't existed before.

"I'm *invested* in that women's division," Kim said. "My goal is to see these women have a perfect match. I'm direct, but when I have a critique, I always follow up with a positive. If you don't get that appreciation, it really impacts your confidence, which you're already struggling with because of the physical aesthetic part of this business."

Kimber Lee said that, in a short time, her career was altered by Kim's influence: "She'll tell you these subtle ideas the average person just wouldn't think about. I'll have a half-baked thought about something I want to do in my match, and she'll change the order so everything makes sense. She understands that women are still proving themselves, and she knows how to tell you the best way to go out there and kill it."

In the midst of #SpeakingOut, someone unearthed audio of Sammy Guevara on a podcast in 2016. AEW's Spanish God was 22-years-old at the time, and described the thrill of seeing Sasha Banks in person when he appeared on a WWE show as an "extra" — an inexperienced talent generally brought in either to lose or appear in some type of vignette.

"Bro, Sasha Banks . . . oh my God," Guevara raved. "When I was at WWE the other week, I wanted to just go fuckin' rape that woman."

Sammy wasn't being literal. He was using a term he'd probably been unthinkingly throwing around since high school. Still, it was a very bad choice of words. Now, Guevara was an AEW star, and the interview was part of the #SpeakingOut discourse. He knew that there were going to be ramifications. So he got on Twitter and stated the obvious: "I've made stupid, inappropriate and extremely offensive comments in my past. In my idiotic mind, I thought I was being funny in using words and terms that represent nothing but horror and pain. I am truly sorry for my hurtful words and actions, and I will never forgive myself."

He also called Banks and apologized. "We had an open discussion," she said on Twitter. "Words and comments he made, jokingly or not, have absolutely no place in our society! I don't condone or tolerate this kind of behavior. What one thinks is just a side comment can have a massive impact on someone else's life."

AEW had no choice but to suspend Guevara without pay, emphasizing that his future would be re-evaluated following extensive sensitivity training. "I asked him to use that time to try to become a better person, and I think he did," Tony Khan told *Sports Illustrated* upon the star's reinstatement the next month. "He's shown that he's very sorry and he can change. He's spent every day over the past month trying to prove that."

As the controversy faded into the past, Guevara minded his manners — according to one source, he quietly helped young people struggling with suicidal thoughts — and shifted his attention to his in-ring repertoire and on-air persona, growing into one of the most compelling personalities on the AEW roster.

Still, the jitters generated by #SpeakingOut continued to be felt throughout the entire industry. Because of several of its wrestlers being caught up in the storm, along with a taping sabbatical due to COVID, fans speculated over whether NXT UK would close. But in late June, the London-based wrestlers were ordered to participate in a mandatory conference call. NXT UK was going to continue, albeit in empty arenas, Triple H told the roster before stressing that the company had a "zero tolerance" policy regarding verifiable cases of sexual abuse.

In a tweet, Pete Dunne said that the burden was now on the British wrestling scene to implement a different standard. "There will be plenty of you that turn away and quite frankly, I felt like it too. But . . . I hope that eventually we earn the trust back."

While Revolution Pro founder Andy Quildan called for government oversight — indeed, several MPs proposed legislation to end harassment and impose health and safety standards — and OTT drafted a code of conduct that extended even to fans, PROGRESS announced a new management team, including Vicky Haskins, who'd worked in public relations, ring announcing and merchandising, among other tasks in the industry. The company also outlined offenses it would no longer allow, including verbal and emotional abuse, cyber bullying, sexism, racism, homophobia and transphobia. "I've been in the business 16 years," Haskins said in a statement, "and have experienced some of the inexcusable behavior that has come to light recently . . . It is of the utmost importance that we provide . . . a welcoming environment that is safe for everyone who comes through our doors, fans and wrestlers alike."

Kimber Lee worried that, as time passed, and pro wrestling transitioned away from the COVID era, the lessons of #SpeakingOut would no longer be remembered. "I hope that none of this is forgotten," she said. "I don't want women to be scared to be in dressing rooms anymore."

In the meantime, Brittany Blake believed the industry was safer for women than at any previous time in its history: "I won't name names. But there's not one person I had a problem with who didn't get called out."

Not only were men more hesitant to display predatory behavior, she said, but women now understood the signs of a menacing situation and were unafraid to come together and draw attention to it. "Our sisterhood is stronger."

#SpeakingOut broke just before ECW Press was about to release *Too Sweet: Inside the Indie Wrestling Revolution*. I'd interviewed Starr, Ryan and Scurll about their experiences in indie wrestling, and included their impressions in the book. Although it was too late in the process to remove these, there were questions about whether to replace certain photos. I argued against it. This was supposed to be the definitive story of indie wrestling, and to remove the images would be akin to pretending that Chris Benoit never won a title in WWE, WCW, ECW or New Japan. Pro wrestling history had been murky for so long, and I wanted a chronicle that would withstand time. That included both personal impressions from the players who helped shape the indies, and photos of the more memorable characters. I still think I made the right decision.

But when I read the online comments for *Too Sweet*, I found a tweet from a fan who said that she would have liked to have seen more about women's wrestling. Determined to offer a more balanced perspective in the book you're now reading, I attended a SHIMMER show that was part of GCW's "Collective" in October (more on that later on).

"All those women's wrestling promotions out there, it started with SHIMMER," noted the iconic LuFisto during her induction into the Indie Wrestling Hall of Fame in early 2022.

SHIMMER was founded in the Chicago area in 2005 to give female athletes a platform they might not otherwise receive. "When I started training, SHIMMER was always my goal," said Blake. "Not only were they an all-women's promotion, but they had the kind of wrestling I really loved — the technical, the high-flying, the Japanese influence."

Milwaukee-based wrestler Sierra said that one of the draws for a performer was the overall mood in SHIMMER's backstage area: "It's nice to be in an all-women's locker room. We all love wrestling. There's no vibe of competitiveness. We're here for the show, and we're here for each other."

Explained "The Wild Child" Jody Threat, "When you're in a male-dominated space, you need to foster safe spaces so you can join the wider, male-dominated community with confidence. Society as a whole is starting to evolve into a more fair place. Schools have been implementing policies to fight oppression and create a more equitable standard, and a generation has grown up accordingly.

"Wrestling is not just about being fast and strong. It's art. And if you're going to create, you have to feel free."

CHAPTER 15

SINCE THE TIME I became a professional writer, I've been to the Hoosier State dozens, if not hundreds, of times for, among other reasons, researching my 2015 book, *Too Fast to Live, Too Young to Die: James Dean's Final Hours*, signing copies of the first edition of the WWE encyclopedia that I co-wrote, once to interview a couple who ran a dating service for men attracted to female inmates. But nothing compared to the elation of landing in Indianapolis on Saturday, June 20, 2020, and knowing that I was going to see my first live wrestling show since the pandemic was declared.

As a precursor to *WrestleMania 37* ten months later, the Game Changer Wrestling (GCW) event was outdoors and replete with rules dictating health etiquette. At the Celebration Plaza Amphitheater at White River State Park, there were a mask requirement and easy-to-reach sanitizer stations, while ropes and turnbuckles were cleaned between every match. The "stagger social distance seating chart" that promoter Brett Lauderdale showed me restricted ringside seating to 50 percent while, elsewhere on the lawn, fans could only congregate in groups of two or four, based on "household purchase."

If there was a cluster of chairs in one row, the row behind was empty.

When tickets went online, a total of 250 sold out in three and a half hours. Although lots of space was still available, GCW opted not to admit anyone else.

Backstage, GCW World champion Rickey Shane Page wielded the thermometer gun, personally checking every performer's temperature.

A few of the wrestlers who appeared on the card also wrestled the night before at an Independent Wrestling Association (IWA) Mid-South show that was held indoors. I was told that this was less stringent, with fans sitting close to one another, often without masks. Responding to a photo posted by the promotion of the event, a fan tweeted, "How is this even legal?"

Still, the wrestlers I spoke with were pretty jazzed to be there. Blake Christian had last appeared on GCW's *Acid Cup 2* — the show that featured the social distancing match between Joey Janela and Jimmy Lloyd. During his break, he'd taken time to heal a bad ankle at home and worked on cardio outside. Then, he tested the ankle in a local promoter's ring, while continuing to build up his cardio and taking bumps.

Although the arena was broiling, Christian and his opponent, "Unbreakable" Michael Elgin, held nothing back. During one exchange, Elgin attempted to powerbomb Christian after catching him in the middle of a springboard. Backflipping onto his feet, Christian delivered a clothesline, followed by, in rapid succession, a superkick, elbow and Pele kick. Elgin came right back with a German suplex. But when Unbreakable tried rising from the mat, Christian smashed him with a knee.

"The fans were chanting, 'This is awesome,'" Christian said. "And it was. These people didn't have wrestling for a long time, and we were giving it to them."

Even when he lost, Christian felt triumphant. Elgin took the microphone, complimented his rival for coming a long way in such a short time and encouraged the crowd to shout his nickname, All Heart."

Prior to the pandemic, Mance Warner had punctured a lung and collapsed while coming back through the curtain. When his family took him to the hospital two days later, the doctor asked, "How did you walk in here? You have one lung."

He said that he was out for a month before battling Nick Gage in a death match. "I took off my boots and ran through the thumbtacks barefoot. But I didn't swallow any."

And then, suddenly, there was COVID, and no other way to match that excitement. "The worst part was not being with your friends. I was scared about the business, scared about my future, scared about whether my friends would get sick."

At home, he occupied himself "doing curls and bench presses before drinking beer" and studying vintage wrestling from the 1980s: Bill Watts's Mid-South, Jim Crockett Jr.'s Mid-Atlantic, Fritz Von Erich's World Class, Verne Gagne's AWA. "That's my style," he said, invoking FTR's slogan. "No flips. Just punching, eye pokes, beating each other up. No one was writing these guys' shit. They'd go and fight and say what they wanted to say."

Despite the density of the crowd at the IWA Mid-South event, Warner didn't hesitate before stepping into the ring. "It was hot and crowded," he recalled after his loss to Gary Jay. "But I was so happy to be in there, hitting someone again."

That sense of exuberance carried over to the GCW card the next day. "It feels extremely good to be back," said Effy, the self-professed "sober, queer, punk rock pro wrestler of your dreams." "How cool during Pride Month that I get to work the first big show since everything shut down. And to see this running, with all the precautions, it sets a precedent that other promotions can follow."

During his time off, he'd kept in shape by doing yoga. After three months, though, he said, "It's good to know you remember how to be a wrestler. But, man, I know I'm going to be sore."

When Iowan JJ Garrett read about the card on Twitter, he contacted Lauderdale and volunteered to work the show. He'd spent the lockdown "smoking a bunch of weed, working out and watching Attitude Era stuff on the WWE Network. I haven't had a ring available to me for the past couple of months. It'll be like bumping on concrete, but I can't wait to do it."

One of the more interesting characters on the card was Levi Everett, who wore traditional Amish garb — as a shoot, he insisted, and not a work. "If I didn't dress the way I do, you wouldn't think I was really Amish," he explained. "It's all in the presentation."

To add to the gimmick, Everett had taken to churning butter before his match, as the fans chanted, "Churn, churn, churn."

Born in 1992, Everett missed the Attitude Era, the early days of TNA and the emergence of John Cena, all for a very simple reason. Because of their rejection of the modern world, his family eschewed television — or any device that used electricity generated by public power lines.

While he wouldn't name his order, he specified that he was allowed to catch rides to the arena from non-Amish friends. But, for short trips, "most of the time, it's horse and buggy."

On a typical workday, he trained only after he completed his other tasks, cleaning up the job site where he hammered wooden stakes into the ground and poured concrete foundations, and tended to the animals on his farm.

He'd discovered professional wrestling on a fluke, while riding in his buggy and spotting a sign for an indie show. He parked outside and went in.

"I was fascinated by the fighting," he remembered. "People were jumping high, flying around. I didn't know anything about the business then, but it felt real. I thought, 'This is really something I want to do.'"

There were no training schools in the rural pocket of Indiana where he was raised, so he moved his wife and four children closer to Indianapolis. While the family continued to observe the tenets of their faith, Everett was baptized into the creed of the squared circle.

"I'm not sure if they really get what I'm doing, but they try to, and I try to help them," he said. But once he debuted for the Wild Championship Wrestling Outlaws (WCWO) group in the town of Greensburg in 2017, his parents "shunned me out. I told them this is something I need to do for me. But they always said, 'no violence,' and I broke that protocol."

Only when the bell rang was he able to put his life conflicts into perspective. "It's something weird. The outside world exits me, and there's this explosion I feel inside that I've never been able to feel anywhere else."

As I sat under a tarp, shielded from the sun, watching the crew prepare for the 4:30 pre-show prior to the 5 p.m. broadcast on FITE TV, I asked Lauderdale why the event was starting so early. "I didn't want to pay for the lights," he answered.

My attention went back to the ring, where a Joey Janela lookalike — who occasionally wrestled as The Bad Boy's "cousin," Kung Fu Janela — was sanitizing the ropes. Then, ring announcer Jay Rose was stepping between the strands, microphone in hand. "I have to get this out of the way," he began. "We're in the middle of a damn pandemic. I don't know if you know it . . . In order for other professional wrestling shows to exist in this space, we have to do this safe . . . If you have a mask, please wear it . . . even though it's hot as hell . . . Please take every single precaution . . . Please."

If there were any COVID cynics in the crowd, they were keeping their opinions to themselves. Like many indie shows I'd attended, this had a progressive vibe, and a punk rock look. When I circulated the amphitheater, I met people who'd driven to the event from as far away as New York, California and Florida. Even so, Lauderdale estimated that 90 percent of the spectators were from the Midwest, most of them GCW followers as opposed to pedestrians wandering through the park and happening on a wrestling show.

"Let the whole world see," Rose continued to cheers, "that the pandemic hasn't killed the spirit of indie wrestling."

Before the action began, fans stood for a 10-bell salute to Hana Kimura and Danny Havoc, a recently-departed death match legend who'd taken part in a GCW tour to Japan earlier in the year.

In addition to the requisite brawling, aerial maneuvers and technical moves, there were aspects of the card that reminded people of the times in which they were living. Wrestlers walked through the crowd bumping elbows rather than slapping hands. Following his win over Jimmy Lloyd, Alex Zayne approached the timekeeper's table, extended his hands and received a long squirt of sanitizer. Tre Lamar and Lee Moriarty both wore Black Lives Matter shirts before colliding.

Prior to his intergender match with Allie Katch, Effy announced that two LGBTQ talents were sharing the ring in the semi-main event. He congratulated Allie on recently coming out as pansexual, but quickly reminded her, "I'm the old gay. You didn't break down the closet door."

To underscore this point, he attempted to drag a door into the ring, with the fans intoning, "Closet door. Closet door."

Allie kicked it in his face.

The two then went slap for slap. Depending upon which one was delivering the blow, the crowd alternated with shouts of "new gay" and "old gay."

Surviving a Frankensteiner through a door propped up on two chairs, Allie won the contest with a DDT.

She later told me that Effy's remarks about taking risks as an openly gay pro wrestler were grounded in truth. "I was never persecuted. But even among the older generations of gay people, there was some internalized homophobia. For me, pro wrestling is a platform. I want fans to see people who look like them, and are like them, and feel more comfortable within themselves."

The only time I saw the fans blatantly disregard social distancing precautions was when death match master Nick Gage charged the ring for his clash with Nate Webb. Unhinged by the sight of Gage, fans raced toward him, bumping bodies with the indie legend, while others assembled around the mat, pounding it. In the middle of everything, one fan had a seizure.

Reversing course, Gage went out of wrestler mode, and knelt beside the woman, checking on her.

The ring announcer asked the crowd for "peace and silence" — he didn't want unnecessary noise to aggravate her condition — and the fans largely complied. With Gage looking down on her, she slowly seemed to come back to her senses. When sirens were heard in the distance, spectators moved their chairs to other parts of the grass and cleared a wide path for the EMTs.

As the woman was placed onto a gurney, Gage returned the ring, watching the medical team from his perch on the middle rope.

"I was waiting there, all ready," Nate Webb told me. "I'd helped put the show together because this is my hometown. Nick comes out, I was all excited to start the match and then, we had this long break and I had to wait for the ambulance to leave. But when the lady on the stretcher passed by me and gave me a thumbs-up, I got back into myself again."

During the interruption, FITE TV had aired a loop of promos. As soon as the feed resumed, so did the pounding of the ring apron. Webb emerged from an elevated section of the amphitheater, while fans clapped and stomped along to his entrance music. As he mounted the ropes and turned to the crowd, Gage shoved him into the audience, pounded him with a chair and put him through a door positioned at ringside.

The audience was getting the main event it wanted. The pair rumbled across the lawn. Gage held his opponent over a gate, threatening to throw him into the river below. Webb fought back, delivering a back-breaker onto the grass. Smashing Webb with a cooler, Gage handed a fan two chairs to hold up, then rammed Nate's head into the metal.

The finish came after Gage executed a package piledriver from the second rope through a chair. As soon as the bell rang, though, the victor pulled up his foe and raised his arm. "It feels good to be back with you crazy fuckin' fans," he proclaimed, reminding them that while he had been serving time for bank robbery a few years earlier, their letters kept him inspired.

He then promised to continue wrestling until he was dead. And if you knew anything about his real life — he once literally died after a match and was revived on the way to the hospital — that wasn't fake news.

Webb replied by praising his adversary and inviting fans to an after-party at a newly opened pub downtown. "Who wants to drink some shots?" he yelled.

Since New York City was still closed to this type of socializing, I was open to the suggestion — although a bit cautious about getting too close to anybody. When I arrived, I was relieved to see a handful of outdoor tables and ended up having a pretty decent conversation with Kyle the Beast (KTB), who'd lost earlier in the night to AJ Gray. Someone had a Polaroid camera, and I ended up with a souvenir, a blurry photo with a masked Effy and bare-faced Levi Everett to commemorate the best day most of us had had in a while.

CHAPTER 16

THE GCW SHOW was an aberration, a boisterous infusion of regularity at a time when few were sure if a successful vaccine would ever be developed and the majority of small wrestling promotions were struggling. Several months into the pandemic, Tommy Dreamer had no choice but to put his House of Hardcore group — which had featured AEW names Luchasaurus, Marko Stunt, Private Party, Best Friends and Orange Cassidy; former Ring of Honor and Impact World champion Eddie Edwards; and WWE Hall of Famers Rikishi and The Godfather — on hiatus. "My company is pretty much non-existent anymore," he told me. "How can you run a show when you don't even know if you can go indoors, and you can only sell 200 or 250 tickets tops without getting people sick? What if the situation gets worse, and you have to cancel at the last minute? And COVID testing is an added expense for an indie."

In L.A., the esteemed Santino Brothers Wrestling Academy, whose former students included Ronda Rousey, Jessamyn Duke, Jake Atlas, Big Swole and Brody King, was relegated to offering classes online, as the re-opening of its in-person dojo continued to be delayed.

Every summer, Montreal's International Wrestling Syndicate (IWS) staged a show at a local music festival, exposing metal fans to a wrestling product that was different from what they might have spotted while turning channels. "The Quebec scene was the best it had ever been," said IWS cofounder PCP Crazy F'N Manny. "Even with something like 20 wrestling promotions, everybody was selling out."

But once the coronavirus hit, the music festival was postponed and the company had to stress over whether there was enough video in the archives to fill time on its cable TV show. "Everybody has been really understanding," Manny said. "But there's still pressure to produce original content because the big companies have something new on TV every week."

With or without TV, he continued to feel assured that his fans would stay loyal. Two hours after learning that the 2020 festival would not be taking place, Manny was walking down Rue Ste.-Catherine in Montreal's East End when he was approached by a 72-year-old woman who'd been following the local scene since the Grand Prix and Les As De La Lutte (All-Star Wrestling) promotions were hot shotting each other during their wrestling war in the 1970s. With tears in her eyes, she asked, "Do you promise? Do you promise that, when this is over, you'll put shows back on?"

The absence of live events left some companies with no choice but to merge. In July, it was announced that Japan's Pro Wrestling NOAH — founded in 2000 by former All Japan Pro Wrestling titlist Mitsuharu Misawa, who convinced 24 of the company's wrestlers to defect — and DDT were joining GanPro Wrestling and the Tokyo Joshi (women's) group to form a single company, CyberFight. The organization's goal, its president Sanshiro Takagi said, was overtaking New Japan.

As time went on, though, the mission statement was revised — to the point that, in 2022, a third night of *Wrestle Kingdom* was added specifically to feature New Japan athletes doing battle with talent from NOAH.

Although cutbacks related to the pandemic reportedly halted WWE's plans to start a Japanese brand, the company did purchase EVOLVE, a highly respected indie promotion whose performers had included future WWE signees Daniel Bryan, Apollo Crews, Austin Theory, Johnny Gargano, Ricochet, Oney Lorcan, Cedric Alexander, Drew Gulak, Mia Yim and Bobby Fish, as well as the Young Bucks, Eddie Kingston, Ethan Page and Zack Sabre Jr. Started in 2010 by Gabe Sapolsky, who learned the business from Paul Heyman in ECW, cofounded ROH and was considered one of the best bookers in the industry during the group's early years, EVOLVE and WWE developed a working relationship in 2015. The league funneled a number of stars to NXT, while the WWE Network presented an EVOLVE special, opposite an AEW show, in 2019.

Still, the company's financial issues escalated with COVID-19, particularly the cancellation of the cards it had planned for the week of *WrestleMania 36*.

Several EVOLVE stars would quickly transition to NXT: Harlem Bravado, Leon Ruff, Anthony Henry, Joe Gacy, Curt Stallion, Josh Briggs, even referee Jake Clemons. Brandi Lauren's name was rebranded Skyler Story and Anthony Greene became August Grey. In November, Ruff defeated Johnny Gargano to become NXT North American champion.

But WWE's acquisition brought at least one legal challenge with it. Former UFC fighter Matt Riddle had signed with EVOLVE in 2015, beating Sabre for the group's title three years later. He was set to make his *SmackDown* debut in June when his name was linked to #SpeakingOut.

A female wrestler who'd appeared in EVOLVE said that, in 2018, the two were in a van with three other wrestlers and a videographer when Riddle asked for sex after the others fell asleep. When she refused, she claimed, he grabbed her by the throat, and she gave him oral sex to diffuse the situation.

Instantly, fans began posting about the accusations on social media, and Riddle was quick to respond. In one exchange, he wrote, "You don't need to be my fan/friend but try not to believe every story you hear especially with no proof."

The fans countered with a question: what would motivate a woman to lie about something so traumatic? "Why does anybody lie?" Riddle replied. "She has been harassing me for years and I've had to change my number 3 times and I almost got a restraining order against her but didn't wanna ruin her career."

An attorney representing Riddle soon entered the conflict, alleging, "Our firm had drafted a pleading against this performer to seek an injunction for cyberstalking in the Circuit Court for Orange County, Florida." The lawyer called the woman's story "completely false and another attempt to harass and humiliate" Riddle and his wife.

The WWE wrestler later posted a video statement on Twitter, maintaining that he'd had an extramarital affair with the accuser, and she became bitter when he ended it.

Addressing the woman directly, he said, "I have never in my entire life sexually assaulted a man, woman or anybody . . . I never assaulted you. That story about that van trip, and the driver being asleep and me forcing you . . . it's a fabricated story because you're still mad."

Talking about his infidelity was embarrassing, he added, but the circumstances left him little choice. "We had a fling. I started to get sad and depressed because I was lying to my wife . . . I told my wife about you and us. I tried to end it. I blocked you. I blocked your social media . . . I got a new number. You got my new number and kept messaging me."

He said that his accuser then began turning up at hotels where he was staying and asking his friends about his whereabouts. "At this point, you have to realize, if you don't think you're stalking or harassing me, you're crazy."

Speaking directly to his fans, he contended that, when the woman "didn't get her way," she manipulated the #SpeakingOut movement "to try and ruin my career."

In October, the woman announced that she'd sued Riddle, Gabe Sapolsky, EVOLVE and the company's new owner, WWE. At a news conference, her attorney, John Chwarzynski said that there had been a "multitude of sexual assaults committed [against the accuser] by Matt Riddle." After the first one in 2017, Chwarzynski alleged that Riddle boasted to Sapolsky and two others now associated with WWE, who "tacitly approved."

Another charge was that, at Riddle's insistence, EVOLVE and WWE eventually punished the woman by refusing to book her on cards, even though she appeared online as a "social media ambassador" for EVOLVE's final show in March 2020.

Zoning in on the industry's most dominant company, Chwarzynski stressed, "The WWE has painted a picture over the course of the years that female performers are to comply with certain rules. The WWE, since its inception, has hypersexualized female performers and they've profited from male aggression against these female performers."

Reportedly, Riddle had previously warned WWE about potential issues with his accuser, prompting the company to do its own investigation.

A statement from WWE noted that the organization had not been officially sued but intended to fight vigorously if that occurred.

WWE and Sapolsky were later removed from the lawsuit after a judge ruled that there was no proof that either was connected to the claims against Riddle. The suit against the wrestler called the Original Bro was dropped in July 2021. "The parties have put this in their past and are focused on the future," Chwarzynski told TMZ.

He did not disclose whether a financial settlement had been reached out of court.

The closest AEW and NXT came to a full-on death match was in early July, when both companies presented two consecutive weeks of shows with pay-per-view themes. On July 1 and 8, AEW staged *Fyter Fest*, originally created as a spoof on the much-ridiculed Fyre Festival, a high-end music event in the Bahamas that fell apart, as attendees were housed in the types of tents provided to victims of natural disasters and served a "gourmet" cuisine of sandwiches. At the very same time, NXT aired the *Great American Bash*, a spectacular designed in 1985 by Dusty Rhodes for Jim Crockett Promotions and eventually appropriated into the WWE pay-per-view calendar.

Although both shows appeared on cable television, NXT tried bolstering the pay-per-view mood by limiting commercials. For its part, AEW promised prizes to the first 10 people who tweeted a specific hashtag during its picture-on-picture breaks.

On the July 8 program, former Impact World champion Brian Cage was scheduled to challenge Jon Moxley for the AEW crown. Cage was a recent AEW acquisition, debuting at *Double or Nothing* in May, where he was the surprise final entrant in what was billed as a "Casino Ladder Match." With Taz in his corner, Cage won the bout, earning a shot at Moxley's title.

"Obviously, I wish I had my first match in front of a sold-out arena," he told me. "But I still felt pretty good. The reaction to me online was overwhelming."

About a week before the clash, Cage learned that AEW wanted to pair him with Taz, the onetime "Human Suplex Machine" who realized, at a fairly early stage of his career, that he could turn a phrase as well as he bumped. Since 2000, he'd been a staple at the announce table — for WWE, TNA and, now, AEW.

"We didn't know each other," Cage said, "but, right away, we started to brainstorm ideas. We both like to talk. But he's seen a lot in the business and understands it. When he looks at a situation, he sees possibilities I don't."

After following AEW from the time of its launch, Cage was anxious to tangle with Moxley. But in late June, the champion's wife, WWE announcer Renee Young, became sick and lost her senses of taste and smell. Even before her COVID test came back, she knew that she had the virus.

Moxley tested negative and isolated himself in a different part of the house from his wife. But he'd been with Renee for several days before the diagnosis and couldn't take the risk of going to Daily's Place and infecting his fellow wrestlers. He'd stay at home, he said, and take other tests, refusing to interact with people until he could confirm that he was well.

The battle with Cage would have to be delayed. "Jon Moxley can get slammed on a car, crawl through tacks and fall through the stage," tweeted Tony Khan. "But it's every bit as cool that he came forward & told us that he had secondhand exposure to COVD. We test everyone here at #AEWDynamite, but Jon protected everyone onsite like the great champ he is."

The pair would finally meet on July 15. In the interim, though, Taz awarded his charge with the unofficial title he wore in ECW, the FTW — for "Fuck The World" — belt. "We pulled that out at the last minute," Cage said backstage before an indie card. "But that title means a lot to him personally, and he will *not* let me travel with it. And that's why it's not here."

Both *Fyter Fest* events raised money for Florida's First Coast Relief Fund and the Feeding Northeast Florida food bank, established charities that had shifted focus to COVID-19 response. In terms of the shows' content, Orange Cassidy's main event with Chris Jericho on July 1 sent a message that, despite an entertaining gimmick that worked on the indies, the "freshly squeezed" grappler — who billed himself from "wherever," and deliberately executed lackadaisical soft chops and kicks before firing up — was worthy of being elevated.

"He proved a lot to the wrestling world that he can be a main event star and that he belonged with Chris," Khan told the *New York Post*.

In terms of ratings, though, the *Great American Bash* enabled NXT to pass its rival. Some observers theorized that the shift was due to #SpeakingOut, and AEW watchers — who tended to be more plugged in to wrestling intrigue on social media — turning on the industry. The reality was that NXT put on some pretty absorbing matches. On July 1, NXT women's champion Io Shirai retained her title over Sasha Banks. WWE was clearly using its main roster players to boost the NXT talent, as *Raw* women's champion Asuka also made an appearance, blowing mist into Banks's face to prevent her from cheating. The next week, the brand's longest championship reign ended when NXT kingpin Adam Cole dropped the title to North American champion Keith Lee. With his victory, Lee became the first competitor to hold both belts at the same time.

After losing for three straight weeks, though, AEW regained the ratings lead. But in October, NXT beat AEW again — this time when WWE decided to offer another pay-per-view themed card on a regular broadcast, *Halloween Havoc*.

FTR's Dax Harwood said that the beneficiaries of the dueling programs were the people who loved wrestling. "Guys, if you're burying one company over the other, you're completely missing the fun," he tweeted the night after the two weeks of *Fyter Fest* and the *Great American Bash* ended. "I watched both shows from last night and we are lucky, as fans, to get the wrestling we get! In 1997 I LOVED the Hart Foundation [in the World Wrestling Federation] and I LOVED the n.W.o. I hope you guys can do the same."

CHAPTER 17

IN JUNE, NEW JAPAN held its first show since suspending its schedule in late February. Although fans were not admitted into the building, by July, the company was confident enough to perform at 33 percent capacity. Not only were strict social distancing guidelines enforced, but spectators were forbidden from shouting either insults or praise — even when masked — lest they spread airborne germs.

Eventually, New Japan incorporated a new technology into its performances — the same used at Japanese baseball and soccer events — permitting fans to emote by pressing buttons generating either cheering or booing noises. It didn't sound exactly like a live crowd — and keep in mind that Japanese audiences were not particularly renowned for expressing themselves — but at least the mood was genuine.

Backstage, wrestlers were allowed to remove their masks to eat, but required to bring their own packed and labeled food instead of lining up at catering. With so many foreigners unable to travel to Japan, the decision was made to expand the Bullet Club — a group traditionally dominated by gaijin — with native-born performers.

Some 3,900 fans were in Osaka-jō Hall on July 11 when Evil beat Kazuchika Okada in the finals of the New Japan Cup tournament, earning a shot at the unified IWGP Heavyweight and Intercontinental Championship the next night. Evil and titleholder Tetsuya Naito had been partners in the past, and, at the tournament's conclusion, the champion came to the ring to acknowledge the challenger. Unexpectedly, Evil threw up the Bullet Club sign and attacked his former ally, then exited with the faction — proudly declaring himself its newest member.

A day later, the Bullet Club interfered throughout the match. The end came when another intruder interceded. After jumping Naito, the masked man assisted Evil in securing the pinfall and the titles. The trespasser then revealed himself to be veteran Dick Togo, who would also be initiated into the Bullet Club and second Evil in his championship defenses.

New Japan fans were uncertain about how to react. Outside interference in important title matches was something observers expected in American wrestling. Although this device had been incorporated into New Japan plotlines, a sizeable number of followers considered it below the dignity of the sports-oriented product on which the company gained its reputation.

Without question, Evil's skills were respected, but he did not have the same main event aura as Naito, Okada and other past IWGP Heavyweight champions. Likewise, Togo was popular among hardcore Japanese fans. But given the fact that he was nearly 51 years old, there were questions about whether he belonged in a faction as esteemed as the Bullet Club. To some fans, New Japan was watering down the Bullet Club, indoctrinating people with the haphazardness that WCW exhibited when it allowed journeyman Louie Spicolli, referee Nick Patrick and the Hulkster's real-life nephew, Horace Hogan, into the nWo.

Of course, you wouldn't know that if you were sitting in Osaka-jō Hall. Remember — the Japanese fans were told not to boo. And they didn't.

In the United States, the promotion's American wing, NJPW Strong — launched in 2019 so the company could build a following on the other side of the Pacific Ocean — began running empty arena shows in June, broadcasting the cards worldwide on the organization's streaming service, NJPW World, as well as FITE TV. Performers were required to take COVID tests and quarantine for several days before the tapings. Here, the Bullet Club was represented by its New Zealand–born leader, Jay White, along with Chase Owens, KENTA, Tama Tonga and Tanga Loa. Although some of these wrestlers would eventually travel to Japan — secluding themselves for two weeks before taking part in any in-ring activity — the American shows featured such stateside talent as David Finlay — Fit Finlay's son — Rust Taylor, Alex Zayne, Blake Christian, Flip Gordon, Brody King, Rocky Romero, Tom Lawlor and Alex Coughlin.

Karl Fredericks, who'd been one of the first trainees at New Japan's L.A. dojo, entered into a U.S.-based feud with Jeff Cobb. "I'm pretty happy with the New Japan stuff we're doing in the U.S.," Cobb told me in August, as we sat across from each other in a suburban Illinois restaurant that allowed limited-capacity dining. "As long as I'm working for New Japan, I'm happy. I like that style, and I have a lot of unfinished business there. These NJPW Strong shows are keeping me in the spotlight."

After becoming one of the most coveted athletes in the business, Cobb was initially taken by surprise by the COVID shutdown. "Let me figure something out," he said, pulling out his phone and examining its calendar. "Fifteen weeks without wrestling. It was rough. Training in quarantine isn't like being in the ring."

Still, he tried to use the time productively, working out with Norm Turner, who'd been Matt Riddle's strength and conditioning coach when the Original Bro was in MMA. Always a powerhouse, Cobb said that he stopped lifting the "heavy stuff" to engage in more functional training, including "rigorous, hellacious sprints" to improve his endurance between the ropes.

When NJPW Strong renewed its schedule, he stepped into the ring with Tanga Loa for an empty arena match in Southern California and took a backdrop that "hurt like hell. Oh my god. I don't know why I thought that would be a good spot. When you're doing this three or four times a week, your back gets calcified. This was like bumping for the first time."

The next month, he flew to Mexico to receive stem cell treatments at a Guadalajara clinic. "I'd partially torn my labrum," the cup-shaped rim of cartilage lining and reinforcing the ball-and-socket joint of the shoulder. "It had been giving me problems for several years. If you watch some of my New Japan matches, you'll see I always had my shoulder taped up."

The regenerative therapy that Cobb received had yet to be approved by the Food and Drug Administration (FDA) in the United States. The procedure included a placenta implant inserted into his stomach, and a 50-million stem cell injection with a multivitamin intravenous drip. "From what I was told, [the process] calls upon your body to build more stem cells, doing construction in places that need rebuilding. All the stem cells were collected from umbilical cords and after-births. So no babies were hurt."

Within three days, Cobb noticed a difference. "My shoulder felt great. I was able to do exercises I had never done before."

He was ready for whatever came next, returning to Asia in September after appearing on several more NJPW Strong broadcasts, alongside Sterling and Logan Riegel. Despite the frustration of watching the pandemic stall their careers, the pair were grateful for the association with New Japan and mindful of the progress they'd made since their beginnings in the Kansas City area.

Growing up in the 1990s, the brothers had heard tales about the stars of the old Central States territory — Harley Race, Rufus R. Jones and Bulldog Bob Brown, among others — but didn't appreciate the region's wrestling past until they started training and researching that history themselves.

Since they innately understood that they were cruiserweights — the twins began their careers at five-foot-nine and about 180 pounds each — the two were drawn to WCW, where an array of lighter athletes combined technical wrestling with enterprising ring strategies: Eddie Guerrero, Dean Malenko, Chris Benoit, Chris Jericho, Rey Mysterio. "A lot of our friends watched the WWF and wondered why we didn't," Sterling said. "But we were just into the cruiserweights, man."

Logan considered the opening bout of *Starcade '98* , a Triangle Match between Mysterio, Juventud Guerrera and Billy Kidman for the WCW Cruiserweight Championship, a life-changing moment. After Kidman retained the title, he was immediately challenged by Guerrera and another match commenced. Kidman eventually won with a shooting star press.

"I had vague memories of watching wrestling before this with my dad, but this was the first match I watched bell to bell," Logan said. "Now, we went back, buying tapes, catching up, learning the background of all these guys until we found some tapes of Rey from Mexico. It was after the whole tape trading thing, but we got them on eBay. It was like finding a treasure."

When the World Wrestling Federation purchased WCW in 2001, the victorious company ran an *InVasion* pay-per-view featuring the stars of both promotions, as well as ECW. The brothers tuned in but were so disappointed that Mysterio hadn't been signed that they boycotted the organization. It was only when Rey became a *SmackDown* regular in 2002 that they returned.

At the time, *SmackDown* was pretaped, and, by going online, the boys discovered that they could learn the match results before the program even aired. "I'd go to school and smarten up the other kids," Sterling said.

On their backyard trampoline, the two began putting together matches. "We understood that wrestling was a choreographed thing," Sterling said. "Our father had taught us to do flips, so we always knew we could do high spots," somersaulting from the trampoline onto each other on the lawn. "Only we didn't know what a high spot was."

At Lee's Summit High School, they enhanced their acrobatic skills by competing on the dive team. "It was one of the least popular sports," Sterling said. "There'd sometimes be six people in the crowd. It prepared us for the indies in a weird way."

At that point, the twins were considered skinny and small. But after graduating and attending classes on the Longview campus of Metropolitan Community College, they began to scrupulously work out, imagining themselves looking like such jacked-up WCW performers as Buff Bagwell and Scott Steiner.

Transferring to the University of Central Missouri, both enrolled in a public speaking class. When the teacher asked about everyone's goals, Logan spoke about becoming a pro wrestler. Although most of their classmates scoffed, one student mentioned that he knew someone who owned a ring in Raytown, Missouri. "I wish I'd gotten into this business a different way," Sterling said. "The ring felt like it was being held together with duct tape. We really didn't get trained there. And later on, we had to relearn everything they taught us. We just kind of wrestled each other."

The duo discussed traveling to Texas to train at Booker T's Houston-area Reality of Wrestling school but weren't ready to uproot their lives.

Even with their limited experience, though, promoters began asking them to appear on local cards, starting in 2015. "We didn't know a lot of the fundamentals," Sterling said. "Luckily, we were athletic enough to hit the moves we knew. We kind of got lucky. We were twins. We were in good shape. We could do flips."

At a certain point, they were befriended by Mike Sydal, who'd later appear with his own brother, Matt, in AEW. During long car rides "he told us how to dress when you show up at an arena," Sterling said, "how to walk to the ring before your match, how to talk to promoters, how to get yourself over against bigger opponents and the different things we could do with guys our own size."

Gradually, the Riegels learned tag team psychology — when to tag in and tag out, the best times to use double team maneuvers. Their finishes included a Doomsday Blockbuster, with Sterling coming off the ropes to deliver a flying guillotine while Logan held a foe on his shoulders. Noted Sterling, "We're not the biggest guys, but my brother is really strong and can get most wrestlers up, no matter how big they are."

Another move they favored was the pendulum DDT. The sequence would begin with Logan facelocking an opponent while leaping up and wrapping his legs around Sterling's shoulders. Sterling would then thrust his brother's legs into the air and step back, while Logan plummeted downwards, driving their rival's head into the mat.

Slowly and steadily, the Reigel Twins were building their brand. At one stage, a youth pastor they knew mentioned that he was acquainted with Shawn Michaels, who'd become a born-again Christian in 2002 and occasionally spoke at churches. On the minister's suggestion, the Heartbreak Kid agreed to do a FaceTime call with the twins. "We were at a very early stage of our career, where we were trying to do the craziest move of the night in every match," Sterling said. "And Shawn told us that longevity was the key. If you can't do the crazy moves because you blew out your knee, what's the point?"

The novelty of receiving career advice from a legend like Michaels instilled the twins with confidence. Recalled Logan, "We were looking on Instagram and seeing guys who got started at the same time as us, people like MJF and Flip Gordon, and thinking, 'We're all going to be going places.'"

In 2016, the Riegels were earning extra money by donning suits and working the door at a Kansas City night club when a well-groomed, light-skinned Black man introduced himself. "I'm starting a wrestling company," Major Baisden told the twins, "and I want to sign you guys."

Logan was cynical. "He was talking about paying us like $50,000 a year. And we're like, 'You're so full of shit.' But he brought us to his office and talked to my parents and said, 'I didn't have enough money to buy the Royals, so this is the second-best option.'"

Baisden, who'd be described in the press as a "serial entrepreneur," believed that interest in WWE was declining and the time had come to return to the age of the territories. His concept involved starting branches of his National Wrasslin' League (NWL) in Kansas City and St. Louis, utilizing hometown talent in each region and staging family-friendly inter-city clashes. After buying existing promotions in both locales, he declared that he intended to expand to 30 cities — including former regional hot spots like Houston, Los Angeles, Memphis and San Francisco — and operate on a budget of $250-million annually within 10 years.

The 24-year-old Riegels were the NWL's first signings. Blaisden rechristened them Jet and Jax Royal and named the tandem Royal Blood. In addition to their yearly salary, they received housing in a corporate complex, health insurance and a 401K plan.

The company's training facility contained two rings and, according to Logan, $80,000 worth of weights. Before the NWL had generated a dollar, the Riegels and the other wrestlers under contract were training daily from 9 a.m. to 4 p.m., with a lunch break in between. After another break, the talent would work out some more before calling it a day.

Blaisden "was living his Vince McMahon fantasy," Logan said.

And like McMahon in the '80s, he quickly earned the ire of aficionados with an allegiance to the regional outfits he hoped to displace. "Indie fans hated him," Logan said, "because he was taking away and signing up the wrestlers at the promotions they loved — especially in St. Louis, where there was a lot of loyalty to the local groups."

Bizarrely, Blaisden also resisted publicizing the NWL online. "He was against YouTube," Logan said. "He only wanted to do syndicated TV. He loved the fact that he owned a film and didn't want to give it away for free. But in the digital era, no one wanted to watch Saturday night wrestling."

In 2017, the budding magnate predicted that, within a year, the NWL would be averaging approximately 600 fans per show and running up to a dozen shows a month. And on the surface, the cards appeared to be crowded. Even in cold weather, attendees were seen lining up outside each event.

But a large proportion of the tickets were free — given out at anti-bullying events the NWL sponsored at area schools. Like so many before him, Blaisden was in over his head. The company was declining before it ever ascended.

For austerity purposes, the entire office staff was terminated, and wrestlers recruited to fill their positions. When Blaisden finally conceded that YouTube might not be such a bad idea, the Riegels were placed in charge of editing the videos.

The talent also worked construction, converting the training center into a new NWL Arena. "We put in flooring," Logan said. "We built the bleachers like Lego pieces. But a few days before our first show, when we already had the chairs set up, the owner called us all in for a meeting and said he couldn't do it anymore. He was done."

The company officially ceased operations on April 12, 2018. "Was it really that bad?" Logan asked. "He took a bunch of indie guys in the Midwest and gave us a bunch of money and medical and dental insurance for two years, and let us eat, drink and sleep wrestling. But man, it's still the weirdest thing to talk about. There was so much money dumped into it. When some of these guys become famous in wrestling one day, it'll be a much bigger story."

While the Riegels had been busy in the NWL, the wrestling scene was moving forward. Immediately, the twins found work in other places, Metro Pro and Journey Pro in Kansas City, St. Louis Anarchy and Glory

Pro in St. Louis, AAW in Chicago, and promotions in Iowa, Colorado, Texas and California.

Even the best times were tempered with cautious thoughts. "If you're working the indies all the time, even if you're paying your rent and buying nice things, you can also get injured," Logan said. "So we realized how short your time in the business can be. And a lot of your money goes back into wrestling. You meet workers all the time who've been at it for 20 years and never got their due. At the same time, it can all change in one day, and we knew that."

Just before the pandemic, the pair observed that the industry, as a whole, seemed to be creating a greater emphasis on tag team wrestling, the result they believed of AEW making the division an important part of its brand. After a tryout with New Japan at the company's L.A. dojo, the pair cleared a critical career hurdle. "We look at the business as a sport, and so New Japan, to us, was always the best of the best," Logan said. "When they wanted us in their system, it was surreal."

They were booked as part of the New Japan lineup in Tampa on the week of *WrestleMania 36* when the shutdown occurred.

Sterling happened to be in England visiting his girlfriend — whom he'd met when she was an au pair for a congressman in Kansas — and opted to remain until his options widened. "There weren't any wrestling shows in the U.S., and the gyms were closed everywhere." He switched his workouts to outdoors, running to maintain his cardio.

When the gyms opened back in Missouri in May, Logan took a job as a personal trainer. "All I was doing was working out," he said.

Although he had access to a ring, he minimized the time he spent between the ropes to allow certain injuries to heal. "Getting in the ring before an actual show is what's most important for me, visualizing the match and memorizing spots."

With his brother away, he resisted pressure to start pursuing a singles career. "I'm a tag team wrestler. That's how my brain is wired. Singles wrestling and tag team wrestling are two different worlds for me."

From opposite sides of the Atlantic, each sibling followed the escalation of COVID-19 and despaired over the future of the industry. "There was a point," Logan admitted, "when I asked myself if I'd ever wrestle again."

Yet, it was too late to turn to another interest or lifestyle. When NJPW Strong resumed, the Riegels were invited back. By early 2021, they were in the main event.

"Before COVID-19, I was in this weird stress level where we had to get signed somewhere," Sterling said. "But this whole thing reminded me why I loved wrestling. It's about having fun, being myself. And if that's my goal, I know it will lead me where I need to be."

All the Riegels needed to do was look around the NJPW Strong dressing room to find kindred spirits whose stories and ambitions matched their own. After the disappointment of his *WrestleMania 36* week, Chris Dickinson continued building his following in NJPW Strong, as well as ROH.

"There were people who saw the pandemic, packed their bags and went home," he told me. "And I couldn't be that way. I used the time to become a way better professional wrestler," training in submission grappling with former UFC Heavyweight champion Josh Barnett and Davey Boy Smith Jr., a former WWE competitor and son of the late British Bulldog. "When I had nothing to do, I'd watch six hours of wrestling at a time. Even during the worst days, it could only get better, right?"

Danhausen already had a presence on Patreon, an online platform that allows "patrons" to send money to videographers, musicians and other artists whose content they follow. "I knew I'd do fine financially," he said. "I'd set myself up to have an entertaining character who people would want to watch."

His offerings included food and movie reviews, interview segments with Nyla Rose, Lance Archer, Allie Katch, Ethan Page and other wrestlers, and a mini-series centered around his improv bits. In one episode, he dissected the science of chewing Bazooka gum. Effy joined him in another video to promote a new piece of merchandise.

Because of the difficulty of shipping from Canada, he arranged to have stores around the United States mail out his t-shirts, towels, Halloween masks, enamel pins and other items. He sold stickers to supporters north of the border. "I tried to release things that I would buy personally, and I think the fans could read my sincerity," he said. "I felt like they really wanted to help the wrestlers out during this period."

He picked up extra money by sending greetings to followers on Cameo. "Instead of wrestling four times a week, I began making more content."

Ricky Morton had to learn about technology that didn't exist at the height of his career. "I didn't know that much about social media until the coronavirus," he said, "and I did good off of it." Along with selling old Rock 'n' Roll Express merchandise, the WWE Hall of Famer presented a YouTube show featuring matches between the students at his Chuckey, Tennessee, wrestling school.

"It feels like it did when I was starting out," he asserted. "We keep heat on the heels. I can make you believe if I want to."

Like Morton, Thunder Rosa told me that the shutdowns gave her little choice but to turn her energy to social media: "I was forced out of my comfort zone. I was so used to looking out at the crowd, listening to them and connecting with them that way. Now, I had to connect with them emotionally on a small screen and make them forget their reality in the middle of a pandemic."

Brian Pillman Jr. credited Pro Wrestling Tees, the Chicago-based website for wrestling t-shirts and other merchandise, with helping him earn money when there were no bookings. Then, in early July, The Good Brothers, Luke Gallows and Karl Anderson, held a combined wrestling and comedy show outdoors in Atlanta, and Pillman was invited to participate. Over the next two days, he'd work in Tennessee for 127 Pro Wrestling in Grimsley and Kross Fire Wrestling (KFW) in Sevierville. A week later, he wrestled at three other shows in Alabama.

"The south was the first place to open up," he said. "Some people in the crowd wore masks. But down there, no one wants you telling them what to do."

As the summer progressed, he became a regular with AEW, eventually forming the Varsity Blondes with Griff Garrison and Julia Hart.

In August, Danhausen flew to Indiana to do two shows for Black Label Pro. He'd been working out in the gym he'd built on his back porch with Speedball Mike Bailey, a top name on the Montreal indies, and the night before the first card, went over some moves with fellow wrestlers Isaias Velazquez and Kylie Rae. "They taught me how to do a tilt-a-whirl into a submission attempt. And I said, 'I'm going to use this tomorrow.' And it felt great because people hadn't seen me do it before.

"There were way less people there than I was used to, and a lot of thoughts were going through my mind. Would they still care? But nothing dwindled. In fact, I felt like I was better in the ring, probably because I'd spent so much time training."

As per the rules in Canada, he quarantined for two weeks after returning home. On social media, he explained that the country's restrictions limited the number of dates that he could take in the United States. But he spent the time in isolation cranking out more exclusive content, and the orders increased.

On Halloween, he proclaimed that he'd signed with Ring of Honor. "Now, it's time for them to rue the day," he said in a video.

Although the company was conservative about taking health risks — requiring more than 100 wrestlers and staffers to quarantine in single rooms at a Baltimore hotel and go through three rounds of COVID testing before TV tapings at the empty arena at the University of Maryland's local campus — ROH had not been demure about continuing to build its roster.

Rather than becoming a free agent, Flip Gordon made the decision to re-sign with the company due to its alliances with other promotions and willingness to meet his financial demands. "When someone wants to make you a millionaire," he told *The Wrestling Inc. Daily* podcast, "you dedicate time to them."

After a five-year absence, Mike Bennett and his wife, Maria Kanellis, returned, as well. Before being laid off by WWE, they'd taken part in a storyline in which a pregnant Maria berated her spouse, claimed he wasn't the father of her child and forced him to allow her to pin him for the WWE 24/7 title. As an added insult, the company required Bennett to use Maria's surname.

Ring of Honor clearly viewed him differently, reuniting him with old partner Matt Taven, with whom Bennett had held the company's tag team belts as well as the IWGP Tag Team Championship.

The NWA also positioned Bennett as the top contender for Nick Aldis's crown. "The story is that this is part of Mike's road to redemption," Aldis explained to me, "and I'm the cagey NWA champ."

During his time off the road, Aldis focused on tasks he couldn't normally do with a busy wrestling schedule, including his exercise regimen. "Everything's harder with free weights — balance, engaging different muscles. So I concentrated on that." To enhance his cardio core strength, he practiced more yoga.

Although his wife, Mickie James, was signed to WWE at the time, both were home more than in the past. "The number one killer of marriages is the time apart," Aldis said. "Before this, we'd have maybe one day a week to concentrate on each other, and a lot of the focus would be on our child. Now, we had time to talk to each other and listen to each other about our perspectives on professional wrestling.

"The fact that I never worked for WWE meant that I had a fresh set of eyes. She knows production. She knows graphics. She's worked for the market leader, and I wanted to learn from that."

Just as Aldis was growing accustomed to his pandemic routine, though, the NWA was thrust into the middle of the #SpeakingOut movement. In this case, the target was the group's vice president and production chief, Dave Lagana, who was accused of making sexual overtures toward a female houseguest while they were sleeping in the same bed in 2010. When she rolled away from him, she said, Lagana stopped.

"I did not touch her in the way she claimed," he wrote on Twitter. "I never touched her like that, and I never would have."

Nonetheless, he decided to resign from his position at the NWA because "I didn't want to involve the men and women of the National Wrestling Alliance during this time." As a result, the production of NWA content temporarily stopped.

"It was a devastating blow to the NWA," Aldis said. "In some ways, it was worse than COVID-19. Dave contributed so much, but there was no other option than for him to step away. The accusation creates a situation where you end up in some form of purgatory."

Immediately, there was online speculation that Lagana's departure meant the end of Billy Corgan's wrestling experiment. "It's very demoralizing to see people who are supposed to be your biggest fans taking so much pleasure in your hardships," Aldis said. "'Oh, things are really tough for the NWA. Billy's going to pull the plug.' I had a bulging disc for two years but didn't take time off. And when I saw people revel in our difficulties, I sort of wished they understood that. People don't watch TV anymore because they're so fascinated with what's being said on Twitter. It's definitely the part of the industry I enjoy the least."

Before the September debut of the NWA-affiliated United Wrestling Network's weekly television program, it was announced that Bennett would challenge Aldis. While the role that the number one contender played in WWE was never mentioned, there was no mistaking the implication. "I need to restore the dignity to my family," Bennett said online. "I need to restore the dignity to my name. The only way I can do that is to beat you for that prestigious World Heavyweight Championship."

Bolstering Bennett's credibility, Aldis appeared on the *This is the NWA* podcast and countered, "I want the lion. I want the man who thinks that he can take out the king of the jungle. I want that because that's what's best for business. And it's also what's best for me."

To build interest in the upcoming match, the NWA revived its documentary-style series, *Ten Pounds of Gold*. With Lagana gone, most of the editing was personally done by the champion.

"I had to pivot and learn another skill set," Aldis said. "I always had one eye on working in production eventually. This is another example of making good use of the downtime during COVID."

He compared the story arc on these programs to "a stripped-down version of wrestling booking. Yes, it's a predetermined endeavor. But there's authenticity so the audience can suspend its disbelief."

When the two finally collided on September 15, Bennett's talents had been re-established, while his motivations for snaring the gold were believable. The two wrestled a credible match, with Aldis catching his foe in the air, trapping him in a cloverleaf and sitting down on him. Bennett struggled to make it to the ropes on several occasions, but the champion dragged him back to the center of the mat. Eventually, Bennett appeared to pass out from the pain — like "Stone Cold" Steve Austin in Bret

Hart's Sharpshooter at *WrestleMania XIII* — as the referee called for the bell.

Aldis retained the Ten Pounds of Gold. Despite the long coronavirus sabbatical, fans were reminded that his reign stood at 694 days.

"In the end, no matter how cinematic the build-up might be, an important professional wrestling match is like a big money prize fight," he pointed out. "There's no guarantee that it will be satisfactory to watch. So you have to perform in the ring to make it stimulating and engaging."

CHAPTER 18

"PUT YOUR MASK on, old man."

On the football field at Marian Catholic High School in Chicago Heights, Illinois, a heel manager known as Frank the Clown was shaking his rainbow wig and hurling insults at fans spread throughout the gridiron and bleachers in socially distanced pods. The date was August 7, 2020, and more than 500 people were there to watch the card presented by the Warrior Wrestling promotion. It was the first professional wrestling event with spectators in the state of Illinois in five months.

Referring to a recent spike of COVID cases in the Sunshine State, Frank threatened, "I will cough on you. I came from Florida."

Standing alone in the first row of bleachers, Steve Tortorello took in the scene with a look of satisfaction. Not only was he the promoter for Warrior Wrestling, he was also an alumni of Marion Catholic — and the school's current principal.

Located 30 miles south of Chicago, the city was once largely Italian-American and known for manufacturing freight cars and auto parts. While the Ford Motor Company still ran a metal stamping plant in 2020, sections of the city suffered from high crime, unemployment and poverty, typified in rows of abandoned and dilapidated buildings and overgrown lots.

When Tortorello and I spoke, he pointed out that Marian Catholic drew kids from 75 separate zip codes. The majority — 40 percent — were African American, while 30 percent were white, 15 percent Hispanic and the remainder from a variety of other ethnic backgrounds. Although 60 percent were Catholic, there were also Muslims, Buddhists, Hindus, Baptists, Jews and Taoists.

With the nuns who occupied teaching positions largely retired, labor costs at the school had gone up, as well as tuition. It now cost $13,000 annually to educate a student there, and many were on scholarship — the endowments raised through events like Warrior Wrestling.

At this particular show, the clusters of family and friends were separated from other groups by a distance of five yards. Concession stands were closed; fans were required to bring their own snacks. When the crowd arrived, no one was there ripping tickets and handing them back. Rather, all purchases were made in advance, and attendees gave their names at the door. During the meet and greets, tables separated the performers from their followers. If a fan had a piece of merchandise, the wrestler signed it with his or her own marker. Photos were generally taken with a spectator standing some six feet in front of the talent and snapping a selfie.

It was Jeff Cobb's first indie since the pandemic was declared. "I missed being in an environment like this, where fans could react to you," he said. He also liked that the gate receipts were going toward education, and the promoter wasn't some shyster or money mark — a guy who recently experienced a financial windfall and was now going to blow it on a wrestling promotion — but a decent man who was trying to do better for his community.

Even with Frank the Clown's taunts, it was a good vibe.

Steve Tortorello didn't grow up expecting to go into the wrestling business.

After being raised in Tinley Park, about 25 miles away, and graduating from Marian Catholic in 2004, Tortorello attended Notre Dame. While majoring in American Studies, he joined the Alliance for Catholic Education, which trains potential teachers by sending them to schools in disadvantaged communities. Dispatched to East L.A., Tortorello was able to bond with the Mexican-American parents over their shared interest in professional wrestling. But even though he'd followed the World Wrestling Federation during the Hulkamania and Attitude Eras, he knew little about lucha libre. Invited to an event in a mechanic's garage, Tortorello stood with a group of parents who broke down how lucha differed from the type of wrestling he knew. In a six-man tag match, for instance, each team is headed by a captain and victory is attained when either the captain or two members of the opposing squad lose. Also, rather than tagging in, any participant can enter the ring the moment his or her partner touches the arena floor. Wrestlers in other parts of the world have traditionally worked the left side of an opponent's body — in order for comebacks to be staged with the stronger right arm. In Mexico, the arrangement is generally opposite.

Eventually, someone told Tortorello about PWG, where he was exposed to a more extensive array of styles and performers.

While teaching during the day, he began training at the Mach-1 Wrestling school at night. "I was falling in love with education and wrestling at the same time," he recalled. In fact, his thesis at Notre Dame dissected the phenomenon of professional wrestling in the U.S. from World War II until the present day.

Following his graduation, he returned to Marian Catholic, teaching English and social studies as he worked on his master's degree in administration. When the principal retired in 2014, Tortorello applied for the position.

With his hiring, he became Marian Catholic's first leader who hadn't studied in a convent.

Given his other passion, it made sense that he'd turn to wrestling to raise funds. But he wanted his promotion to be known by a name rather than an acronym, "like the New Deal. All these letters get hard to remember after a while. Warrior Wrestling sounded good. It sounded so good, we were sure someone else had the trademark. But when we looked into it, nobody did."

He estimated that only a small percentage of the student body were wrestling fans. "About 30 of these kids think I'm the greatest principal ever. The other 970 never watch wrestling, and it doesn't mean anything to them."

The first card took place in May 2018 and featured names like Jake Hager, Eddie Edwards, Chelsea Green, Deonna Purrazzo, Nick Aldis, Tessa Blanchard and Alberto El Patron (formerly Alberto Del Rio in

WWE). The show broke even — not bad for a first-time promoter — and Tortorello decided to try again at the end of the summer.

Rey Mysterio appeared on the second show. Even among Anglo fans, lucha libre tended to have a strong following in the Chicago area, so Rey's appearance caused a sensation. He was booked for the event by Konnan, the inaugural CMLL World Heavyweight champion and ex-WCW star, who, along with former CMLL competitor Sam Adonis, helped open the door to Mexican talent in Warrior Wrestling.

This particular event — held on Labor Day weekend 2018 — took place the night after *All In*, when Mysterio was already in town, alongside such wrestlers as Rey Fenix, Penta El Zero Miedo, Dr. Britt Baker, Colt Cabana and Brian Cage. Despite the expense of using the marquee talent, the card drew 970 fans and turned a profit.

In February 2020, Tortorello began planning the group's May show, enquiring about the availability of stars. Even when the pandemic was declared in March, he wondered whether the coronavirus would still be a threat two months later. "After *WrestleMania* was cancelled," he said, "we realized we weren't going to have another show this school year."

It was Eric Hamilton, a former classmate of Tortorello's at Marian Catholic as well as an ex-teacher there, who came up with the concept of an outdoor card. For the better part of a year, Hamilton had been urging the principal to make use of the school's football stadium when the weather was warm. In late June, when Illinois governor J.B. Pritzker announced that the state would allow outdoor events with safety guidelines, Tortorello began querying talent.

"As you know, a lot of guys had dates open," he said. "At the same time, we had to operate on a smaller budget because we needed to have social distancing, and we didn't know how many people would be willing to come."

But when word spread, there were enough fans who believed that — since the spectators weren't being jammed together in an indoor setting — the risk was negligible.

The school cafeteria was converted into a dressing room in which competitors could repair to different sections and avoid close contact.

When I entered, I noticed that numerous people were masked. At this point, the concept of a live event was novel, and I heard some of the wrestlers talking about how they'd spent the past few months.

Steve Manders, who came to the ring in an old-fashioned cowboy gimmick — hat, vest, cowbell — had gained a reputation for "tearing it up" during the pandemic, taking every available booking, and gaining a following through appearances for promotions like IWA Mid-South, GCW, AIW, Southern Championship Wrestling (SCW) in North Carolina, New England's Beyond Wrestling and Zero1 USA in Central Illinois. "You can never be complacent," he said. "You have to put in the miles."

As I circulated, I heard the performers exchanging opinions on what they'd been witnessing in the wider wrestling world, including a short-lived WWE experiment called *Raw* Underground.

Earlier in the week, during an episode of *Monday Night Raw*, the cameras cut away to a dingy warehouse setting, where scantily-clad women were dancing and a ring was set up without ropes. This was WWE's version of a fight club, and Shane McMahon — Vince's son, who hadn't been seen on TV for 10 months — was the master of ceremonies and onscreen matchmaker, stressing that "anything goes" in the shoot style confrontations. Much of the attention was on Babatunde Aiyegbusi, a hulking NXT competitor who'd been born in Poland, the son of a Nigerian father and Polish mother. Now branded Dabba-Kato, the former Minnesota Vikings signee sported a white undershirt as he demolished two unknown opponents — one after the other.

The idea seemed to be using the alternative environment for Performance Center talent and overlooked main roster players to establish their credentials as legitimate tough guys. But as the segments continued week after week, fans began to view *Raw* Underground as something that wasn't as counterculture as it portrayed itself to be. Despite the buzz backstage at Warrior Wrestling, curiosity quickly diminished. By October, *Raw* Underground had disappeared from the show — forgotten until a new character named Commander Azeez made a surprise appearance at *WrestleMania 37*, and viewers recalled that he was the same guy as Dabba-Kato.

At Marian Catholic, fans were in a buoyant mood, cheering loudly when Tre Lamar wore his face covering to the ring before his fast-paced match with Isaias Velazquez, and jeering after Frank the Clown pulled down his mask to tell a fan, "You're stupid." As the ring crew wiped down the ropes between bouts, the audience encouraged them with chants of "*san-i-tize, san-i-tize.*"

Joey Janela had a stirring back-and-forth confrontation with Impact's Jake Something and revealed that he hoped to continue the feud all over the indie circuit. The idea, he said, was creating angles separate from what people saw on AEW each week. "It's hard to put all your acts on a two-hour show, so a lot of people get left off," he explained. "It's especially tough for me after being one of the main guys on the independents. Fortunately, I'm still allowed to work the independents and have been given a lot of freedom by Tony Khan to do what I want creatively."

At the autograph tables, I watched as one fan after another asked Janela about a crazy bump he recently took during a wild GCW clash with Lio Rush on the Atlantic City, New Jersey, boardwalk. "That's how it works," Janela maintained, referring to the fan curiosity. "People care about what they see in an indie match on the internet, sometimes more than something they see on television. I don't know if mainstream wrestling fans like me. But indie fans love me."

There was a good deal of history between Janela and Rush. Before either man was signed to a major promotion, they engaged in a memorable rivalry in CZW in 2016. In one encounter, Rush was draped across a ladder propped against the side of the ring and The Bad Boy crashed onto him from the ceiling beams. In Atlantic City, Janela tried a similar exploit, scaling a building alongside the boardwalk before coming down on the recently released WWE performer.

"It was awesome," Joey said, "one of the most frightening things I ever did. Lio was laying across a table, and when I landed on him, I hit my head on the boardwalk. But I had to do it. I needed to get it out of my system."

In Chicago Heights, the wrestlers on the Warrior card were working hard to create their own memories. The Rascalz — Dezmond Xavier, Zachary Wentz and Trey Miguel from Impact — had a thriller against

Alex Zayne, Blake Christian and Benjamin Carter. Initially, the main event was supposed to pit Brian Cage against Jeff Cobb. But the match was spontaneously turned into a Fatal Fourway, also involving Lance Archer and Sam Adonis. In the end, Adonis — the younger brother of WWE commentator Corey Graves — did the honors for the other three, taking the loss after getting pulverized and pinned by Cage.

Then, as instructed, fans picked up their cushions and lawn chairs and left in an orderly manner, still masked and doing their best not to crowd anyone else.

What I didn't realize was that I wasn't the only one scrutinizing these kinds of outdoor shows. According to the *Wrestling Observer*, Tony Khan also kept close tabs on the live events I attended in Indianapolis and Chicago Heights. My motive was compiling research for this book. Khan's was bringing an audience of actual wrestling fans to his cards at Daily's Place.

I'm sure that Tortorello was gratified to learn that the AEW president was particularly impressed by the way Warrior Wrestling managed to keep its fans safe.

At the next *Dynamite* card, a small number of spectators were admitted into the amphitheater in Jacksonsville. They were in a separate deck from the talent gathered around ringside, and a staffer passed through the various pods to ensure that everyone was wearing a mask. Some 150 fans were on-hand for the show, but the goal was expanding to the point that Daily's Place — at least in the short term — would be operating at 10 to 15 percent capacity. As at Warrior Wrestling, AEW kept people apart with floor markings. Despite the fact that Daily's Place is an open-air venue, industrial coolers were utilized to increase circulation.

For the time being, AEW would operate "like a wrestling territory with a weekly audience," Khan told UPI.com. "I'm really proud of that."

It was May when AEW added the TNT Championship to its list of titles, with Cody Rhodes defeating Lance Archer in the tournament finals. Cody proclaimed himself to be a fighting champion, willing to defend the belt against anybody. Over the next few weeks, fans watched him war with Sonny Kiss, Jake Hager, Jungle Boy and Marq Quen of the tag team Private Party. He also took on athletes who weren't signed to AEW, including Eddie Kingston and Ricky Starks, both of whom were eventually awarded contracts with the company.

Both men had been affiliated with the NWA. Just before the pandemic was declared, Starks lost the NWA World Television Championship, while Kingston was one of the most captivating speakers on *NWA Power*. To the outsider, it seemed like AEW was handpicking the NWA's best performers at a time when the organization was vulnerable. But Nick Aldis pointed out that the two were in an entirely different category than him. "I have a six figure salary that I get whether we're on hiatus or not. Eddie's been at this a long time and deserves to get paid too. Ricky had signed a short-term contract with the NWA but was there for any promoter who wanted him afterwards. Both of them were too good to just wait around for things to get back to normal, and Tony Khan wasn't going to let that kind of talent get by him."

Kingston, in particular, drew attention the moment the camera was pointed in his direction. Without script writers crafting a persona for him, he tapped into his hard luck upbringing and lean years in the business to pull fans into his plotlines.

Raised in a predominantly Irish Catholic environment in the Woodlawn section of the Bronx, just over the Westchester County line in the city of Yonkers, Kingston was bullied incessantly because his relatives hailed from both the Emerald Isle and Puerto Rico. "I learned about racism in like second grade," he told the *New York Post*, "being called a spic, 'spic-ghetti,' 'spic and span.' By sixth, seventh grade, I was like, 'Well, next person who makes fun of me, I'm going to start swinging."

Although he received acceptance from his African American neighbors, it infuriated him that most of the Irish or Puerto Rican people he knew refused to recognize him as one of their own. By middle school, he was boxing, applying the discipline he learned from his father, who worked overtime shifts at a job he disliked to support his family. Still, it took a while to develop the self-restraint that prevented him from punching out his tormentors. By high school, he was one of the most dangerous guys in the neighborhood.

After training with Mike Quackenbush and Chris Hero at the CHIKARA Wrestle Factory in Philadelphia, Kingston felt the sting of rejection again. At six-foot-one and 290 pounds — 50 pounds heavier than he'd be in his debut match in AEW — his appearance seemed a little too beefy for a television superstar. His authenticity — as a speaker and believable character in the ring — led to good runs with TNA and ROH, but his career was always up and down. Although he worked for 25 different promotions in 2019, his "big mouth," by his own admission, regularly weakened his career prospects.

He'd curse out promoters, as well as wrestlers who seemed to wield power on the indies. "To me, if you're a scumbag, just because you've been in the business 'X' amount of years, I'm not going to show you respect," he told the *Post*.

After 18 years in the industry, he considered retirement, but wanted his baby nephew to see him in the ring. Recognizing the zeal he applied to his matches, as well as his exceptional abilities on the mic, WWE reportedly was interested in him as a Performance Center coach. But there were statements Kingston still needed to make between the ropes.

Then COVID-19 hit. As travel restrictions were imposed, the 38-year-old veteran had to rush back from Europe to his home in Orlando, Florida. The bookings had dried up. To pay his mortgage, he sold off his ring gear and was considering moving in with his parents when he was invited to challenge Cody for the TNT belt in July. Although the champion retained, Kingston did what came naturally and showed his heart, winning admirers who'd never seen him before. He and his girlfriend were in the car together a few days later when AEW called to see if he was interested in becoming a contracted performer.

"I was like, Damn. I was going to be broke and homeless and back living with my parents. It hit me then. I just started bawling in the car and apologizing for crying. That whole New York tough guy thing — I can't let anybody see me cry."

While he didn't secure an AEW contract, Midwestern indie icon Warhorse saw his status skyrocket after his TNT Championship challenge against Cody a week after the Kingston match.

In promotions like Fully Loaded Wrestling (FLW), Zero1 and Black Label Pro, Warhorse aroused audiences with basic maneuvers like a clothesline or double stomp from the top rope. "They're simple but effective," he said when I met him at the Warrior Wrestling card, where he received one of the loudest ovations of the night.

After pumping himself up backstage with music by the band Eternal Champion, known for its sword and sorcery lyrical themes, he'd make his entrance — in face paint and a denim vest — rocking his head back and forth like a 1980s headbanger and making longhorns with his fingers. He cited his inspirations for this routine as the Ultimate Warrior, Sting and the Road Warriors; the band KISS; and Lobo, the interstellar mercenary from DC Comics. "There hasn't been a really cool heavy metal wrestler in a long time."

The confrontation with Cody would expose him to hundreds of thousands of new fans, and Warhorse was nervous about making the right kind of showing. As soon as he arrived at Daily's Place, he found Cody backstage, but the TNT champion was caught up in tasks associated with being an EVP. In between, though, the two managed to have a good back-and-forth conversation.

"I pitched a bunch of things, and Cody agreed with about 90 percent of them. But even while we were talking, people kept interrupting us. When we got in the ring, it didn't matter. He remembered everything. There's also something about the way Cody works — his communication is very physical. The way he was leaning his body told me what he wanted us to do, and I never felt lost or out of place.

"He gave me way more than I intended."

For instance, at one point, Cody was applying the figure-four, but Warhorse dramatically twisted on the mat and reversed the pressure. The challenger also stunned Cody with a big dropkick and a series of running clotheslines in the corner. Warhorse harbored no illusions about scoring an upset and winning the title, and, after submitting to Cody's figure-four, he returned to the dressing room feeling satisfied.

There were 14 other matches to tape that day, and Warhorse found a spot for himself in the group of wrestlers gathered around ringside, scrutinizing each encounter and taking mental notes.

At different points, he went over his match with Cody, Dustin Rhodes, Matt Hardy and AEW backstage producer Dean Malenko. "With their critiques and advice," he said, "I knew what to work on when I went back to the indies."

In September, the NBA playoffs forced AEW to reschedule its broadcasts to different nights on the TNT network, while NHL coverage on USA resulted in NXT also being shifted. The shuffle put a temporary hold on the Wednesday Night Wars, since, during this brief interval, the programs stopped running head-to-head. Without direct competition, each brand rated well. In fact, fans who normally watched AEW tuned into NXT, and vice versa.

Which begged the question, What was the point of the Wednesday Night Wars anyway?

Opined Joey Janela, "Some guys are into a ratings war. I'm not. I'm friends with 85 percent of the people on the NXT roster and am really glad they got the opportunities they did. Personally, I'm just glad to see wrestling thriving during a pandemic."

Chris Jericho, on the other hand, was anxious to continue the competition, hawking a "Demo God" t-shirt, and cutting promos in which he took personal credit for AEW consistently winning the key 18-to-49-year-old demographic.

On *Being the Elite*, the Young Bucks crowed about NXT drawing an older viewership. In one skit, Matt Jackson despaired over not pulling more viewers over 50 years old. In response, Nick Jackson recommended hiring more stars from the 1990s.

"We've already tried that," Matt lamented.

During an interview with Alex McCarty from talkSPORT, Jericho justified the gloating: "They came on Wednesday just to mess with us ... Don't worry about our company. We're not worried about you. We don't have a screen up that shows what's going on every moment on NXT, like they do, watching *Dynamite*.

"Leave us alone. Do your own thing. Go to Tuesdays. Grab an extra 250,000 viewers. Finally, get your demo where it needs to be because it's pretty embarrassing on a Wednesday night to go up against us. The 'Demo God' thing is not a gimmick. It's real."

But Triple H maintained that NXT had Wednesdays first, debuting new episodes on the WWE Network before moving over to USA. "I'm happy where we are," he insisted in September during a media call. The ratings war, he continued, was "not a concern to me . . . We go out to put the best show on . . . every week with the talent that we have, which I consider to be the best in the world."

CHAPTER 19

The early days of 2020 had been dark ones for the World Wrestling Entertainment corporation. In February, it was reported that revenues and profits fell short of Wall Street estimates. Live event income had dropped 13 percent in 2019 as the company presented fewer cards and, on the average, drew smaller crowds. During the final quarter of 2019, WWE Network subscriptions fell by 10 percent. Less than 24 hours after co-presidents George Barrios and Michelle Wilson were ousted in January, WWE's stock fell to an 18-month low.

Like The Good Brothers and FTR, though, Barrios and Wilson would remain a tandem, even outside the WWE umbrella, starting a capital management company that pledged "growth and value creation across the media, entertainment and sports ecosystem."

With all the corporate jargon, the whole thing sounded like an Ultimate Warrior promo to me — *"Do you, Hulk Hogan, kick the doors out, kick the cockpit door down, take the two pilots . . . dispose of them, Hulk Hogan?"* — but, obviously, these guys understood a lot more about business than I did.

And so did Vince McMahon.

While others wilted during the pandemic, WWE posted its most profitable quarter, quadrupling profits, increasing WWE Network subscriptions and consumer product sales and — by taping shows on successive days in a smaller building than the arenas that generally hosted *Raw* and *SmackDown* — saving money on TV production and travel. With sports bars closed and *WrestleMania* parties cancelled, fans stayed at home, not only watching the Showcase of The Immortals in their living rooms but breaking the pattern of cancelling their subscriptions after the event ended. Add Trump's corporate tax breaks, and the company ended up contributing a lot less to the U.S. treasury than during the Obama years.

As Bray Wyatt's father, Irwin R. Schyster, reminded in 1994, "Nothing in this world compares to the power of taxes, not even death."

Interestingly, the furloughs and layoffs didn't factor into WWE's profits that quarter since — as part of their severance — many of those employees continued to receive their salaries into the summer. But when those payments ended, the company made an even greater profit.

By early 2021, McMahon was able to tell his investors that the company had generated more revenue in 2020 than at any time in its history, topping $100-million in profits for the first time ever. During the lockdown, licensing — as in WWE games — increased. And even without live events, and the costs of transporting people and merchandise to arenas around the world, fans couldn't go without their Braun Strowman slippers, New Day "unicorn" shorts and *Raw* Women's Championship bottle openers.

During a February 2021 earnings call, McMahon was asked about going back on the road again. "We're going to have live events," he answered, "but will the live events make any money? Are we going to have 20 percent [capacity], 30 percent, 40 percent to where you break even? I don't think anyone has a handle on exactly what's going to happen."

When capacity did reach 100 percent, it appeared that the company was leaning toward a different business plan. Rather than promoting separate, non-televised *Raw* and *SmackDown* cards, WWE presented talent from both brands on what were called Supershows. At least at the outset, the new strategy seemed to make sense. After all, what was the point of riding the highway and wearing yourself down — eating shitty food, fighting with your spouse via text and working through injuries — when the same money could be made by working a limited number of dates?

It might mean that fans in certain markets got to see WWE less, or perhaps factored travel to the company's larger events into their lifestyles. Or maybe the indies would fill the voids created by the scaled-down WWE schedule, meaning more business for everybody. Either way, the post-pandemic industry would look different than what had been there before.

Beyond WWE, Vince McMahon had lapsed into an old habit of trying to disrupt American football.

Back in 2001, McMahon and longtime ally NBC Sports and Olympics chairman Dick Ebersol had started the XFL — the name was conceived by my friend Barry Werner, publisher of the World Wrestling Federation's magazines at the time — primarily to harass the NFL. NBC had lost the broadcasting rights to the league three years earlier, so this was an opportunity for Ebersol to lure back football fans. Fueled by the success of the Attitude Era, McMahon was convinced that he could present an edgier product than aficionados were accustomed to watching each Sunday. Rather than over-regulation, McMahon promised, the XFL would present "smash mouth football." Cheerleaders were encouraged to dress provocatively, and there would be no prohibition against dating players. In fact, there might even be a place in the XFL where the romances could receive screen time.

"We will make America great again."

At that point, everything associated with the World Wrestling Federation was on fire, and interest was initially high. The Rock cut a promo at one game, and *Monday Night Raw* announcers Jim Ross and Jerry "The King" Lawler did some play-by-play. But football fans didn't necessarily want a wrestling show, and the action wasn't gimmicky enough to hold wrestling fans. Plus, the quality of play was far below the NFL's. At the end of the first season, the XFL folded.

McMahon called his effort a "colossal failure."

But in the decades that followed, people began to remember the XFL with a touch of nostalgia, particularly after a 2017 ESPN documentary on the league. Vince had had two decades to study the sports landscape and zoned in on the interest. After establishing a separate company to distinguish his project from WWE, McMahon announced that a revised version of the XFL would return in 2020.

As with the original, the season would commence after the Super Bowl and continue until April, but the carny gimmicks of two decades earlier were discarded. If you were a safety on the Houston Roughnecks and happened to shtup a pom-pom girl, you kayfabed. Players were discouraged from making political statements, like kneeling rather than saluting during the national anthem, and Vince intended to stock his league with "quality" competitors who hadn't had issues with the law.

Best of Irish luck to you with that.

Rules were changed to add to the drama of the game without cheapening the sport. After a touchdown, for example, rather than kicking for an extra point, a team had three options: running a play over the goal line from two yards, from five yards or ten— for one, two or three points, respectively. If the defense managed to cause a turnover and take the ball to the opposing end zone, the score would be equal to the number of points initially attempted by the offense.

The St. Louis Rams had returned to Los Angeles in 2016, but the people in the Gateway City still loved their football. The XFL would give them a new team to adore, while New York, Dallas, Washington, DC, Houston, Seattle, Tampa and L.A. also received franchises.

When someone tweeted that Riyadh should also be gifted a squad, given WWE's regular visits to Saudi Arabia, CM Punk replied with a name — the Bone Saws, a reference to the way dissident journalist Jamal Khashoggi had been dismembered inside the Saudi consulate in Istanbul.

While this type of banter could not have pleased many in Stamford, the fact that the league was generating a social media buzz did. It had taken the NFL too long to grasp the importance of online platforms, but WWE was adroit at the discipline of generating interest before an event and keeping the people's attention by posting highlights.

Yet, despite being renowned for working interminable hours and avoiding sleep, observers wondered whether McMahon possessed the stamina and focus to manage both operations. Unlike in 2001, Vince could occasionally miss a WWE broadcast and depend on the reliable hand of Triple H to shepherd the program through. If the chairman's primary focus became the XFL, there was speculation that Triple H's influence would widen. In that case, hardcore fans hoped the in-ring standards and character development would more closely resemble NXT.

A total of 3.3-million viewers tuned in for the first XFL game on February 17, and the reaction was almost universally positive. As expected, ratings declined once the curiosity factor was exhausted, but not precipitously. Predicatably, St. Louis embraced its new team, with 29,554 attendees setting a league record on week three.

But outside forces were starting to interfere. In early March, it was reported that a vendor at CenturyLink Field in Seattle had tested positive for the coronavirus after the February 22 game. Of the 12 COVID deaths in the United States at this point, 11 had been in Washington state. And although the state's public health department said that the risk of the vendor spreading the illness was "low," fears were escalating.

By March 11, the day WHO declared a pandemic, no one was talking about ratings anymore. Plans for the upcoming game between the Seattle Dragons and Los Angeles Wildcats were abruptly changed; the two teams would now meet in a venue without fans. The next day, XFL commissioner Oliver Luck announced that there wasn't going to be any game that coming Sunday; the league was suspending play. Ticket holders would be issued refunds or credit toward 2021 season matchups. Any XFL player with an opportunity to sign with an NFL team was urged to do so.

Within 24 hours, an unnamed official told *TMZ Sports* that the XFL was filing for bankruptcy. With tens of millions of dollars in revenue wiped out by the coronavirus, the league seemed to be finished for good.

Almost immediately, Luck and McMahon were embroiled in a lawsuit. Luck said that he left his executive position at the NCAA with the understanding that he would get paid regardless of whether the start-up succeeded. The day before the XFL closed, he maintained, he was fired. Accusing the WWE mogul of "wrongful termination," Luck demanded the guaranteed portion of his contract.

McMahon filed a countersuit, arguing that he had good reason to sack the commissioner, most notably for signing Antonio Callaway. Back at the University of Florida, the wide receiver, along with six teammates, agreed to enter a pretrial intervention program in exchange for the dismissal of felony credit card fraud charges against them. In 2018, while a member of the Cleveland Browns, he was issued a citation for marijuana possession and driving with a suspended license. The marijuana charges were later dropped, and he ended up paying a fine for the license violation. Still, he was suspended for several games in 2019 for violating the NFL's substance abuse policy.

Although both the Miami Dolphins and Kansas City Chiefs would employ Callaway after the demise of the XFL, from the beginning, McMahon had emphasized that he didn't want fans turning on the league because of players' off-the-field troubles. "Luck knowingly and deliberately deceived me repeatedly throughout the Callaway situation," the WWE chairman said in court documents.

At one stage, a group of unsecured debtors charged that McMahon was trying to rig the bankruptcy process in a way that would allow him to buy back the league. Vince swiftly condemned the "inflammatory rhetoric and unsubstantiated accusations," telling the *Atlantic*, "I don't know why that's out there, making me out to be the bad guy, [saying] that I'm going to buy the XFL back for pennies on the dollar, basically."

In the few weeks before the pandemic took hold, the XFL performed respectably, McMahon said, and he hoped a bidder stepped forward to save the league. But it wouldn't be him.

It would be Dwayne "The Rock" Johnson.

Despite the similarity to the 2009 storyline in which Donald Trump purchased *Raw*, this was a shoot. There was no secret arrangement in which "the most electrifying man in sports-entertainment" would play XFL boss while McMahon pulled the strings behind the scenes. Rather, Johnson, a third-generation pro wrestling icon who capitalized on his WWE fame to become one of Hollywood's highest-paid actors, saw that the XFL's television partners, FOX and ABC, liked what the league had accomplished and were still interested in airing games. So he, along with business partner and ex-wife, Dany Garcia, and the investment group RedBird Capital — which had ownership stakes in the New York Yankees television network, YES and the French soccer team Toulouse FC — decided to purchase the XFL.

The intention was to have players back on the field by 2023. The revamped XFL would partner with the NFL on training and health programs, while sharing game trends and data on such topics as playing surfaces and equipment.

Reportedly, The Rock's vision of the XFL mirrored much of what he saw in WWE: possible reality shows based on the teams and personalities in the league, as well as weaving players into the plots of his HBO program, *Ballers*.

Interestingly, as a young man, The Rock's career goal had not been pro wrestling but the gridiron. But after being cut by the Calgary Stampeders of the Canadian Football League (CFL) in 1995, Dwayne Johnson made the decision to pursue the family business. He now said that the team did him a favor because it opened the door to his mat and, ultimately, mainstream stardom.

"It's funny how sometimes life comes full circle," he observed.

CHAPTER 20

AFTER *WRESTLEMANIA 36*, both fans and WWE officials looked toward *SummerSlam* with cautious expectation. With COVID cases expected to decline when the weather was warm, the prospect of holding the August pay-per-view in front of live fans was not implausible. But Boston — the city where *SummerSlam* had been scheduled — wanted no part of it. Mayor Marty Walsh banned all parades and festivals for the entire season, including Labor Day celebrations on September 7. An indoor show at the TD Garden, not to mention *NXT TakeOver*, *Raw* and *SmackDown* cards on the days surrounding it — along with the 2020 Hall of Fame ceremony that had originally been scheduled for *WrestleMania* week — was out of the question.

Reportedly, WWE searched the southern states, where coronavirus restrictions were more lenient, but could not come up with an arrangement that worked. Yet again, the decision was made to hold a major pay-per-view in an empty arena. The difference was that WWE had now upgraded from the Performance Center to the ThunderDome at the Amway Center, creating the illusion of a full house.

When the event took place, the company encouraged ThunderDome watchers to express enthusiasm over what was transpiring on the opposite side of their screens. The truth was that they didn't need much prompting. Despite the virtual circumstances, it felt like a privilege to play a role in the biggest card of the summer. Canned noise notwithstanding, the fans seen shouting on the LED screens were doing so with sincerity.

In Japan, live shows continued in starts and stops. On August 15, the first match was slated to begin at a Stardom card in Osaka when news filtered backstage that someone on the roster had tested positive. Before the bell even rang, the promotion shut the event down and cancelled dates for the rest of the month. Every wrestler in Stardom was immediately tested, resulting in one more positive diagnosis. Anyone who'd associated with the two wrestlers was also instructed to self-quarantine for 14 days.

There was no such attentiveness exhibited at the yearly motorcycle rally in Sturgis, South Dakota — site of the WCW *Hog Wild* pay-per-view in 1996. Although attendance was down from past years, 460,000 people still were on hand, many of whom went proudly maskless. In both Minot and Sioux Falls, partygoers attended a concert by Chris Jericho's band, Fozzy, leading to a testy online exchange between the Demo God and people who thought that he was setting a poor example.

"The reason why the shows have happened is because these states of North Dakota and South Dakota have low COVID cases," Jericho argued on YouTube, insisting that the concerts were either outdoors or in places with limited capacity. "We hand out masks at the door, the temperature checks. We stay on the bus all day. The Fozzy crew and camp have been tested."

Although no one could link the cases to Fozzy, according to one report, 290 coronavirus cases across 12 states — including one death — were tied to Sturgis. Jericho would later test positive himself. He said that he exhibited no symptoms and quarantined for 10 days. During this period, no mention of his condition was made on AEW programming. How or when he got COVID remained unclear.

When I met Kyle Hessler at the Warrior Wrestling show, the former MMA fighter invited me to the Independent Pro Wrestling Expo he was holding on the last weekend of August outside of Fort Worth. Unlike the events I'd attended in Indianapolis and Chicago Heights, there would be no fresh air to whisk away microbes. With temperatures projected in the 100-degree (Fahrenheit) range, he'd rented an air-conditioned indoor space for the two-day event at the NYTEX Sports Centre, a youth hockey facility in the suburb of North Richland Hills.

He wasn't planning on being reckless, he assured me. The wrestlers were to be given antibody tests. There would be eight feet of space between lockers. Social distancing was required during meet and greets and merch purchases.

In the end, I stayed home. I admit that, in the course of the COVID era, there were times when I convinced myself that writing this book was so essential that the forces of the universe wouldn't dare conspire to infect me. But I also realized that I was taking a risk every time I boarded a plane or rode the subway. Friends pointed out that I had a tendency to lean into people when I talked and, occasionally, pulled down my mask while making a point. So far, I'd been okay. But, look, if The Rock and Chris Jericho could get COVID, why couldn't I?

Much as it galled me, in this one instance, I chose not to push my luck.

As it was, Hessler was a newbie promoter. He wanted his story chronicled in the book. So — while I believe that there is no journalistic experience that can match a first-hand interaction — I knew that I could call him after the expo, and he'd pick up the phone and answer my questions.

"Did everyone follow the rules?" he said a few days after the event. "No. But I'd say 95 percent did."

In the few hours I spent around Hessler in Illinois, I learned a few things about him. Although he didn't preach to me, I could tell that was he was a man of faith. For one thing, he listed "Christian" as one of his attributes on his Twitter page. That's always a telltale sign. I also overheard him having a conversation with Lance Archer about the religious journey they shared. Perhaps, I speculated, this was why he decided to hold an indoor — albeit, scaled-down — wrestling convention in a pandemic.

For the Lord God is a sun and a shield; the Lord bestows favor and honor. No good thing does he withhold from those who walk uprightly.

Well, that's not really how Hessler looked at it. He understood his vulnerabilities, and he certainly didn't want to get run out of the business for hosting a super-spreader event. But he also saw an opportunity in a period when people were pretty unsettled about being cooped up at home. "Wrestling is more cost-effective than boxing or kickboxing," he explained. "In Texas, you're not dealing with an athletic commission, so you don't have the same insurance issues you have in other places. We tried to snatch up that market of people who wanted to attend a fan event after everything was cancelled."

And, to be honest, had the expo been in Brooklyn or Queens, I probably would have stopped by — whether I was invited or not. Entertainment and wrestling reporter Chris Van Vliet hosted three live podcasts — with Gangrel, Jazz and Jake "The Snake" Roberts. And there were a lot of good, young wrestlers involved whom I would have enjoyed seeing in an indie setting before they were grabbed by one of the larger promotions: Ryan Justice, Jastin Taylor, Miranda Gordy — daughter of the late Freebird, Terry "Bam Bam" Gordy — Erica Torres, Chandler Hopkins.

As someone who hadn't done this before, Hessler expected to run into some problems, and did. He'd purchased a brand-new ring, and on the first night, one of the ropes fell off. "There are things you just don't think about when you promote your first wrestling show," he said. "We taped it up and moved it, so it was the bottom rope now, and we thought everything was going to be okay. But then, Ace Austin put his hand on it, and it snapped again."

On night two, Nick Aldis defended his NWA belt against "Real Deal" Nobe Bryant, who'd qualified for the title shot by winning a battle royal the day before. Despite his workouts during his sabbatical, Aldis became winded. "I blew up sky high," he admitted. "You can't replicate the cardio you do in a gym with what you experience in the ring. And when you're wrestling, especially after you've been away for a long time, the adrenaline can blow you up so fast, and that starts messing with your head. I had to slap on one or two chinlocks [and rest] But, when the finish comes, you have to have something in the tank. And I did. Even though I won, my opponent ended up looking like a star. That's what the NWA champ always did for his opponent, and that's what I wish more people would do today."

Given the social distancing protocols, Hessler had hoped to populate the 2,700-capacity arena with 500 fans. But the numbers were disappointing — 150 on night one and 250 on night two. Still, the promoter met attendees who'd come to the event from as far away as California,

Florida and Maryland. "It kind of proves that there were people out there who really wanted that fan experience," he reflected.

In the ring, nobody phoned it in. After Madman Fulton, a former NXT competitor who was appearing in Impact at the time, learned that his opponent, Garrisaon Creed, had flown himself down to the expo at his own expense, the veteran asked his foe to execute a German suplex. Then, Fulton sold for everything he was worth. "You see someone who's in Impact doing this for a new guy, and you take notice," Hessler said. "Fulton just gave Creed way more than he had to. It shows that if you handle yourself a certain way, people in this business — the real professionals — want to do something to reassure you that it's worth it."

Ultimately, Hessler was proud of what he accomplished. "It took a lot of gusto to try this with everything else that's going on. We took a real big swing at it. We didn't knock it out of the park, but nobody got sick, and every person I met there was having a good time."

A week after the Independent Pro Wrestling Expo, the NWA was represented again in a far larger setting when Women's champion Thunder Rosa challenged AEW titlist Hikaru Shida at *All Out* on September 5. This was different than Eddie Kingston and Ricky Starks joining the promotion since Rosa was still an active member of the NWA. Rather, the purpose of her match was bringing new attention to the storied organization.

"I hadn't really thought about reaching out and booking Thunder Rosa," Tony Khan said on the *AEW Unrestricted* podcast, "and I was with Kenny Omega and when we were talking contenders, he thought Thunder Rosa would be great, but she works for the NWA. I said, 'You know what? I bet we could work something out.'"

His instinct was correct. "Billy [Corgan] said all champions should be fighting champions," Khan continued, "so why wouldn't their champion come in and challenge for our title?"

This time, it was Shida playing the role traditionally reserved for the NWA champion, scoring the win after a running knee, but making Rosa look so good that AEW fans wanted to see her again.

"Obviously, this was something that was needed," said Rosa, who eventually became a part of the AEW roster. "It did benefit women's wrestling," she paused and laughed, "and it benefitted me."

The relationship between the two leagues continued after Rosa dropped the NWA Women's Championship to Serena Deeb in October. At *Full Gear*, Deeb defended the NWA strap on an AEW pay-per-view, her victory over Allysin Kay a form of retribution after WWE released the gifted athlete from her Performance Center coaching job, as part of the company's cost-cutting measures earlier in the year.

The woman who'd later market herself as "The Professor of Professional Wrestling," Deeb referred to the dismissal as "the best thing that ever happened to me."

Khan characterized the prominence of NWA stars on AEW cards as a "win-win for both companies," and said that he hoped to encourage affiliations with other promotions. "There are a lot of stages between me saying this and this happening," Aldis observed. "But if Tony and Billy can put their egos aside and make a real deal, maybe they can combine forces and take on Vince McMahon."

Confident in its long-term television deal, AEW continued to acquire talent, aware that, at some point, the promotion would expand from the two hours fans were accustomed to seeing every Wednesday. After sending out a tweet about wanting to wrestle the Young Bucks, the aptly named Top Flight — Darius and Daunte Martin — were brought in to battle them on *Dynamite*. Matt Sydal — who, as Evan Bourne, had held the WWE Tag Team Championship with Kofi Kingston — said that he was "holding on by a thin thread" to his career when he received calls from both Ring of Honor and AEW.

The latter appearance received the most attention — for all the wrong reasons. Announced as a surprise entrant at *All Out*'s Casino Battle Royal, Sydal tried impressing viewers with a shooting star press, and instead slipped on the top turnbuckle and landed on his back.

"I was so lucky I didn't get injured," he told Chris Van Vliet. "I can say I've jumped off that top rope thousands of times and zero times have I had a slip like that. That was the first one. It was also the first time fireworks exploded in the background. There are a million excuses, but I'm not going to make them. It just didn't go well. What did go well was when I slipped, I basically reached back with my arm and the rope was there and basically, it kept me from turning over on my head."

WWE was equally prolific, scouting the indies, international promotions and amateur ranks for names with the potential to remodel the industry. Lucky Kid, who'd wrestled Timothy Thatcher, Ilja Dragunov and WALTER in wXw in Germany, was announced as an NXT UK addition in 2021, alongside William Regal's son, Bailey Matthews, Anglo-Indian standout Tony Gill and Meiko Satomura, a former PROGRESS women's champion and the cofounder of SENDAI Girls' Pro Wrestling in Japan. In February, NXT picked up Taya Valkyrie, the longest reigning Knockouts champion ever — rebranding her Franky Monet — and Jennifer Michell Cantu Iglesias, the daughter of Mexican wrestler Bronco and a weightlifter who had hoped to compete at the cancelled 2020 Olympics.

The class also included Parker Boudreaux, a former University of Central Florida right guard who resembled Brock Lesnar enough to be mistaken for his son, and ex–Baltimore Ravens signee Bronson Rechsteiner, the real-life offspring of former World Wrestling Federation and WCW star Rick Steiner.

Both were slated for big things in NXT going into 2022, as well as some repackaging. Boudreaux became Harland, and Rechsteiner was billed as Bron Breakker.

Bobby Stevenson, an NCAA qualifier who'd gained a competitive edge by working out with Lesnar — a fellow University of Minnesota alum — entered the NXT Performance Center around the same time. His brother, U.S. Olympic hopeful Gable Stevenson, would appear at ringside next to Stephanie McMahon at *NXT TakeOver: Stand and Deliver* in the build-up to *WrestleMania 37*, and was widely expected to sign with WWE after the international competition.

When the postponed 2020 Olympics took place in August 2021, Gable won the gold. The next month, he announced that he'd signed with WWE.

Five of the guys I saw glisten during that memorable six-man tag match at Warrior Wrestling ended up in WWE as well.

The year had been a mixed blessing for Ben Carter, a British-born graduate of Seth Rollins's Black and Brave Wrestling Academy. After a notable outing against Scorpio Sky on *Late Night Dynamite*, an AEW broadcast that aired after the NBA playoffs in September, Carter was diagnosed with COVID-19. He quarantined and posted his concerns online about pro wrestling opportunities missed. But when he recovered, WWE was ready to sign him, rebranding him Nathan Frazer.

His tag team partners in the Warrior bout, Blake Christian and Alex Zayne were both signed by NXT, and respectively renamed Trey Baxter and Ari Sterling. But because NJPW Strong taped its shows so far in advance, Zayne was still on their program after joining WWE.

Yet, when I attended GCW's first card at New York's storied Hammerstein Ballroom in January 2022, Christian and Zayne were back to their old names and on the show, each the victim of the tornado of WWE layoffs in 2021.

Dezmond Xavier and Zachary Wentz of the Rascalz were gifted the handles Wes Lee and Nash Carter. Citing family challenges, the third member of the trio, Trey Miguel, opted to remain with Impact.

To use a cliché, Lee and Carter — now calling themselves MSK — had the proverbial rocket strapped to each of their backs. On February 14, they toppled the Grizzled Young Veterans (James Drake and Zack Gibson) to win the finals of the Dusty Rhodes Tag Team Classic at *NXT TakeOver: Vengeance Day*. After a Triple Threat with the Grizzled Young Veterans and Legado Del Fantasma (Joaquin Wilde and Raul Mendoza) at *Stand and Deliver*, they emerged as NXT Tag Team champions.

Once again, as the saying went, the indies mattered — whether there was a pandemic or not.

CHAPTER 21

ACCORDING TO ONE study, as many as 40 million Mexicans — one-third of the population — were exposed to the coronavirus in 2020. The devastation was felt in every corner of Mexican society, including the subculture of lucha libre. It is believed that, out of a community of between 5,000 and 7,000 luchadores, at least 150 died from COVID. With a president who continued to embrace supporters in public appearances while downplaying the need for containment measures, Mexicans felt a certain stigma about losing relatives to the disease.

Among the luchadores who'd pass away from the virus: Golden Bull, Dragon Chino II, El Matemático II, Angel o Demonico, Estrella Blanca Jr., Super Bracito.

Because of their dependance on box office revenue — pay-per-view in Mexico never reached the level it did in other countries — a group of luchadores, representing several companies, staged a protest in Mexico City in March 2021, calling for arenas to open at 30 percent capacity. Authorities were unmoved.

The Box y Lucha Commission, the governing body that sanctioned championships and ensured that wrestlers could not revert to their old gimmicks after losing their masks in the ring, suggested that luchadores start looking for other work. But when you've been training to do one job since your early teens, outside opportunities are slim. Former CMLL Mexican National Tag Team co-titlist Atlantis Jr. — who continued to study even after he began preparing to enter the ring at age 12 — used the time off to earn a college degree in animation and digital arts. Most of his peers, though, had fewer choices.

In between selling flowers that grow on the chinampas — artificial, floating islands in Mexico City's Xochimilco borough — three brothers began staging wrestling shows there. "We said, 'Why not?'" the eldest sibling, Ciciónico, told the Associated Press. "We have the ring. We have the chinampa. We have everything. So we decided to bring this beautiful sport to this gorgeous landscape."

At one point, the weight of the ring almost sunk the craft it was on. But disaster was averted, and the show continued.

Other wrestlers attempted to attract a following online, live streaming matches for $12 and charging $3 for replays.

Still others used their knowledge of Mexican pro wrestling history to sell protective face coverings modeled after the masks of legends El Santo, Blue Demon, La Parka, Dr. Wagner and Black Taurus.

CMLL World Heavyweight Champion Ultimo Guerrero and his wife, women's star Lluvia, opened a hamburger truck adorned with their images, setting up shop on the same block as a chef who lost his job at a Cancun resort and was now selling cochinita pibil — a traditional roast pork dish — to anyone who happened down the sidewalk. The stand drew neighbors as well as fans who traveled long distances to patronize the titlist.

Guerrero, whose mother was a street vendor of floured tortillas called gringas, was not the only luchador who chose to enter the food industry. Shocker had begun driving a lucha-themed taco truck the year before to help pay for jaw surgery, then kept it going. Pimpinela Escarlata opened a fried chicken restaurant. Rey Bucanero started an ice cream and waffles stand. Frequent Guerrero opponent Olímpico retired in 2020, living instead off the proceeds of his crepe business.

"We thought we were eternal," he told the *Los Angeles Times*. "We never knew something like this could happen."

When the newspaper interviewed Guerrero, he mentioned that, physically, it was easier to stand behind a grill than take bumps in the squared circle. Since the pandemic started, he'd been able to wean himself off painkillers. "My body doesn't ache," he said. "I feel good."

In addition to earnings from their side gigs, licensed wrestlers received small loans from the government to help them through the lucha drought.

Through the Box y Lucha Commission, a number of supermarkets provided food donations. Boxes of meals were also funneled to talent after an auction of wrestling masks and costumes.

Promotions had to be innovative as well. After tapings started again, AAA supplemented its empty arena broadcasts with cards from the Plaza de Toros in Tlaxcala, the country's oldest bullring, situated alongside the bell tower from a 16th Century convent, and from the Hotel Hacienda Santa Maria Xalostoc, on the grounds of a plantation built in the 1500s. The purpose was showcasing historical sites for lucha fans, a deal the promotion brokered with the government.

And when vaccinations started in the COVID-ravaged nation and authorities were anxious to ensure that the public turned out en masse at inoculation sites, such luchadores as Ciclón Ramírez Jr., El Hijo de Pirata Morgan and Bandido were recruited to lure people to the locations.

In Europe, where fresh waves of COVID were forcing renewed lockdowns, NXT UK came back from hiatus in September, announcing a tournament to crown the victor of the brand's Heritage Cup. Unlike other championships in the company, the winner would receive a trophy rather than a belt. In a unique nod to British wrestling history, the matches were conducted by rules adhered to by stars like Big Daddy, Mick McManus, Johnny Saint and Catweazle in the 1970s when *World of Sport* was a popular ITV staple. Bouts were two-out-of-three falls and broken up into six three-minute rounds. The inaugural NXT UK Heritage Cup champion was A-Kid, an electrifying Spaniard who'd competed in PWG and PROGRESS, among other places. In 2018, at age 20, he became the youngest wrestler to participate in a match that received a five-star rating from the *Wrestling Observer*, following his clash with Zack Sabre Jr. for Madrid's White Wolf Wrestling (Triple W) league.

Denmark's BODYSLAM! Wrestling promotion re-opened on September 19, with a card in the country's second-largest city, Aarhus, located on the east coast of the Jutland peninsula.

The group was started in 2105 with a corps of five Danish athletes who'd learned enough about the craft "not to embarrass themselves," according to Kristian Buus Nielsen, who cofounded BODYSLAM! Wrestling with his brother, Søren. Supplementing the cards was a contingent of Swedish wrestlers who'd previously worked in Germany, as well as Britain's All Star league, which had started in 1970 and continued to promote shows in theaters, town halls and holiday camps.

"We're just a dot on the map of a larger wrestling scene," Nielsen told me.

Even so, the company's story was typical of indie promotions everywhere in 2020. The year began with high expectations. The group had 19 shows planned, including a combined event with wXw in Germany. "Theoretically, it could have ended up on their [streaming] network," Nielsen said. In June, BODYSLAM! Wrestling was to be part of a music festival lineup, exposing its brand to hundreds of potential fans. Talent would include Holidead, an eerie female performer from the U.S. who claimed to wrestle demons "in and out of the ring," and twins Patrick and Chris Vörös, Canadians who also did comedy on TikTok.

The country's wrestling scene could be traced to 1992 when "The Great Dane Bear" Asbjørn Riis returned home after training at Jesse Hernandez's School of Hard Knocks, a California academy whose alumni would also include Awesome Kong, Frankie Kazarian, Candice LeRae and Rocky Romero. "He was about the size of Hulk Hogan and even had the mustache," Nielsen said. "He said he'd wrestled in front of 10,000 fans in L.A. There was no way to fact check him. He'd appear at fairs, ripping phone books in half and inviting kids to give him snapmares."

With no notable rivals, Riis appointed himself the caretaker of Danish wrestling, introducing a Saturday morning television program that showcased WWF and WCW matches starting in 1993. Using colloquialisms from the small island of Mors, where he was raised, Riis entertained viewers with his commentary, uttering phrases like "Vi må ikke håbe han har fået gule ærter til aftensmad" — "Let's hope he didn't have yellow pea soup for dinner."

In 1994, he opened a training school, while staging small cards around Denmark.

In the town of Viborg, some three-and-a-half hours from Copenhagen, the Nielsen brothers missed Riis's peak years on local television and discovered pro wrestling by playing Nintendo 64 in the late 1990s. They first became regular mat watchers when WCW's ancillary program, *Thunder*, began airing on a small cable station. "At that time, the internet was becoming bigger," Nielsen recalled. "I got on a message board for Danish fans, and people were talking about all this wrestling we never heard of."

While they probed the mat wars' history, the siblings enquired about shows in their area. The choices were narrow, but the pair managed to attend a number of backyard wrestling events.

Ultimately, they became acquainted with Riis. "He is not training people properly, but no one knows how to train for wrestling," Nielsen said. "Everyone just knows he's a guy who has a ring."

The Nielsens attended two sessions before a group of attendees fell out with the The Great Dane Bear and splintered off. This was not an uncommon scenario; despite the miniscule quantity of performers, Danish pro wrestling would become ridiculously factionalized. In this instance, Riis found himself without a key piece of equipment. "One guy keeps the ring and still to this day, he has it in his barn," Nielsen said. To compensate, trainees simply worked out their moves on mats.

Meanwhile, the brothers became affiliated with a trainer who'd managed to acquire "a huge, defective ring from Northern Germany. The spring underneath is crooked. There's no give. There's no padding. It was just two layers of carpet."

Cards consisted of self-trained talent. As a student, it was Kristian Nielsen's job to set up the chairs and cue the entrance music at shows in the central Danish town of Langå. "We would draw 150 fans for guys in sweat pants and t-shirts."

Eventually, some German talent found their way to the events. "They're not so great, but they know things we don't know, and they start teaching things here and there."

Then, a few Brits associated with Norwich's WAW group turned up. "I'm not sure how they found us. I'm the guy who sets up chairs, so nobody tells me. But I remember seeing a 15- or 16-year-old Paige at some of the shows." The future NXT women's champion was the daughter of WAW promoters Ricky and "Sweet" Saraya Knight, and had already been bumping around English rings for a few years.

Just as he was ready to launch his own career, though, Nielsen hurt his shoulder. As a result, he opted to pursue promoting, along with a straight job as a graphic designer — a common side gig, for some reason, for people in the wrestling business. Meanwhile, frustrated with the quality of coaching in his homeland, Søren Nielsen traveled to the Detroit area in 2008 to train at Truth Martini's House of Truth school. With an alumni list that included Alex Shelley, Jimmy Jacobs, Rhyno and Zach Gowen, the academy was adept at preparing talent for the rigors of promotions like New Japan and WWE. When Søren returned home, he finally understood how to work.

The Danish scene was still small, but slowly, more wrestlers from other countries were arriving and imparting wisdom. The future Sami Zayn, El Generico, visited Scandinavia and conducted seminars for less seasoned performers in 2011. On another tour, sessions were led by Robbie Dynamite — a five-time British Mid-Heavyweight champion in All Star, as well as a TNA competitor — and Rampage Brown, an English, former WWE trainee. "I remember Robbie Dynamite explaining getting heat and making comebacks," Nielsen said, "and it blew people's minds. They never heard that before."

Still, Danish wrestling couldn't resist its tendency to cannibalize itself. In 2010, a group called Wrestling.dk peeled off from an organization called Danish Pro Wrestling, which had been only drawing between 50 and 100 fans a card. This extreme example of what Freud termed "the narcissism of small differences" split the audience even further.

"When BODYSLAM! Wrestling started, our rivals would put on shows the same day," Nielsen said, "and everybody lost money."

The company's goal was playing rock venues, but, with no track record, the shows generally took place in gyms. Little by little, though, the promotion began to gain a small following, turning Copenhagen into its strongest market with four cards a year, staging two annual shows in Aarhus, and drawing 400 in the town of Aalborg each January. In between, there were spot shows in towns around the country.

"You can't run one place too much because there aren't enough wrestling fans to go around," Nielsen explained. "At every show, you try to attract non-fans who just want to drink some beer, shout and have a good time. That's three-quarters of the audience at our shows, and they don't think about wrestling again until we come back."

Over the years, the company began to feature genuine indie stars, among them Lucky Kid, Speedball Mike Bailey, Chris Brookes and Shigehiro Irie. Future NXT UK competitors Joseph Conners and Flash Morgan Webster also made appearances. A Swedish wrestler performed as Harley Rage, a parody, at least in name, of eight-time NWA World Heavyweight champion Harley Race — avoiding heat from the rest of the industry because of the Scandinavian scene's obscurity. In March 2020, Danish standouts Michael Fynne, Peter Olisander and Emeritus (Søren under a skull mask) participated in wXw's 16 Carat Gold weekend, the last major event for the performers before the WHO declared a pandemic.

The Vörös twins had just arrived in the country and had to fly back to Canada at their own expense, then immediately go into quarantine. The pair made the best of a bad situation, chronicling their ordeal while expanding their following on TikTok.

"Everything happened fast," Nielsen said. "We saw that Italy was shutting down. Then, gatherings of more than 500 people were banned in Denmark. We cancelled our shows but thought that everything would be fine by August."

Instead, the promotion had to wait until September and even then, costly adjustments needed to be made. "The venue we picked normally seats 350 people, and we only admitted 105. It was weird. We were glad to be back but, financially, it was hard to make it work."

Besides testing the wrestlers, BODYSLAM! Wrestling consulted with lawyers about a floor plan. "Actual lawyers," Nielsen noted with astonishment in his voice. "There was just so much extra red tape. But people volunteered to help out. 'We'll do anything. We miss wrestling.' In the end, it was worth the shot.

"It's not the same, but it's better than nothing," he told me while coronavirus anxieties were still high. "People lost their jobs. Will they even have money for wrestling tickets? Hardcore fans prioritize that.

And our local guys want to get in the ring and work. Will it ever return to what it used to be? We built everything from the ground up. It would suck if we had to start over."

One story I never expected to hear was that, while larger leagues in Europe were grounded, a group called SLAM! Wrestling Finland was continuing its pre-COVID plan of expanding into Estonia.

"When everyone else was frozen with fear, I decided, 'Why don't we swim upstream, against the tide and get the attention?'" promoter Michael Majalahti told me. "Only dead fish float downstream."

For the better part of three decades, Majalahti had been grinding out a living as a wrestler and musician, primarily in Europe and Japan, billing himself as "The Canadian Rebel" StarBuck. "It has nothing to do with the coffee chain," he explained. "I had a band called the Stoner Kings, and we all took gimmick names to incorporate the spirit of pro wrestling into indie rock. Dirk Benedict played a character called Lieutenant Starbuck in *Battlestar Galactica*, and he was a man's man. It wasn't about coffee."

The son of Finnish parents, Majalahti was raised in Timmins, Ontario, where his father preached the gospel at a Pentecostal church. "Jesus is my lord and savior, and I'm proud to let the whole world know," StarBuck said, adding that he viewed the story of SLAM! Wrestling Finland as his "testimony."

Like BODYSLAM! Wrestling promoter Kristian Buus Nielsen, Majalahti studied graphic arts. He was driving a bottled water truck in Western Canada in 1992 when he met wrestling manager Abu Wizal, who mentioned that Steve DiSalvo, who'd worked Stu Hart's Calgary-based Stampede Wrestling promotion as "Sadistic" Steve Strong, was launching an operation in the same region. "I thought I could get in with my artwork," Majalahti said. "But Steve liked my voice and thought he could use me as a ring announcer and commentator."

Soon he was training with former Intercontinental champion and future WWE Performance Center coach Lance Storm, debuting against him in 1994.

Eventually, Majalahti returned to Ontario and was working indies in Eastern Canada when his father contracted a bacterial disease at a religious convention. Upon hearing that his parents were moving back to Finland while his father recovered, Majalahti made the fateful decision to go with them.

Rather than relocate to the cosmopolitan city of Helsinki, the family instead settled in Vilppula, a place Majalahti described as "the suicide capital of Finland." There, he managed to find graphic arts work, along with occasional wrestling gigs in the UK.

To wrestling fans, there were few associations with Finland other than Tony Halme, a boxer and UFC fighter who'd been trained for pro wrestling by Verne Gagne in the U.S., did an MMA gimmick in New Japan and, as Ludvig Borga, wrestled in the WWF, starting in 1993. Borga was portrayed as a Finnish nationalist — which he was, later serving in parliament as a member of the right-wing True Finns party — but the shtick didn't really hit any chords with American audiences. After being released by the WWF, Borga exported the routine to Austria and Germany, capturing the CWA World Heavyweight Championship in 1995. Unfortunately, he was plagued by drug, alcohol and mental health issues; after a search of his parliamentary office uncovered illegal steroids, his trial was broadcast on Finnish TV. In 2010, two days after his 47th birthday, he died of a self-inflicted gunshot wound.

Yet, despite his name recognition, few, if any, Finns took up pro wrestling because of him. "He never coached anybody," Majalahti pointed out, "he only had a seven-year career, and he wasn't a real craftsman in our game. Today, you mention his name, and a lot of young people go, 'Huh? Who was that?'"

Even in 2002, after WWE began running on the Finnish entertainment network Subtv, the average fan was more interested in Triple H, Chris Jericho and The Rock. When the company toured the country and drew more than 10,000 fans to Helsinki's Hartwall Arena, Majalahti realized that it was time to flaunt his wrestling skills in his ancestral homeland.

After a successful series of matches with Norwegian wrestling promoter Erik Isaksen, he formed a partnership with a businessman named

Patrik Pesola to start a group called Valhalla Pro Wrestling. The local talent included a disproportionate number of bar bouncers who learned how to bump and sell at a training facility in Kerava, but a few names stood out, particularly Johnny Merlyn and Easyrider. The premier card in 2003 featured celebrated imports like AJ Styles, Shane Douglas, Sabu and future WWE Cruiserweight champion Kid Kash, as well as athletes from Spain and Norway.

Unfortunately, the funds Pesola used to bankroll the venture instantly vaporized.

"For the first show, we had a ramp, a full TV crew, the works," Majalahti said. "And Patrik lost a shit ton of money on it. The next month, we promoted something called Baltic Brawl. We rented an 8,000 capacity ice arena, but only 1,500 fans showed up. Not only that, but he blew 44,000 euros on bus stop ads. Sting was supposed to make an appearance, and we paid half of his advance up front. But we couldn't afford to pay the second part, so he stayed in the U.S. When the event finally took place, it was so bad, we didn't even have a camera crew."

To the promoters' great relief, a group of ambulance attendants happened to be present. As a result, former WCW competitor Allan "Kwee Wee" Funk's life was probably saved.

Funk and Mike Saunders were teaming up against Elix Skipper and Sonny Siaki when Siaki attempted a split-legged moonsault. The positioning was off, though, and Sonny's knee went crashing into his opponent's face. "Funk had blood squirting everywhere like a fuckin' horror movie," Majalahti recounted.

It would take four extensive surgeries to repair the damage.

By the end of 2003, the calamity had become a metaphor for Valhalla's challenges, and the company folded.

Still, Majalahti was determined to learn from his mistakes. "I now look back on what happened to Allan Funk and I say, 'This is where Finnish wrestling started.'"

Certainly, those who experienced the wonder of professional wrestling in the country were not ready to let it go. With the demise of Valhalla, a collection of former trainees began holding events for fans they'd met on internet forums. In 2004, Majalahti started working with another ex-student who'd launched a group labeled Pro Wrestling Finlandia. The next year, he headlined a card against former ECW star Steve Corino that packed 500 fans into an appropriately sized venue and blew the house away. Starting in 2006, he was associated with an organization called Fight Club Finland, laboring behind the scenes, as well as in the ring.

From working on the fringes of the wrestling industry, Majalahti drifted closer to the center. Recognizing the same abilities that Steve Strong spotted in Calgary, WWE recruited the multilingual Canadian to do play-by-play on the company's Finnish broadcasts on the Eurosport network in 2009. Although the assignment ended in 2015, Majalahti maintained his relationship with the corporation, performing promotional tasks during Nordic tours.

As indie opportunities were exploding in 2018, he took another shot at starting his own operation, launching SLAM! Wrestling Finland. "I am the Vince McMahon of this company. I am the main shareholder. I have total autonomy.

"If I sell a wrestling show to a motorcycle festival or something like the American Car Show, which we have every year, I will bring a roster from all over the world that suits the audience."

These have included future NXT UK women's champion Meiko Satomura, former ECW and WWF star Yoshihiro Tajiri, ex-AEW competitor Ivelisse, Matt "Son of Havoc" Cross, who worked in ROH and Lucha Underground, and Tom LaRuffa — who used the name Sylvester Lefort in NXT and Basile Baraka in TNA. Among the Scandinavian attractions: Polar Pekko, Jami Aalto and Viktor Tykki from Finland, and Ken Malmsteen from Sweden.

Said Majalahti, "My philosophy is that when I sell a show to a customer, that customer should have a say in what they want to see on the card. And customers' needs are diverse. But I make sure they get what they want so they come to me again the next time."

Always, the plan was to expand further into the Baltics, particularly Estonia, which has a large Finnic population and is the birthplace of George Hackenschmidt, who is credited with creating the bearhug and began his celebrated championship rivalry with American Frank Gotch in 1908. "In Estonia, George Hackenschmidt is a source of national pride," Majalahti explained. "There's a Hackenschmidt tournament every year on the amateur level. There's a deep emotional connection that makes Estonians interested in wrestling."

The promotion was planning to present nine cards in both Estonia and Finland in 2020. But once the pandemic was declared, Finland limited gatherings of more than 10 people. "I lost six out of nine shows once corona hit," Majalahti griped to me in November. "The other three got shuttled to 2021 if COVID doesn't fuck it up again."

But like WWE, AEW and other promotions, SLAM! Wrestling Finland managed to enhance its identity by presenting events that were unique to the era. In June, the company staged a card dubbed Quarantine Combat. Only 50 fans were admitted into an old oil silo to watch four matches. "We made it into a VIP event. And the oil silo was really cool, with a lot of echo so you could really hear the bumps."

On Halloween, the group was in the Estonian capital of Tallinn. Only 200 spectators were allowed into a nightclub that usually welcomed 1,000 for a combined rock and wrestling event. "I took a financial loss, but it's still a win. The media was impressed that we were taking a risk, and every outlet covered it."

In the post-COVID era, he predicted more of the same. "We have a good reputation," he said. "[All Japan Pro Wrestling founder] Giant Baba was known for making handshake deals and always living up to his promise. My father taught me the same philosophy. The good Lord has offered me doors of opportunity, and I'll use that to hold the torch of truth."

CHAPTER 22

"IS THERE ANY meaning in my life that the inevitable death awaiting me does not destroy?" the British writer Ian McEwan once asked.

In pro wrestling, the answer was affirmative. With or without COVID, there was going to be a long list of wrestling losses in 2020, but the majority of those were accompanied by warm feelings and admiration for the performers' legacies. Of the casualties, the standout names included the "Wild-Eyed Southern Boy" Tracy Smothers, "Bullet" Bob Armstrong, famed ring announcer Howard Finkel, Rocky Johnson — from whom his son, Dwayne's ring moniker was inspired — Joe "Animal" Laurinaitis of the Road Warriors, *Royal Rumble* creator Pat Patterson and Danny Hodge, arguably the most gifted athlete never inducted into the WWE Hall of Fame during his lifetime.

James "Kamala" Harris never really saw anything wrong with his gimmick. A onetime sharecropper from Mississippi, Harris was a large, rotund Black man who portrayed a jungle savage, wrestling barefoot in face paint and a leopard-print loincloth, wielding a spear and war mask and slapping his large belly when he became excited or agitated. He enjoyed memorable feuds with Hulk Hogan, the Undertaker, Andre the Giant, the Ultimate Warrior and others, and — when he broke character around friends and used his actual speaking voice — described his shtick as "fun." In the modern era, both he and whoever was responsible for booking him would be instantly cancelled.

Time had not been kind to Kamala. He suffered from a multitude of health problems, including diabetes, which resulted in the amputation of both legs. In early August, he was undergoing kidney dialysis when he contracted the coronavirus, either from another patient or staffer. Too debilitated to fight the illness, he died of a heart attack on August 9 at age 70.

Despite the way his gimmick was perceived at the time of his death, Kamala was both well-remembered by spectators and well-liked by his fellow wrestlers. When a GoFundMe account was set up to help his family with funeral expenses, Chris Jericho — who'd previously provided the funds to prevent the legend from being evicted from his home — promptly donated $5,000.

But all this was overshadowed by the emergence of another Kamala Harris when, two days after the headliner's passing, Joe Biden announced his vice-presidential pick.

In recent years, as I watched the ascension of her political career, I periodically wondered if the California senator knew that she shared a name with the Ugandan Giant. Although as of this writing, I've yet to meet her in my capacity as reporter, I'm not sure how I'd even broach the topic if I did. However, I do know that the grappler was well-aware of his political namesake, posing for photos with a "Kamala for President" shirt adorned with a cartoon of his face-painted countenance.

The new Kamala quickly obscured the large shadow cast by her predecessor, becoming only the third woman ever chosen by a major party for the number two spot on a presidential ticket — after Geraldine Ferraro and Sarah Palin. With Biden advancing in age, Harris's detractors were quick to allege that she'd manipulate him behind the scenes and pervert American policy to suit her personal agenda.

Trump wasted little time labeling the duo "Sleepy Joe" and "Phony Kamala." In a Trump campaign advertisement that aired shortly after her selection, an announcer pointed out that Democratic voters had rejected Harris during the primaries because "they smartly spotted a phony. But not Joe Biden. He's not that smart."

The insults continued when the presidential candidates debated each other for the first time in September. Talking over Biden and moderator Chris Wallace, Trump labeled the former vice president a socialist and predicted that the most extreme left-wing elements of his party would control him. At one point, Biden told his rival, "Will you shut up, man?" At another, he complained, "It's hard to get any word in with this clown."

Throughout the campaign, the president had portrayed Biden's adherence to mask guidelines as a sign of weakness. "It gives him a feeling of security," Trump said at one rally. "If I was a psychiatrist, I'd say this guy has some big issues."

At the debate, Trump continued the onslaught. "I don't wear a mask like [Biden]. Every time you see him, he's got a mask. He could be speaking 200 feet away from it, and he shows up with the biggest mask I've seen."

The next day, at a rally in Minnesota, the president's family was observed flouting the scientific community's recommendations about face coverings. This despite the fact that, in June, eight White House staffers had tested positive after an Oklahoma gathering where mask restrictions were not enforced. One of the guests at that event, Herman Cain — a 2012 Republican primary candidate and co-chairman of a group called Black Voices for Trump — would later die of COVID.

One day after the Minnesota rally, close presidential advisor Hope Hicks tested positive for the virus. Following a fundraiser at a Trump-owned golf club in New Jersey, the president tweeted that he and his wife were being tested.

On Friday, October 2, with just 32 days left in the campaign, the president and the first lady announced that the tests were positive.

Trump's doctor, Sean Conley, described the couple's symptoms as "mild," and said that they would convalesce at the White House. Later in the day, there was a change of plans, and Trump was flown via helicopter to Walter Reed National Military Medical Center. He was wearing a suit and still acted as if little was wrong, proclaiming that he planned to use a special office suite at the hospital to work.

Over the next three days, at least nine other presidential associates would reveal that they also had COVID, infuriating doctors who insisted that Trump and his allies were irresponsible for holding "chaotic events" where attendees were vulnerable to airborne exposure. In China, the state-run *Global Times* appeared to take pleasure in the president's condition. "President Trump and the first lady have paid the price for his gamble to play down the COVID-19," tweeted editor-in-chief Hu Xijin.

But Trump refused to betray even a hint of regret. On October 4, the still infectious leader insisted on climbing into an SUV and taking a quick motorcade ride around the hospital, potentially endangering the health of the Secret Service agents accompanying him. He also boasted that, of the more than 56,000 tweets he'd composed since 2009, the coronavirus announcement was the most "liked ever."

While the president recovered, a small but fervent segment of indie wrestling fans were preparing to go to Indianapolis for The Collective, GCW's assembly of various small promotions that was initially supposed to take place during *WrestleMania* week. Unlike the GCW card I'd attended in the summer, this wasn't technically an outdoor show. Still, the location at the Marion County Fairgrounds was large and airy. A ring was perched in the middle of a cavernous agricultural building, and the doors were kept open, allowing the wind to circulate through. Approximately 450 people were scattered throughout a space meant to hold 2,000.

For three days, starting on October 9, spectators came to watch an assortment of primarily Midwestern groups, including AIW, Glory Pro, Freelance Wrestling, Black Label Pro, Paradigm Pro and SHIMMER, along with the Southern Underground group from Nashville, and special events like Josh Barnett's Bloodsport — a shoot-style attraction organized by the former UFC Heavyweight champion — and the postponed version of *Joey Janela's Spring Break*. Although GCW always took pride in being an outlier, it had acquired enough legitimacy that the Marion County Council and City of Indianapolis issued the group a formal proclamation, declaring the gathering "Indie in Indy Weekend."

Of course, COVID remained in everyone's thoughts. While I reclined in my seat at one point, a woman with an official badge peeked into my row and reminded me to make sure my mask was covering my nose. Ace Austin showed up in an elaborate face covering for his match with Jordan Oliver — an upside-down version of the jaguar veneer once worn by Konnan in Mexico. The mask remained on for a few minutes until Austin, breathing heavily, pulled it down, rolled out of the ring and slid out a door from under the mat. The weapon would later work against him when, following a cloud cutter, Oliver delivered an RKO through the portal and scored the pin.

"I work for Impact," Austin explained the decision to shield his face, "and I don't want to get sick and lose my position to someone else. So I wear the mask to protect myself, but also to send the message to take COVID-19 seriously."

A high point of the weekend was Effy's Big Gay Brunch, an event celebrating the industry's LGBTQ talent, as well as allies willing to play along. Traditionally, merely implying that a wrestler might be something other than heterosexual served one distinct purpose: drawing cheap heat. There had always been gay performers in the game, of course, but many of them chose to remain closeted.

Chris Jericho had been part of a group of young wrestlers in WCW that included Chris Kanyon, who took his own life by overdosing on antidepressants and Seroquel, a drug used to treat bipolar disorder, in 2010. "I pretty much knew that Chris was gay," Jericho remembered on his podcast, *Talk Is Jericho*, "but he never said it. Back then, everybody was going after the chicks, and he never went after a girl. Nobody cared."

Still, Kanyon resisted coming out to his group of friends. "That made him very depressed," Jericho said. "I read his book . . . after he passed away about how lonely he was because he would have to go meet a guy at a bar and not tell anybody. I just wish he would have told us."

By contrast, Effy never denied his sexuality. He had the luxury of time, debuting after Kanyon's death, and understood the destructive repercussions of hiding in the closet. "We can't stop our progress even if some people aren't ready," he said. "I started as a heel, so even though the majority of the crowd hated me, LGBTQ people would show up and say I made them feel safe being in the arena. It's not like wrestling fans changed. It's that people like me brought in new people who didn't know they were welcome here."

In July, NXT star Tegan Nox posted an item on Instagram declaring that she was in a committed relationship with a woman. Before making the decision, she spoke with Sonya Deville, who described both the positive and negative reactions she received when she revealed that she was a lesbian. "My family knew, but my fans didn't," Nox told *Newsweek*. "So she helped me bring it out to the public."

Nox estimated that 99 percent of the feedback she received was positive.

Like Effy, Nox was wrestling in an era that was vastly different from the way it had been when Kanyon launched his career in 1992. It wasn't until 2015 that the U.S. Supreme Court struck down bans on same-sex marriage in all 50 states. In November 2020, DC Comics introduced a nonbinary hero called Kid Quick who used they/them pronouns and was described as a gender-fluid version of the Flash.

Effy's match on the Big Gay Brunch card was baked with the camp elements his fans had come to expect. Although his scheduled opponent, Priscilla Kelly — later Gigi Dolin in WWE — cancelled, spectators were overjoyed to see her replaced by Marko Stunt, the five-foot-two-inch AEW personality known as Mr. Fun Size. Despite being the son of a missionary, Stunt seemed to revel in the decadent theme of the show, whipping Effy with a cat o' nine tails early in the confrontation. Effy gained the edge by hurling a chair into his rival's face as Stunt dove through the ropes onto the arena floor. But when Effy grabbed a Bunsen burner, Marko killed the momentum by biting his foe's dick.

Strapping a ball gag around his opponent's head, Stunt held Effy in a camel clutch and smacked him in the ass while the crowd chanted, "Make him gay-er."

Reaching below the ring, Marko then produced a rubber penis. Effy fought him off with a vertical suplex, then tried to make the Arkansas native suck the object. Stunt managed to slip away and bring out a wrestler dressed as a love doll.

The intruder fared poorly. Effy pummeled him and propped him up on a door positioned between two chairs. But when Effy ascended the ropes, Marko pushed the trespasser away, clambered up after the "sober, queer, punk rock pro wrestler of your dreams" and suplexed him through the door. With Effy sprawled out over the splintered wood, Mr. Fun Size tied up his rival for the pin.

In Mexico, Cassandro was among the most enduring exoticos — male luchadors who appropriate feminine traits into their gimmicks. The subject of a 2018 documentary, Cassandro struggled with physical and emotional pain throughout his career, wrestling with dozens of broken bones and metal pins in his body and enduring the fury of fans when he was awarded a match with Universal Wrestling Association (UWA) World Welterweight champion El Hijo del Santo in 1991. The performer found the reaction so painful that he slit his wrists with a razor blade, but he was saved by fellow exotico Pimpinela Escarlata, who found Cassandro in the bathroom. But even in a macho society like Mexico, perceptions changed, and Cassandro eventually came to be regarded as a beloved icon of lucha libre.

In the main event, Cassandro was matched against AEW star Sonny Kiss, a bleached blond African American who used both male and female pronouns to describe themself. As part of their gender fluidity, Sonny changed in the female dressing room but competed on the male roster.

In AEW, Kiss had formed a tag team with fellow Jersey native Joey Janela. Janela told me that he took great pride in the fact that their gender identities never played in a role in how they were portrayed on television. "This has never happened in wrestling — a person like Sonny and a person like me, with no hint of a romantic relationship. We're friends just pushing each other to do better. And that's pretty much the way it really is. We know each other for years and relate on a lot of levels."

When I asked Kiss about the partnership, they described the tandem's car rides. "We listen to Limp Bizkit. We listen to Korn. It's beyond wrestling. It's beyond being an ally. It's two people with a great connection."

At one point, Janela referred to the pair as the "New New Midnight Express," an allusion to the legendary duos of Bobby Eaton and Dennis Condrey, as well as Eaton and Stan Lane, managed by Jim Cornette from 1983 onward. (The original Midnight Express, formed in 1980, consisted of Condrey and Randy Rose and resurfaced in Jim Crockett

Promotions in 1988, managed by Paul Heyman.) A lawyer representing Cornette — who'd recently tried to trademark the name with Condrey, Eaton and Lane — swiftly sent a cease and desist letter to AEW.

The team was never called the New New Midnight Express again. Janela later claimed that the whole thing was a rib designed to irritate his perpetual antagonist, Cornette.

Just prior to his clash with Kiss at Effy's Big Gay Brunch, Cassandro drew a roar by parading around the arena in a pink robe with a massive train, while Kiss balanced himself on the top turnbuckles and performed a split.

It was an acrobatic match with Kiss responsible for many of the theatrics. But despite being 50 years old, Cassandro did not rely on his younger opponent to do all the work. At one point, the legend walked across the top rope while holding Kiss in an arm bar, then sent him to the arena floor with a flying head scissors and delivered a plancha. Kiss was equally crafty, hanging Cassandro upside down in the corner and executing a somersault. Ultimately, though, Cassandro took over, zapping his opponent with a dropkick from the top rope and winning with a reverse sunset flip from the turnbuckles.

With the crowd clapping rhythmically, the pair embraced before Sonny bowed to the LGBTQ pioneer. Effy then rushed to the ring, grabbed the microphone and praised Cassandro for "teaching all these children how to work, how to be a professional and how to be star."

At this point, the other wrestlers on the card were surrounding the ring and pounding the apron. With a wide grin, Kiss lifted Cassandro into their arms, and the renowned exotico wrapped his legs around his vanquished opponent.

"With AEW, I feel like the representative of the LGBTQ community in today's world," Kiss said backstage. "But this is the trailblazer. I *wanted* to put him over. Why wouldn't I?"

While *Raw* Underground was being phased out, at The Collective, Josh Barnett's Bloodsport seemed to have mastered the concept. The matches incorporated elements of MMA and traditional catch wrestling, and victory could only be attained via knockout or submission. The thing was a work, of course, but it certainly felt authentic.

The action was preceded by a ceremony in which all the participants entered the ropeless ring, forming two straight lines — with opponents positioned across from one another. Then, Barnett — looking every bit as intimidating as when he held the UFC title — walked between the competitors and took the microphone, addressing the challenges of the times and promising a night of "heart, soul and violence."

In the main event, Jon Moxley clashed with Chris Dickinson. By virtue of sharing the ring with the AEW World champion, Dickinson was elevated to the spot where his followers believed he long belonged. As he lumbered through the curtain, he had the aura of a guy who could headline the Tokyo Dome or Madison Square Garden, pacing at ringside, climbing the stairs and throwing up his fist to a big pop.

Not only was Moxley endorsing Dickinson with this match, he was ratifying the importance of The Collective. He passed through the curtain in a black hoodie, determinedly taking a sip from a water bottle then splattering the contents on the ground. Every head shake by the eccentric performer generated a response. Holding his arms apart, Moxley sent vibrations through the audience by wiggling his fingers. Moxley applauded when Dickinson's name was announced. When the announcer introduced the AEW champ, the titlist blew a kiss to the crowd — and the indies.

Both men looked trim, as if they'd trained to get into fighting shape, and the exchanges were intense and believable. Moxley slapped Dickinson on the break, and Chris slapped back, the sound reverberating off the bleachers and ceiling. Dickinson surged at one point, kicking at Moxley's legs, flooring him, then delivering a hard foot to the back of the head. After executing two belly to back suplexes, Dickinson followed up with another high kick, mounted his rival and pounded him with forearms. Moxley didn't wilt, recovering to blast Dickinson with a knee strike and trapping him in a rear naked choke hold.

The referee signaled for the bell as fans chanted for both men. The official thrust the winner's arm into the air, but Moxley was limping across the ring, selling the earlier beating from Dickinson. Moxley took the microphone and thanked the fans. Then, he and Dickinson shook hands and exchanged a few words.

I was too far away to hear what they said but imagine that Chris thanked Moxley for his generosity in the ring, and the AEW titlist expressed gratitude to his foe for having the kind of match that likely drove both of them to professional wrestling in the first place.

Joey Janela's Spring Break was the flagship of the weekend, the event that established GCW as the indie promotion to catch on *WrestleMania* week and the reason that The Collective was able to draw in so many companies. GCW World champion Rickey Shane Page opened the card, surrounded by his entourage. The back story was that he was engaging in non-title matches to hold onto the gold but felt bold enough to issue open challenges when nothing was at stake. A few guys accepted but were quickly terrorized by Page and his flunkies. Then Danhausen came out, only to receive a beating as well.

Shane was brimming with confidence until Orange Cassidy emerged from the back, startling and crowd and triggering a loud ovation. Although Cassidy had logged a lot of time in GCW before emerging as an AEW star, none of the promotional material had mentioned him, and the novelty of seeing him in this intimate setting delighted the fans as much as Moxley's appearance.

Keeping his hands casually in his pockets, Cassidy launched his body at Page, flourishing until Rickey Shane's cohorts tripped and ganged up on him. The "freshly squeezed" attraction shook off the blows and threw some orange juice into one of his tormentor's eyes. Going on offense again, he ascended the turnbuckles and dove onto his adversaries — once again with his hands in his pockets. Then, out of nowhere, Cassidy shocked Page by cradling him for the three-count.

The rest of the card flew by quickly — with fans treated to a talent list that included the Rascalz — soon-to-be NXT Tag Team champions MSK — future ROH World titlist Jonathan Gresham, Impact's Alex Shelley and Inner Circle members Santana and Ortiz. Janela engaged Ricky Morton in a bloodbath, busting open the legend with a chair shot and punching the wound. Morton rebounded, hitting The Bad Boy with a running dropkick followed by a Death Valley Driver on the ring apron. The finish saw Janela trap Morton in the figure-four. Straining his aging body, Morton shook from side to side and turned himself over, reversing the pressure and scoring the win.

Fans were so elated, I saw several literally run around the ring in circles. As with his tag team partner, Sonny Kiss, Janela had done the right thing by putting over a squared circle sovereign and the people loved him for it, chanting his name as loudly as they cheered Morton.

Before Janela and Morton stepped into the ring, Donald Trump had already held his first public event since his diagnosis.

Earlier that morning, hundreds of guests stood on the South Lawn as the president — in a blue surgical mask with bandages visible on his hands — addressed them from the White House balcony. Although more supporters than usual were sporting face coverings, social distancing was not enforced and none of the attendees were tested for COVID-19.

Without mentioning that he'd likely received the best treatment on Earth — reportedly a combination of oxygen and steroids — the president predicted that the virus was "disappearing." Vaccines would be available soon, he promised, and the United States was well on the way to defeating "this terrible China virus" — a reference to the country where COVID began and a term many believed inspired hatred against Asian Americans.

By Monday, October 12, with three weeks remaining before the election, Trump was back on the campaign trail. "They say I'm immune," he declared at an airport hangar in Sanford, Florida. "I feel so powerful. I'll walk in there and kiss everyone."

He specified that he would not discriminate because of gender, cutting a promo that would have gone over at Effy's Big Gay Brunch. "I'll kiss the guys and the beautiful women. I'll give you a big, fat kiss."

In the weeks after The Collective, at least three wrestlers who'd been in Indianapolis tested positive for COVID-19, sparking waves of angst and condemnation, depending upon the sensibility of the person digesting the information.

"There are people who have valid concerns, and I respect them," promoter Brett Lauderdale told me. "And there are people who take joy in being part of a mob and saying we don't care about the fans or the wrestlers. I saw tweets that said I should be arrested for manslaughter. And there was another that said WWE, AEW, Impact and Ring of Honor should all sue me for jeopardizing the industry.

"Obviously, we were trying to do things as safely as possible. Maybe some people were more careless than they should have been. But most of the ones I saw were being pretty safe. I was busy that weekend and couldn't babysit everybody. But you were there. You saw that precautions were being taken. But after every event, I ask myself, 'What should I have done better? What should I do differently next time?' Maybe I should have put up more signs to tell people to wear masks."

Lauderdale conceded that he was particularly worried about the incomplete data the public was receiving about the virus. "It's a pandemic, and we don't know everything about it. There's a chance, even if you wear a mask and gloves, you can get infected. It's the world we live in right now."

I was among those fearing a larger outbreak. And I admit that, after spending so much time around the GCW crew during the writing of this and my last book, I was distressed by the notion of the coronavirus damaging the livelihoods of people I'd come to like. Already, COVID-19 had crushed The Collective the week of *WrestleMania 36*. If more wrestlers and fans fell ill, the decision to hold The Collective in October could potentially drive GCW out of business.

On October 21, AEW pulled Joey Janela from his *Dynamite* match with Kenny Omega because his opponent at a recent indie show, AJ Gray, had tested positive. Gray had also been at The Collective.

In response, one fan sent a tweet to AEW, asking, "Can't you just pay your guys enough to not do indy shows for a year. An indy show is the exact opposite of any situation that is safe for COVID."

An incensed Janela wrote back, "Moron, I wasn't doing indie shows for the money. I was doing it for the ring time and the love of the business. My paycheck is more than enough, and [I] would've done indies for free."

As it turned out, Janela never came down with the virus. Nor did any additional people associated with the Indiana event. But for several weeks, Lauderdale could barely concentrate on anything else. "I kept checking my phone every few minutes, hoping that the number wouldn't go up to 100," he admitted. "And even now, we don't know when those people got infected. It could have been before, it could have been afterwards, and it could have been during."

CHAPTER 23

PRO WRESTLING MEANS telling a story, even if that particular story doesn't turn everyone on.

With the cinematic match now institutionalized, AEW presented its most unusual vignette on the October 21 episode of *Dynamite*. The company had been stretching out a story about MJF possibly joining Chris Jericho's Inner Circle for months. In front of each other, Jericho and Maxwell Jacob Friedman were absurdly deferential. But the two heels were clearly suspicious and contemptuous of the skills the other could bring to a partnership.

The two would battle, merge their energies, then spectacularly combust. Before that, though, they decided to stage a spectacle that even WWE's writers would be afraid of presenting to Vince.

It all began after MJF saw the movie *Rocketman*, in which Elton John's life was recreated in song. As the on-air angle with Jericho intensified, Friedman suggested that he and Jericho sing the tune "Honky Cat" together. Few other pairs could pull this off. But Jericho was already the lead vocalist for Fozzy, and, in addition to playing football and competing as a swimmer at Long Island's Plainview High School, MJF had participated in student concerts in a boy's group called Acafella.

Jericho had a better idea. Why not do "Me and My Shadow," a song performed by Frank Sinatra and Sammy Davis Jr. on American television in 1962? Once MJF agreed, Jericho set about acquiring the rights to the song, composed by Al Jolson, Billy Rose and Dave Dreyer in 1927. Members of the Jacksonville Jaguars cheerleading squad were recruited as dance partners. Le Champion later said that he was inspired by the

Blues Brothers, the 1980 flick in which Dan Aykroyd and John Belushi would engage in elaborate dance routines, then stop and continue whatever they'd been previously doing.

The pair spent a day in rehearsal, then the next day shooting the sequence until 2 a.m. AEW music producer Mikey Rukus recorded all the music himself, playing each instrument by ear. Jericho was in the edit room on the day of *Dynamite* for 10 hours, cobbling together the best parts and mixing the audio, conferring with attorneys about an unexpected rights issue that suddenly emerged and completing the final version 22 minutes before it was slated to air around the world.

The Broadway-style performance — dubbed "Le Dinner Debonair" — began with the pair drinking wine and eating steak before bursting into song and doing a choreographed dance segment with several cheerleaders. Just as Frank Sinatra and Sammy Davis Jr. had altered the lyrics to reference Bobby Kennedy and JFK, the 2020 version included insults specifically aimed at Orange Cassidy, Matt Hardy, Cody Rhodes and Jon Moxley.

Tweeted Broadway actor and Tony Award–winning producer Alex Boniello, "This is good. I hereby relinquish my Tony Award to @IAmJericho and @The_MJF."

The *New York Times* would call the duet one of the best theatrical performances of 2020.

Jericho pointed out that the quarter beat NXT by 11 percent in total viewers and 98 percent in the 18-to-49-year-old demographic. "Just saw the minute by minute ratings for #LeDinnerDebonair," he crowed on Twitter, "& I'm stoked that almost 800k checked out our song and dance . . . Add over a million views on Twitter & it looks like our experiment paid off."

Jim Cornette saw no reason for acclaim. "I do not have words," he said on his podcast, comparing the routine to *Gomer Pyle* actor Jim Nabors singing on *The Carol Burnett Show* in the 1960s. Jericho was a "past-his-expiration-date, oversized canned ham," the manager said. Cornette was even more disappointed in Friedman.

"MJF had it. The one guy, the one guy on their entire roster that not only had it, but he was still young enough to use it. The one heel that knew and worked and talked like he was supposed to be and he's blown the image."

The Louisville Lip was not alone in his opinion. To a section of the fan base, AEW was a wrestling company — like New Japan or ROH — that had taken a vow to deliver a "sports-oriented" product. "Le Dinner Debonair" proved that the company was not ill-disposed to also doing "sports-entertainment."

Interestingly, while these charges were being leveled, WWE was presenting its most emotional feud in years.

After portraying Roman Reigns as a company ambassador, filling a role previously occupied by John Cena, there was irony in the fact that it took a pandemic — when all fan noise on television was artificially generated — for WWE to finally heed public demands to depict him as a villain. As the "Head of the Table," the man who proclaimed that he supported the rest of his Samoan wrestling family through his hard work and superior ring acumen, Reigns was able to reveal that edgy part of himself that refugees to AEW and Impact claimed he always showed backstage. Rather than covet admiration from WWE's PG-13 audience — a position that drew scorn — the WWE Universal champion demanded obedience from members of his clan.

This meant that he expected cousin Jey Uso to acquiesce to his demands, whatever they might be. When Uso resisted, attempting to be his own person, Reigns declared that he had no choice but to punish his kinsman in the ring.

Uso said that many of the words that passed between the two on television were untouched by the people in the writing room. "They can't write how he feels about me, and I feel about him," he said on the *Gorilla Position* podcast. "We got to the level where they trust us and let us do our thing. It feels good to finally get to that level where they took the chains off us."

If that wasn't enough to fire up the masses, Uso continued, Roman now had Brock Lesnar's advocate, Paul Heyman, in his corner.

"When Paul Heyman is in the mix, you know it's going to be lit . . . The man is a creative genius."

To fans who enjoyed cheering for the cool heels, Roman had exceeded all expectations. But they'd always liked the Usos as well, regardless of how the company was depicting them. In the ring, the pair told their tale with plausible physicality, facial expressions and a narrative that took on new dimensions as the battle wore on.

Near the conclusion of their "I Quit" match at the *Hell in a Cell* pay-per-view in October, Reigns burst into tears after his cousin refused to succumb, forcing the aggressor to become more brutal with each blow. Finally, Jey's brother, Jimmy — sidelined with a leg injury — crawled under the ropes and tried to reason with the champion.

A sorrowful Reigns gripped hands with his cousin and apologized for allowing the situation to escalate. "I don't even know who I am," he wept. "I'm sorry."

Moments later, Roman grabbed Jimmy and trapped him in a deadly guillotine choke, forcing Jey to finally quit the match on behalf of his twin.

But the Samoans had always been a ruthless bunch between the ropes. As the victorious titlist made his way up the entrance ramp, he was met by his father and uncle, WWE Hall of Famers Sika and Afa of the Wild Samoans tag team, who presented him with a lei and acknowledged that Roman truly was the clan's "Tribal Chief."

In the White House, the president was also weaving captivating narratives.

Trump repeatedly claimed that his enemies were over-emphasizing the danger of the coronavirus to diminish his support before Americans voted on November 3. If, by some fluke, Biden ended up winning, the alarming prognostications about the illness would disappear, Trump contended. "ALL THE FAKE NEWS MEDIA WANTS TO TALK ABOUT IS COVID, COVID, COVID," he tweeted on October 27. "ON NOVEMBER 4th, YOU WON'T BE HEARING SO MUCH ABOUT IT ANYMORE."

In the course of researching this book, I heard a few people associated with the wrestling business make the exact same assertion.

COVID fears had prompted election authorities to make contingencies for people nervous about gathering in crowded polling spots to cast their ballots. This was not a normal election, and it was understood that it would take days to count the mail-in, drop-off and early ballots. Trump insisted that mail-in voting was "corrupt" and urged supporters to go to the polls on Election Day to prevent Democratic saboteurs from throwing out or disqualifying their votes. Predictably, when the tallies began coming in, the in-person ballots had the president leading in many parts of the country. But in the days that followed, as the mail-in and other ballots were counted, Biden began to overtake the incumbent.

By November 5, some of the key battleground states had yet to determine a winner, and the president's campaign was filing lawsuits to prevent ongoing vote counting. Tweeted Donald Trump Jr., "The best thing for America's future is for @realDonaldTrump to go to war over this election to expose all of the fraud, cheating, dead/no longer in state voters."

As part of its "civic integrity policy" Twitter flagged the post for spreading unverified information and hid it.

The next day, Trump declared victory for the second time that week — with the majority of news outlets cutting away from his live speech. The Associated Press clarified that it had yet to declare a winner in the race, "with several states too early to call."

Even some Republicans were critical of Trump's actions. "A sitting president undermining our political process and questioning the legality of the voices of countless Americans without evidence is not only dangerous and wrong," said Congressman Will Hurd of Texas, "it undermines the very foundation this nation was built upon."

In the midst of all this, AEW made the decision to allow 1,000 socially distanced and masked fans into Daily's Place on November 7 to watch Jon Moxley defend his championship against Eddie Kingston at *Full Gear*. Tony Khan suggested that the scaled-down audience was a small step toward normalcy — even if, on a larger level, there was nothing ordinary about what was transpiring in America.

Earlier that day, the president had announced that his attorney Rudy Giuliani would hold a press conference at the Four Seasons in Philadelphia. But the hotel sent out a tweet emphasizing that no political event was scheduled there. Because of an apparent mix-up, Giuliani instead held his briefing in the suburbs at a place called Four Seasons Total Landscaping, situated between a crematorium and adult bookstore.

As Giuliani was insisting that the Democrats were attempting to steal the election, a reporter informed him that Biden had been declared president-elect.

"Don't be ridiculous," the man once known as America's Mayor shot back.

"We all know why Joe Biden is rushing to falsely pose as the winner and why his media allies are trying so hard to help him," Trump said in a statement. "They don't want the truth to be exposed. The simple fact is this election is far from over. Joe Biden has not been certified the winner of any states . . . It remains shocking that the Biden campaign . . . wants ballots counted even if they are fraudulent, manufactured or cast by ineligible or deceased voters . . . So what is Biden hiding? I will not rest until the American people have the honest vote that they deserve and democracy demands."

To a number of pro wrestling personalities, though, it was the president who was trying to work them.

CM Punk tweeted a photo of himself sarcastically blowing a kiss to Vince McMahon after winning the WWE Championship in 2011 — photoshopping Biden's face instead.

Sami Zayn posted a message to Trump: "Don't let the door hit your ass."

And Kevin Owens, who'd famously dropped the Universal strap to Bill Goldberg in 22 seconds three years earlier, retweeted Trump's victory avowal and followed up with, "And I beat @Goldberg at Fastlane in 2017 to keep my Universal Title."

CHAPTER 24

LIKE BOB BACKLUND, the World Wrestling Federation Heavyweight champion from 1978 to 1983, who'd appear outside Madison Square Garden during the early days of the Hulkamania era and gripe to fans about being pushed aside — "You're still the champ," Bucklund's followers would assure him, to which he'd reply, "I still *feel* like the champ — Donald Trump could not accept that his time had passed.

But Backlund later came to terms with the realities of his vocation — people lose the belt sometimes — and was even rewarded with a brief title reign in 1994. At 74 years old, Trump seemed unwilling to wait to reclaim the top spot.

By December 2, most major news networks were refusing to allow Trump to seize the airwaves and repeat unsubstantiated conspiracies. So the president went on Facebook instead. For 46 minutes, he assailed what he characterized as a meticulously arranged swindle — despite his legal team already losing dozens of lawsuits demanding that the election results be overturned. Even Attorney General William Barr, a man accused of acting more like Trump's defense attorney than the chief law enforcement officer in the United States, told the Associated Press that, although both the Justice Department and FBI had made enquiries, "to date we have not seen fraud on a scale that could have effected a different outcome in the election."

But there was one conspiracy theory that kind of made sense, if you were predisposed to believing this type of thing. Now that Trump had lost, it seemed like there was new vigor in the fight to alleviate COVID — not just in the United States, but around the world — as if the medical

232

community and government elites were trying to signal that everything would be better now.

The United Kingdom authorized use of the vaccine produced by Pfizer and BioNTech on December 2. The premier recipient, 90-year-old Margaret Keenan, received the first of two required injections at University Hospital, Coventry, on December 8.

Three days later, in the U.S., the FDA approved the Pfizer vaccine for emergency use. Within 24 hours, drugs were being shipped to more than 600 sites in all 50 states. On December 14, Sandra Lindsay, an ICU nurse at New York's Long Island Jewish Medical Center, received the first injection in the U.S.

In less than a week, Moderna's version of the serum was also granted emergency use authorization.

By the end of February, more than 20 vaccines would be in development globally.

But distribution would be a long process, and people were still falling ill. On the day that the world's media showed a smiling Lindsay receiving her dose, the U.S. recorded 110,549 hospitalizations — a record high.

After grabbing released WWE talent and presenting consistently good matches throughout the pandemic, Impact appeared to be winning back some fans who'd drifted away during the darker days of TNA. The supporters were not coming in droves, but enthusiasm for the product was higher than in recent memory. Long gone was the time when the company fancied itself as a viable number two to WWE. But at least Impact now had the respect of the wrestling public — even if that public was more intrigued by WWE and AEW.

Still, there were plans to propel Impact higher. Even people who weren't watching its television program would be talking about the promotion and going online to follow developments. And it was all because of Tony Khan and Kenny Omega.

Khan described the strategy as "a shift in wrestling's balance of power."

It began in early December when Impact broadcast an old match between the Young Bucks and the Motor City Machine Guns, Alex

Shelley and Chris Sabin. On the surface, this was not unusual; the company regularly went into its archives to air encounters with stars who'd moved on to other leagues. But given the Bucks' prominence in AEW, fans were left with a feeling that the two promotions were about to enter into a working relationship.

The reality was that Khan had been looking down numerous avenues that had previously been closed. The goal was hitting fans with a variety of tastes and pulling them all to AEW in the process. The same week that the Bucks' match aired, Darby Allin and Cody Rhodes defeated Ricky Starks and Powerhouse Hobbs on *Dynamite*. The losers were not gracious in defeat, with Hobbs running through Allin after the bell. This prompted legend Arn Anderson — Cody's ringside coach — to climb into the ring. Double A managed to fell Starks with a punch before the heels ganged up on the former WWF and WCW tag team co-titlist. In the melee, Brian Cage — a confederate of Hobbs and Starks in Team Taz — and Dustin Rhodes became involved.

Just as Hobbs was about to bash Cody with Cage's FTW belt, the music hit and six-time WCW World Heavyweight champion Sting emerged with his signature black baseball bat, sending the villains scurrying. Sting was 61 years old, but his face paint rendered his age difficult to determine. More importantly, he was a symbol of a time when there was a legitimate alternative to the World Wrestling Federation.

When WCW folded, Sting refused to consider making the jump to WWE — unlike names like Booker T, Torrie Wilson, Diamond Dallas Page, Stacy Keibler and Bill Goldberg — signing with TNA instead. He finally made his first appearance for WWE in 2014 and was inducted into the company's Hall of Fame two years later. But his contract expired in 2020 and his merchandise was taken down from the WWE website.

As he stood in the ring and gave Allin a pep talk — and the "rub" of stardom by establishing their association — fans went online to dissect the meaning of AEW's new signing. Not only did Sting link AEW to WCW's glory period, but his presence sent a message that Tony Khan, not Vince McMahon, knew how to treat and market an icon.

Christmas was coming, and AEW had lots of Sting merch available for fans who'd been increasing their shopping time online throughout the pandemic.

And that wasn't the only thing that happened that night.

In the main event, Kenny Omega dethroned Jon Moxley for the AEW World Championship — with an assist from Impact Executive Vice President Don Callis.

Like Omega and Chris Jericho, Callis was a son of Winnipeg and wore the badge proudly. His trainer was a gravelly voiced, local wrestler called the Golden Sheik. As the Sheik's career was ending, he began managing the younger wrestler and became a father figure. Callis grew close to his mentor's family, particularly the Golden Sheik's nephew, Kenny Omega.

In 1997, Callis debuted in the World Wrestling Federation as The Jackyl, a manager who announcer Jim Ross compared to David Koresh, leader of the Branch Davidians cult during the deadly 1993 standoff with law enforcement near Waco, Texas. Although that tenure was over by 1999, Callis remained a fixture in the business, logging time with ECW and TNA and working as an English-language broadcaster for New Japan before ending up in management at Impact.

According to pro wrestling mythology, it was Callis who convinced free agent Chris Jericho to return to New Japan after a 21-year gap and wrestle Omega at *Wrestle Kingdom 12* — the match that allegedly inspired Tony Khan to launch the company that became AEW.

Callis was at the announcer's table for Omega's challenge to Moxley, purportedly to provide a personal perspective on the number one contender. But when Moxley suplexed his foe into a line of heaters placed at ringside to warm the competitors from the 40-degree weather, Callis left the desk and rushed toward the action. As the champion pulled Omega back into the ring, Callis grabbed a microphone, stepped onto the apron and told the referee that The Cleaner was hurt.

Agitated by the interruption, Moxley shoved Callis onto the ramp. But while the intruder was falling, he dropped the microphone. Immediately, Callis stood and distracted the arbiter, allowing Omega to snatch the object and smash his opponent with it. This was followed by a series of V-Triggers and a One-Winged Angel. Before anyone was fully aware of what was transpiring, Omega had scored the pin and won the championship.

Up until this point, Omega had been a babyface. Now, he and Callis raced through the bowels of Daily's Place with the belt, passing Khan at one point, who attempted to question them about what just occurred. Shortly before they disappeared into a car, they were stopped by AEW backstage interviewer Alex Marvez.

When Marvez asked about the finish of the match, Callis said that more details would be provided on Tuesday.

Marvez noted that *Dynamite* aired on Wednesdays.

That's when Callis said that if AEW fans were interested in learning more, they'd have to watch Impact on Tuesday.

Impact pounced on the visibility. "Tuesdays are the new Wednesdays," the company tweeted.

"Does @IMPACTWRESTLING have your attention now?" Sami Callihan wrote.

In AEW, FTR stoked fan interest in a cross-promotional rivalry. Dax Harwood tweeted "The North" — a reference to two-time Impact World Tag Team champions Ethan Page and Josh Alexander — while Cash Wheeler added "MCMG" — for Motor City Machine Guns.

To the people accusing Callis of helping Omega steal the AEW title, he countered, "You can't steal what you created," reiterating his contention that the company wouldn't exist if it wasn't for him.

During an appearance on the *Living the Gimmick* show on Patreon, Matt Jackson said that he'd been suggesting an alliance with Impact since AEW's beginnings. "There are immediate plans that I can't give away right now," he said. "My dream, if I had my way, is the possible dream matches. How can you not jump ahead and fantasy book?" Although the partnership was just beginning, "there are some big surprises coming, and I'm really excited about it."

On the December 8 Impact, Callis boasted about being the "invisible hand in [Omega's] life." He only became affiliated with New Japan, he claimed, in order to help guide Omega to the IWGP Heavyweight Championship. "It was all part of the plan for me to come to Impact Wrestling like I did." Likewise, he'd orchestrated the scenario that placed him at the announcer's desk when The Cleaner challenged Moxley.

"Why Impact?" Omega said in an interview with the company's play-by-play commentator Josh Mathews. "I'm going to teach you something about myself. As a child, I considered myself a collector. But I had to quit. You know why? Because . . . no matter how many rare comic books I collected, I could never get the . . . rarest, the most valuable prizes in the comic book industry." As a wrestler, his experience was markedly different, he continued. He'd already been the AAA Mega champion when he battled Moxley. Now, he had the AEW World Championship and was planning to add more titles.

That Saturday night, Omega appeared on two pay-per-views at the same time. In a pretaped segment on Impact's *Final Resolution*, he and Callis joked with Karl Anderson of The Good Brothers about a possible Bullet Club reunion. And in a live broadcast from an empty arena in Mexico City's Azcapotzalco section, Omega retained his AAA Mega Championship by routing the Laredo Kid — refusing to shake the challenger's hand after the bell.

Meanwhile, WWE continued to act as if none of these events were taking place, concentrating on its own angles and provoking a blend of beguilement, confusion and repulsion with its final pay-per-view of 2020.

After allowing its talent to be chucked off the roof of its corporate headquarters at *Money in the Bank* and presenting the Eye for an Eye Match between Seth Rollins and Rey Mysterio, the company outdid itself with the Firefly Inferno clash at *Tables, Ladders & Chairs* on December 20.

To folks who aren't wrestling fans, the concept of a ring surrounded by fire is incomprehensible. I know unruly spectators have ignited sections of stadiums at soccer matches in places like Serbia, Poland and Turkey, but that was never with the league's encouragement. Inversely, WWE specified that the Firefly Inferno could not end until either The Fiend or Randy Orton was set on fire.

Here's how Jim Cornette described the stipulation on YouTube: "Unless someone does something incredibly stupid, ignorant, preposterously brainless, without a modicum, a minuscule amount of thought . . . something on a biblical scale of wretchedness" the match could not be won.

The finish wasn't all that notable. As the two battled outside the ring, The Fiend's jacket and pants began burning, and the Viper was declared the winner. Fire extinguishers were deployed, and Orton returned between the ropes, followed by his opponent. When they re-engaged, Orton planted The Fiend with an RKO.

This was when the night took a nefarious turn. Reaching outside the ring, the Apex Predator procured a container of gasoline. Observed Cornette, "Orton gets the gas can, he pours it all over [Bray Wyatt], he goes out and there's a box of brand new, long-stemmed matches sitting carefully placed on the railing."

Taking advantage of that opportunity, Orton flicked a match and soon The Fiend's entire body was consumed by flames.

His third-generation wrestling pedigree notwithstanding, Bray Wyatt wasn't so dedicated to the business that he was willing to actually immolate himself. Reportedly, the match was taped in the afternoon while the producers projected fan faces from previous altercations on the ThunderDome walls, and a dummy was set on fire.

As the show was ending, The Fiend had apparently mended to the point where he was able to tweet, posting an image of a cocoon.

He never specified if he was referring to his own transmogrification or how the industry was mutating, going into 2021.

CHAPTER 25

IN ADDITION TO everything else that it impacted, the pandemic slowed Brexit negotiations. In April, the second and third rounds of talks had been delayed after EU chief negotiator Michel Barnier and his UK counterpart David Frost reported COVID-19 symptoms. With videoconferencing replacing face-to-face meetings, Barnier was unable to continue his travels to European capitals to ensure cohesive positions throughout the coalition.

Imagine Jim Barnett facing the same obstacle while lobbying the NWA Board of Directors to put the belt on Tommy Rich in 1981.

"Mah boy . . ."

"Let's be honest," an EU official told *Politico*. "The political leadership is focused on something else now."

But the deadline remained in place; a new trade agreement had to be reached by the end of the year. With so much uncertainty, carmakers in the UK were stockpiling auto parts, concerned about the possibility of high tariffs. British airline executives worried about the way new regulations would alter routes throughout Europe. Europeans employed in Manchester and Cardiff and Edinburgh feared being detained if their paperwork wasn't in order.

On December 11, after weeks of intensive discussions, Prime Minister Boris Johnson said that there was a "strong possibility" that a deal might not be achieved. "I have to tell you in all candor, the treaty is not there yet."

That changed on Christmas Eve when the two sides agreed to an arrangement that allowed trade to continue without extra taxes on goods. The formal separation would occur on January 1, 2021.

Not everyone viewed this as a triumph. Said Scotland's first minister Nicola Sturgeon, "Brexit is happening against Scotland's will." Her goal, she said, was breaking away from the UK and joining the EU as an independent nation.

"Scotland will be back soon, Europe," she tweeted. "Keep the light on."

Even those happy about Brexit were in no position to dash into the street and embrace each other in celebration. While negotiations were in their final stages, COVID surges prompted the government to impose strict "Tier 4" restrictions on London and the country's southeast, shutting shops, gyms, movie theaters, bowling alleys and beauty salons, among other businesses, while people were prohibited from meeting more than one person at a time from another household outdoors. In other parts of the UK, members from no more than three households could gather, and that was only on Christmas Day.

Like the Olympics and European Football Championships, Christmas in 2020 was essentially postponed.

In the wrestling community, what was arguably the most shocking news of the year came on December 26. Jon Huber, the man who'd been Luke Harper in WWE and Dark Order leader Brodie Lee in AEW, died of a non-COVID-related lung ailment.

Lee had not been seen on *Dynamite* since October 7, when he lost a dog collar match, and the TNT Championship, to Cody Rhodes. While he was home in Tampa, selling a gimmicked injury said to have been sustained in the match, he noticed that he couldn't finish his workouts on his Peloton bicycle and was bewildered about his shortness of breath. He was checked into a local hospital and given a COVID test, with negative results. Tony Khan personally followed the developments. By the end of the month, Huber's lungs were no longer functioning, and Megha Parekh, the senior vice president and chief legal counsel of AEW and the Jacksonville Jaguars, arranged for the wrestler to be airlifted to the Mayo Clinic in Jacksonville.

Doctors continued looking for signs of the coronavirus. But all tests — including those for antibodies — indicated that Huber was suffering from something else. As the condition worsened, it was determined that he needed a lung transplant to save his life. The list was long, and the possibility of finding a set of healthy lungs that could be inserted into his six-foot-five-inch, 275-pound body appeared remote.

At one point, Huber's wife, Amanda — who'd previously wrestled on the indies as Synndy Synn — addressed the AEW dressing room and respectfully asked the talent not to share what they knew. Despite the prevalence of social media, no one violated the family's privacy.

But after the broadcast of the promotion's "Holiday Bash" show, which aired in a rescheduled time slot after an NBA game on December 23, Kenny Omega and the Young Bucks came out and offered "Brodie Lee Jr." — Huber's eight-year-old son — a chance to join The Elite. The boy refused, and the Dark Order stormed the ring. The skirmish concluded with Brodie Jr. trapping Omega in a rear naked choke hold and the titlist submitting.

Ring announcer Justin Roberts declared the child AEW World Champion.

At the time, the popular assumption was that the talent was just being playful; the Young Bucks had done shtick with kids at the conclusion of indie shows for years. Only when Jon Huber passed away did it become clear that the AEW roster was trying to bring the family some joy during a traumatic period.

The irony of Huber's death was that the Brodie Lee name was inspired by Bruiser Brody, who was stabbed to death in a Bayamón, Puerto Rico, dressing room in 1988 — another wrestler robbed from the wrestling community before his time.

On Instagram, Bray Wyatt released a statement, in which he called his former teammate his best friend and compared him to Terry Gordy, the quiet, but arguably most skilled, member of the Freebirds. "I'm so godamn pissed," wrote Wyatt. "This isn't how it was supposed to be. It was supposed to be us fat, bald and useless running Wyatt Family spots in high school gyms in our 70s." This was a reference to past-their-prime pro wrestlers playing their old WWE characters at small indies. "Where do we go now? What do I do knowing that I'll never hear your condescending sarcasm as I am riding high? I miss you so fucking much already. I would do anything to just live through our worst moments again . . . I'm hurting so bad. I wish I had a chance to say goodbye . . . Goodbye forever, Brodie. I love you."

Mick Foley — who was quarantined at the time after contracting the coronavirus — and CM Punk vowed to donate 100 percent of their January merchandise sales from the Pro Wrestling Tees company to the Huber family. The New Day would appear at the 2021 *Royal Rumble* in wrestling outfits bearing Huber's likeness and put matching gear up for sale. The funds were sent to a food pantry in Huber's hometown of Rochester, New York.

FTR changed the name of their finisher from the Goodnight Express to Big Rig — a nickname their friend had used on the indies.

The final *AEW Dynamite* of the year, on December 30, featured a run-in by Joseph Ruud, who'd been Erick Rowan in the Wyatt Family before being released by WWE. Chris Jericho was doing color commentary when the surprise occurred and shouted, "It's Erick Rowan!" — only to be corrected by announcer Tony Schiavone, who said, "Erick Redbeard," the non-WWE-trademarked name the performer was now using. The contest, pitting members of the Inner Circle against the Dark Order, also featured an exchange between MJF and Brodie Lee Jr. — who was wearing a mask in the front row and calling himself Negative One.

The altercation began when MJF reached over the barricade and removed the kid's disguise. The villain turned away, spitting on the mask, then spun around to face the audience again. When he did, Brodie Jr. struck him with a kendo stick.

Refusing to break character, MJF would tweet, "Fuck that kid."

After the match ended, Redbeard held up a sign declaring, "Goodbye for now, my brother. See you down the road."

WWE star Sami Zayn posted a photo of the moment, admitting that he was overcome with tears.

Then, Brodie Jr. was inducted into the Dark Order and handed the TNT Championship. Schiavone declared that the boy — who symbolically signed an AEW contract that day, agreeing to join the roster when he grew up — was the titlist for life.

A designer would create a new belt.

"That was beautiful," WWE's Daniel Bryan wrote in a message to AEW after the program. "I cried numerous times. Thank you . . . so much for honoring a man we loved. And thank you for honoring his family in such a special way."

Sadly, the tributes overshadowed the Christmas Eve passing of the great Danny Hodge, 88, the former U.S. Olympian and perennial on-again, off-again NWA World Junior Heavyweight champion from 1960 to 1976. The omission was unintentional and easy to understand. So many of Hodge's peers were already gone, while Huber's friends were active performers, anxious to use whatever visibility they had to honor his memory.

Observing how people in different branches of the industry were venerating her husband, Amanda Huber urged fans to acknowledge that pro wrestlers shared a bond, regardless of where they were working.

"So many people expect myself and my family to hate on @WWE," she wrote on Instagram. "The fact is, we don't. We never have.

"My husband absolutely got frustrated because he wanted more than [WWE] envisioned for him. That didn't mean he hated them . . . WWE gave my husband a platform . . . He got to entertain millions of people. He got to build a beautiful life for our family. He held singles gold there . . . The most incredible thing he took away from his time in WWE was the people. The people he carried with him until his very last days."

She singled out Big E and Cesaro as "people that transcended the lines of friendship into family. People in the WWE watched my kids grow up . . . They became my family, too. The flood of love I've received from WWE is real and it's beautiful.

"In my husband's final moments, the people that surrounded my family were wrestlers. Companies didn't matter."

CHAPTER 26

AS 2020 FADED into 2021, Tokyo let down its guard, causing a spike in COVID-19 cases. On New Year's Eve, a record 1,337 infections were recorded, the highest number since May, and the city requested that a state of emergency be declared there, as well as in the surrounding prefectures. While urging the public to exercise more caution, the central government refrained from imposing a massive lockdown. As a result, *Wrestle Kingdom 15* was allowed to take place with a limited number of attendees in the Tokyo Dome.

For the second year in a row, the traditional January 4 event was expanded to two nights. The decision had little to do with the coronavirus. The formula seemed to work the year before, and — with the 2020 Tokyo Olympics now rescheduled for the summer — the company wanted to begin the year with a grand event to draw more international eyes to the product.

In a normal year, the Tokyo Dome could have accommodated 55,000 spectators. Still, the announced 12,689 who social distanced in the arena on night one, and the 7,801 who showed up on night two sent a signal that, in small increments, the business was opening up.

But it was obviously a very different *Wrestle Kingdom.* A reported 250 foreigners, primarily gaijin who already lived and worked in Japan, attended each night, as opposed to tourists who would have had to have quarantined for two weeks in order to see the show live. And quite a few ticket holders, alarmed over the acceleration of the illness, opted to stay home.

New Japan's largest event occurred as the organization was enduring a shift in management. During a meeting of the board of directors for Bushiroad, the promotion's parent company, in September, it was announced that New Japan's first foreign-born president Harold Mejj would step down the next month and be replaced by Takami Ohbari, the CEO of the outfit's American wing. Mejj, whose decision to expand *Wrestle Kingdom 14* to two nights generated enough revenue for New Japan to sustain itself during the worst days of the pandemic, had previously stated that he'd hoped to continue the rest of his career in New Japan. However, numerous factors weighed against him.

The departure of Kenny Omega two years earlier reportedly played a role. The former IWGP Heavyweight Champion spoke Japanese and considered himself something other than gaijin. Omega resented New Japan turning him heel after he signed with AEW and hoped to continue working in a top position in the organization. But both he and the Young Bucks claimed that, under Mejj, no effort was made to perpetuate the arrangement.

On the Bucks' web series *Wrestlers on the Road Ordering Room Service* Omega said, "It was a bad business decision. I do take it personally, though. I take it personally because a lot of fans were crushed. I think it was very irresponsible to do that."

Several New Japan insiders were alleged to have felt the same way.

Mejj was also blamed for not preserving the company's affiliation with Chris Jericho, reportedly contending that Le Champion was too expensive.

When AEW was formed, overtures were made to do business with New Japan. But, according to the *Wrestling Observer*, the company — under Mejj's leadership — did not view the new league, with its executive vice presidents consisting of guys still taking bumps, as being in the same category. If Tony Khan was interested in talking, according to the *Observer*, he'd have to travel to Japan and take a subservient position in the negotiations.

In a November interview with TSN, Khan said, "I think with Harold being gone, I don't know if [doing business with New Japan] is going to be easier, but I have a feeling it might be."

In terms of storytelling, the events of night one of *Wrestle Kingdom 15* led smoothly to night two. Following a card that saw the Guerillas of Destiny (Tama Tonga and Tanga Loa) upend the Dangerous Tekkers

(Taichi and Zack Sabre Jr.) to start a seventh reign as IWGP Heavyweight Tag Team champions, IWGP Heavyweight and Intercontinental champion Tetsuya Naito lost the "double gold" to Kota Ibushi.

Naito had pledged to put up the title against former champion Jay White on night two. Instead, fans would see the Golden Star in his first title defense.

For several years, Ibushi and Omega had been part of an inseparable unit called the Golden☆Lovers; the implication had always been that the two enjoyed a romance as well as a deep friendship. Given the new political landscape, fans began speculating over a post-pandemic quest by The Cleaner to add the IWGP titles to his AEW and AAA crowns.

This was fueled by a videotaped appearance on night one by Jon Moxley, who'd won the IWGP United States Heavyweight Championship at the previous *Wrestle Kingdom* and never relinquished the strap. Prior to a number one contender's match between KENTA and Satoshi Kojima, the former AEW kingpin addressed the Tokyo Dome audience on the big screen, asserting that — following the coronavirus outbreak — New Japan wrestlers "all hoped and prayed that the United States Heavyweight champion would never return. But I'm the boogeyman, and I will get you eventually."

Fans — in Japan and elsewhere — were still buzzing about the possibilities on night two, when Hiromu Takahashi beat Taiji Ishimori to capture a fourth IWGP Junior Heavyweight Championship, and Ibushi retained the double gold following a 48-minute classic.

In February, New Japan would merge the Heavyweight and Intercontinental titles into a single IWGP World Heavyweight Championship.

At this point, I was beginning to feel like my story was coming to an end. It was 2021, vaccines had been approved and *Wrestle Kingdom 15* provided a hint of how a major card might feel as the world transitioned back to normal.

But the world was not transitioning back to normal. On the day after *Wrestle Kingdom*, January 6, 2021, the United States endured an unprecedented — and some would say cataclysmic — experience, and I realized that I still had a way to go. Not only would this project cover a period spanning two *Wrestle Kingdom*s, two *Royal Rumble*s and two *WrestleMania*s, it would also be the first professional wrestling book to include two U.S. presidential impeachments.

As Congress met to certify the results of November's election, Trump supporters gathered in Washington, DC, for a "Stop the Steal" protest. The president had been sending them mixed messages. At a "Save America" rally that morning, he urged demonstrators to "peacefully and patriotically make your voices heard" and march on the Capitol, while also reminding them, "If you don't fight like hell, you're not going to have a country anymore."

Protestors — waving everything from Trump flags to the Confederate stars and bars — had already breached the flimsy fence surrounding the Capitol grounds when, at 1:30 p.m., a large segment pushed past police and streamed into the building. Several made it onto the floor of the Senate, with two storming the dais to occupy the seats usually occupied by Vice President Mike Pence — dubbed a traitor by many of the dissenters for not backing up Trump's conspiracy claims — and Speaker of the House Nancy Pelosi. Another was photographed in Pelosi's office with his feet on her desk.

Realizing that they were outnumbered, police blocked the door to the House of Representatives, training their weapons on outsiders who tried to enter.

As lawmakers were rushed to safety, more than 150 officers were injured in the melee. Having been doused with pepper spray, Capitol Police Officer Brian Sicknick — a Trump supporter himself — collapsed at his division office later that night and was taken to the hospital. The next day, he suffered two strokes and died.

While the riot was transpiring, Twitter removed three tweets from Trump espousing unconfirmed theories. Another was tagged with the label, "This claim of election fraud is disputed, and this tweet can't be replied to, retweeted or liked due to a risk of violence."

Two days later, the social media platform suspended the commander-in-chief.

By then, he'd taken a slightly more subdued tone, releasing a statement: "Even though I totally disagree with the outcome of the election, and the facts bear me out, nevertheless there will be an orderly transition" of power. He added that he'd been responsible for "the greatest first term in presidential history."

Despite Trump agreeing to step down, the Democratic-led Congress impeached him again for incitement of insurrection. The Senate trial would conclude after Biden was already in power, but Trump's foes hoped that a conviction would bar him from ever holding federal office again. This time, seven Republicans joined the Democrats in condemning Trump's behavior. But in order to convict, 67 votes were needed, and the final tally was 57 to 43.

Although he'd chosen to acquit the former president, Senate Minority Leader Mitch McConnell took to the Senate floor to chastise Trump for his "disgraceful dereliction of duty." The Kentucky Republican blasted his old ally as being "practically and morally responsible for provoking" the Capitol riot.

Trump was anything but repentant. In a 600-word statement, he cut a promo on McConnell, describing him as a "dour, sullen and unsmiling political hack" and forecasting future GOP losses if he maintained his leadership role.

The Capitol insurgency led to a ratings drop that night for both NXT and AEW — proving that, when the occasion was right, even wrestling fans preferred breaking news to the grunt'n'groan circuit. I personally found myself switching channels a lot and was glad I did. On *Dynamite*, the Impact plotline was progressing with a Bullet Club reunion. Omega had just successfully defended his title against Rey Fenix when a vengeful Jon Moxley charged the ring, swinging a barbed wire baseball bat. This prompted the Impact World Tag Team Champions, Luke Gallows and Karl Anderson, to intervene and brutalize Moxley. As more talent ran down the aisle to restore order, the

AEW Tag Team titlists, the Young Bucks, inserted themselves into the action, throwing superkicks.

The segment ended with all five former Bullet Club members wearing their respective belts and saluting each other with the "Too Sweet" hand gesture appropriated by the unit in Japan.

The development had reverberations that transcended continents. Following a victory over Tomohiro Ishii in Japan on February 1, current Bullet Club leader Jay White grabbed the microphone and declared himself to be "real Bullet Club."

He characterized the former members' theatrics as "a cheap rip off trying to recreate the past, to regain some relevance and doing corny reunions so you sell shitty t-shirts."

His comments mirrored that of Bullet Club teammate Tama Tonga, who'd asserted that the guys in AEW and Impact were a facsimile of the unit that was flourishing across the Pacific.

Noting that New Japan still owned the trademark for the faction's name, the Young Bucks sent out a tweet declaring, "The original Bullet Club t-shirt design hadn't been in the Top Sellers List for two years ... until the night we all decided to throw up Too Sweet again. You're welcome."

Even in WWE, founding member Finn Balor couldn't resist expressing enthusiasm. After posting an image of nine past or present Bullet Club partners — including multiple WWE Championship–winner AJ Styles — Balor told the *New York Post*, "There has been a little animosity between some of the brothers lately, and I was just trying to remind everyone that we're all cut from the same cloth." With alumni spread among several companies, Balor contended that the Bullet Club "has the potential to bring the entire wrestling community together, not divide, and I think that's something we should be aiming for."

On January 16, Omega continued the intrigue when he wore a Bullet Club shirt while teaming with The Good Brothers in a winning effort over Impact World champion Rich Swann, Moose and Chris Sabin on the promotion's *Hard to Kill* pay-per-view.

Three months later, at another Impact pay-per-view, *Rebellion*, Omega would unseat Swann for the company's championship, becoming the first wrestler to hold three "world" titles simultaneously since

April 1989 — when Vader added the IWGP Heavyweight strap to the belts he'd already won in the CWA in Austria and Universal Wrestling Association (UWA) in Mexico.

In the meantime, AEW and New Japan appeared to be drawing closer. Following his video proclamation at *Wrestle Kingdom 15*, Moxley was jumped by a masked man on the February 3 *Dynamite*. The trespasser then lowered his hood to reveal himself as KENTA, number one contender for Moxley's IWGP United States Championship. The next week, after Moxley and Lance Archer tangled with KENTA and Omega, the confrontation was broadcast on New Japan's streaming platform — the first time that AEW allowed a *Dynamite* match to be shown there.

Moxley would retain his title against KENTA on NJPW Strong's weekly program.

On *Dynamite*, the champ would also defeat a true Japanese legend, 53-year-old Yuji Nagata — the only wrestler to have won his country's three biggest tournaments (New Japan's G1 Climax, All Japan's Champion Carnival and NOAH's Global League) — in a May 12 defense. Following the victory, Moxley paid homage to the New Japan great, bowing and placing his head on the mat.

Khan compared the burgeoning alliances to opening a "forbidden door" — and even used the term as a Twitter location.

When the AEW founder was asked on the *Wrestle Fetish* podcast about the possibility of working with WWE, he invited the dominant promotion to bring its talent to Jacksonville. "The forbidden door is open anytime," he said. "Just come and knock. If they were to knock on the door, I would certainly be willing to let them in."

And he didn't seem to be joking. Immediately after *WrestleMania 37*, Chris Jericho was a special guest on WWE's Steve Austin–hosted *Broken Skull Sessions*. And Khan wasn't the only one who approved the lengthy interview.

Vince McMahon did too.

CHAPTER 27

WHEN PUERTO RICAN rapper Bad Bunny was announced as a special 2021 *Royal Rumble* guest, few expected him to be anything more than a musical attraction. The lifetime wrestling fan performed a number dedicated to Booker T, as the WWE Hall of Famer stood menacingly in the camouflage outfit he wore as G.I. Bro early in his career. Later, as The Miz was making his Rumble entrance, the heel overturned Bad Bunny's turntable system. But Bunny would receive his revenge later that night, aiding fellow Puerto Rican Damian Priest in the match by executing a dive from the top rope onto Miz and partner John Morrison.

Few realized that Bad Bunny was that nimble — or that WWE had bigger plans for him. In addition to regularly appearing on WWE television for the next few months, he was clandestinely training at the Performance Center — in preparation for a *WrestleMania 37* appearance that some would call the most athletic showing by a non-wrestler at the Showcase of the Immortals.

Although many longtime watchers had been critical of WWE's uneven storylines, the 2021 Rumble served its purpose, building toward the promotion's annual spectacular. The women's Rumble match was won by charismatic Bianca Belair — known for her stunning strength as well as a long braid she occasionally wielded as a cat o' nine tails — setting her up for a title shot at *WrestleMania 37*. On the men's side, 47-year-old Edge continued his inspirational comeback, entering the Rumble in the number one spot and lasting until the very end, depositing old foe Randy Orton over the top rope to claim victory.

In the coming weeks, Edge's character would take a heelish turn. But his professional rebirth made it difficult to boo him as he headed toward the *WrestleMania 37* main event.

For the first time since 2014, the WWE Network would not carry *WrestleMania* in the United States. Instead, the World Cup of professional wrestling was seen on NBC's new streaming service, Peacock — as part of a five-year exclusive rights deal reportedly worth more than $1 billion.

The WWE Network was supposed to help redefine broadcasting, following the groundbreaking tradition set by the company that introduced much of the world to pay-per-view in the Hulkamania era. Now, with cable television in decline, watchers would be turning away from pay-per-view, the logic went, while the public gravitated to streaming. The WWE Network intended to spearhead the trend.

To a degree, this is exactly what WWE did. In fact, the company would eventually move away from the term "pay-per-view" entirely — the way it shed the words "wrestler" in favor of "superstar" and "fans" became "WWE Universe" — referring to these broadcasts as "premium live events." But the number of subscribers never got past a certain level. At the time of the transaction, 1.5 million people were paying approximately $10 a month to watch the WWE Network, while Peacock's parent company, Comcast, claimed its streaming service had 33 million signees.

The monthly cost — not just for the WWE Network, but the movies, TV series and sporting events available on Peacock — was about $5. Which meant that WWE had pulled a pretty slick move, taking in a stupefying amount of money during a pandemic while giving its fans a better month-to-month deal.

From Peacock's point of view, though, the added subscribers made the service even more attractive to advertisers. In fact, if WWE's popularity grew — as the company hoped, given all the new eyes potentially exposed to the product — Peacock might even make back its investment, and more, in ad revenue.

The arrangement solved another problem. For nearly three years, maintaining the technological infrastructure of the WWE Network had been a struggle. Originally, BAMTech, a technology subsidiary affiliated with Major League Baseball (MLB), built the outlet's framework. Then, BAMTech spun off from MLB and became a separate company, which was acquired by Disney in 2018. Since then, there'd been fears that the expense of constant infrastructure updates could come at the expense of new WWE Network programming.

"At the end of the day, we're not a technology company and shouldn't try to be," Stephanie McMahon told CNBC. "We are a content company at our core, and we want to do what we do best."

Although discussions with Comcast were said to have been ongoing since prior to the COVID-19 outbreak, the deal seemed to bear the fingerprints of Nick Khan, who'd become WWE president and chief revenue officer in August 2020 — filling the void created by the departures of co-presidents George Barrios and Michelle Wilson earlier in the year.

Khan, a former attorney, had become intimate with WWE's management team while representing the company as the co-head of television for the Creative Artists Agency (CAA). During his time there, he also negotiated lucrative deals for Top Rank Boxing and the Southeastern Conference (SEC), a college athletic association.

He reportedly celebrated his new position by purchasing a $7.6 million mansion in the exclusive Riviera section of Pacific Palisades.

Their shared surname notwithstanding, Nick was not related to Tony Khan — a disappointment to fans who would have thrilled to see a replication of the front office rivalry between George and Sandy Scott when the brothers were respectively working as executives for Vince McMahon and Jim Crockett Jr. in the 1980s. Tony, of Pakistani descent, grew up cheering for Steve Austin, Bret Hart and Chris Jericho. Nick hailed from an Iranian family and had been partial to the Iron Sheik.

"Cam-e-ra-man, zoom it!"

AEW was not going to pull off any billion dollar deals in the foreseeable future. Still, the promotion was coming up with ways to tweak WWE. In February, Paul "Big Show" Wight — renowned for his mammoth size, along with versatility and sharp wit — parted ways with WWE after 22 years and signed with the upstart company, primarily as a commentator and brand ambassador.

The Young Bucks turned the development into comedy on *Being the Elite*, creating a scene in which Matt Jackson suffers from flashbacks of being chokeslammed through a table by the Big Show while working as WWE enhancement talent. His son reminds him that the incident occurred "back when you were a jobber."

Another longtime WWE personality, Hall of Famer Mark Henry, would join Wight in May, starting at *Double or Nothing*. The former Olympian had a wealth of knowledge that would aid him as an AEW scout and coach. And with his high-profile name, he had the potential to attract lapsed fans. But it felt like, in addition to all that, Tony Khan — the kid who grew up loving Jim Cornette's Smoky Mountain Wrestling and Paul Heyman's ECW — derived a certain joy from annoying WWE.

If there were uncertainties about this, a video he posted in May eclipsed all doubt. Referencing a quote from Nick Khan about WWE engaging in conversations with New Japan, Tony Khan cut a classic wrestling promo.

"Nick, I have to say that if you've been talking to New Japan for two months, then you've gotten a lot done," Tony sneered, mentioning the Japanese talent who'd recently appeared in AEW, as well as Jon Moxley's IWGP United States title defense on *Dynamite*. "I have future plans for the U.S. title, so you've really gotten a lot done in the last two months, Nick. In fact, I think there's only room for one Khan in the wrestling business. It's me. It's Tony Khan. It's not some con man from Connecticut."

Along with the angles tied in to other promotions, the company had been taking steps to generate an energy that reminded fans of the atmosphere that existed in pro wrestling prior to COVID. About 1,300 spectators were admitted to Daily's Place for *AEW Revolution* in March, creating the type of sound that hadn't been heard on a major wrestling show for a year. "What I'd like to do is slowly increase capacity," Khan told the media after the card, "but not put the pods too close together yet. And as we learn more and more about the transmission of the virus, then we can go and make a plan for touring." For the time being, though, it was "too soon to try to pack an arena."

Although the matches ranged from solid to excellent, the pay-per-view was responsible for arguably the most glaring screw-up since the company's founding. But like WWE during the Attitude Era, AEW seemed to be blessed and able to pivot away from the mistake without alienating loyal fans.

As an homage to the Japanese death match scene, Kenny Omega defended his AEW World Championship against Moxley in an exploding barbed wire confrontation. Atsushi Onita, wrestling's premier practitioner of this type of clash in the 1990s, had hoped to lend his credence to the spectacle live in Jacksonville, but because of coronavirus restrictions, was forced to remain in Japan, and sent a video instead. The referee wore a protective suit to emphasize the danger, and announcers built intrigue by emphasizing that the pressure was on the competitors to complete their business within 30 minutes. Because as soon as the half hour expired, the ring was programmed to combust.

Omega and Moxley worked hard to introduce new fans to the exploding barbed wire concept at the same time as they satisfied the purists. Moxley bled early. Omega tried to wrap his foe's legs into a figure-four but instead was kicked, face-first, into the barbed wire ropes, triggering an explosion. Moxley followed up by dropkicking the champ into the spiked strands and delivering a side slam onto a barbed wire-shrouded chair.

The Good Brothers interfered, handing Omega a barbed wire baseball bat that exploded on impact. After driving the challenger through the chair, the titlist scored the win with a One-Winged Angel.

On the big screen, a timer began to count down as the 30-minute mark approached. Omega and his cohorts fled to safety backstage, leaving Moxley prone on the mat. Seeing Moxley's vulnerability, old friend Eddie Kingston apparently forgot about their recent skirmishes and rushed to the ring. With precious seconds ticking away, Kingston used his own body to shield his old ally from the horror that was about to transpire.

But when the timer reached zero, the pyrotechnic display was reminiscent not of the Hindenburg blast but an eruption of sparklers at a toddler's birthday party. Still, Kingston sold it like he'd sustained life-threatening injuries.

Omega was reportedly furious about the underwhelming finale. "It was really deflating to do so much preparation, test the explosions, have them be so impressive in the rehearsal, and then have it be something so different than what was promised," he said in a statement to the *Wrestling Observer*.

Tony Khan later claimed to have received a refund of "like $100,000" from the pyrotechnic company.

Before leaving the ring, Moxley took the effort to address the live audience; as a fan himself, he knew he owed them that much. "We can agree on one thing," he said with his characteristic smirk. "Kenny Omega may be a tough son of a bitch, but he can't make an exploding ring worth a shit."

The comment provoked laugher, lifting the cynical mood.

On the following *Dynamite*, Kingston attempted to explain his dramatic response to the twinkling bursts. "When I went to that ring and I covered my friend," he said with Moxley beside him, "I caught a flashback to . . . the last time I had that kind of panic, when I couldn't breathe. That's when I was sitting in a jail cell, getting ready for court. And I had the guards telling me . . . 'We're going to take you to Sing Sing, boy.' And everything went black."

Appearing to gloat over the mishap, Moxley then ventured, "I don't know who paid for that bomb."

"Impact did," Kingston answered, seeming to enjoy the opportunity to ridicule the company where he'd previously worked. "You know they did."

"Impact paid for the bomb?" Moxley replied. "Yeah, that makes perfect sense."

The irony, of course, was that, had the match taken place at the height of the pandemic — when shows were pretaped and sets closed — the participants could have waited for the technicians to reconfigure the pyro and reshoot the conclusion with all its scorching intent. And no one watching at home would have been the wiser.

Instead, wrestling was going live again. And here we were, complaining about *that*.

CHAPTER 28

ON THE ONE-YEAR anniversary of WHO's pandemic declaration, Americans had been receiving the vaccine for three months, with 33.9 million eligible citizens reportedly protected with either one dose or two. On March 19, President Biden's promised benchmark of 100 million doses administered within his first 100 days in office was reached, ahead of schedule.

With his access to Twitter banned, former President Trump tried remaining part of the conversation, speaking at fundraisers and sending out press releases. A recurrent theme was that he wasn't receiving enough credit for the medical advances. At a speech delivered the same weekend as *WrestleMania 37*, he argued that the inoculation should be rebranded the "Trump-zine."

Europe was still struggling with vaccine distribution and fresh outbreaks of COVID-19. As cases rose in Italy, the government announced that the country would be locked down for the second Easter in a row. In France, 21 million people in 16 areas, including Paris, were restricted to exercising within six miles of their respective homes and banned from traveling to other parts of the nation without a valid reason.

To certain U.S. populations, though — African Americans who remembered how the government allowed Black men in Tuskegee, Alabama, to suffer from syphilis in order to study the effects, undocumented immigrants who feared exposure if they signed up at a vaccination site, religious fundamentalists who believed in giving their fate to God instead of the judgmental scientific community — there was hesitance, if not outright hostility, toward the COVID treatments. WWE attempted to allay some of the trepidation by having stars Daniel Bryan, Bianca Belair, Montez Ford and Rey

Mysterio participate in a public service campaign on YouTube, urging fans to protect themselves against the virus. Perhaps concerned about the backlash from anti-vaxxers, the company disabled the comments section.

Still, promotions that had been sidelined for much of the past year suddenly saw the potential for restoration. In March, as WWE fans were in the throes of *WrestleMania* season, Billy Corgan assured NWA fans that the company would not only survive, but resume broadcasts of *NWA Power*, now on FITE TV.

On March 21, the NWA presented its *Back for the Attack* pay-per-view from GPB Studios in Atlanta. Acknowledging that its watchers also enjoyed WWE, the league scheduled the event early so fans could then watch *Fast Lane*, the last pay-per-view available on the WWE Network. While winning back casual spectators might take some time, the show satisfied loyalists, with Nick Aldis retaining the Ten Pounds of Gold against Aron Stevens then joining the challenger in saluting his mentor, the recently departed Joseph "Jocephus" Hudson — aka The Question Mark. In a number one contender's match, Kamille, a toned, serious woman some compared to a female Nick Aldis, toppled Thunder Rosa to earn a shot at the women's title.

She'd capture the championship from Serena Deeb at the NWA's next pay-per-view, *When Our Shadows Fall*, on June 6.

Prior to *Back for the Attack*, Aldis appeared before the Georgia State Senate to accept a resolution honoring him for his 800-plus day reign and to recognize the NWA for its proud history in cities like Atlanta, Columbus and Augusta. The legislators also declared that the third anniversary of Aldis's win over Cody Rhodes, October 21, would be acknowledged in the Peach State as National Wrestling Alliance Day.

Rusev Day, it wasn't. But if you were rooting for wrestling's smaller outfits to outlast the pandemic, it felt pretty good.

The rumors about the end of the Wednesday Night Wars started in March amid reports that, following *WrestleMania 37*, NXT would switch to Tuesdays. This seemed to have little to do with WWE raising a white flag and to be more of a big picture decision, as the NBC Sports Network was shutting down, which meant some NHL games would be switched to another Comcast entity, the USA Network, on Wednesdays. By the end of the month, the news was confirmed, along with a multi-year deal that would keep WWE's third brand on USA.

This did not mean that NXT would now go head-to-head with Impact, which had been airing on Tuesdays. Rather, *that* show was moving to Thursdays. The shifts created a unique situation in pro wrestling, allowing American fans to watch at least one fresh show — courtesy of WWE, AEW, MLW, NJPW Strong, the NWA or Impact — every weeknight, either via cable or streaming. And Ring of Honor's syndicated programs, televised on different days in various parts of the U.S., provided even greater viewing opportunities.

CHAPTER 29

THE TAGLINE FOR *WrestleMania 37* was "Back in Business" — even though the world wasn't quite "back" to where it had been before. There would still be mask-wearing and pod seating. But the location of the event — Raymond James Stadium in Tampa, where *WrestleMania 36* had been scheduled — would allow WWE to have something of a do-over, even with fewer fans coming from fewer places to the Showcase of the Immortals.

Under the arguably lax conventions in Governor Ron DeSantis's Florida, it would be far easier to present *WrestleMania 37* in Tampa than at the planned 2021 venue, SoFi Stadium in Los Angeles, where California state regulations were more stringent. To keep all parties happy, WWE agreed to hold *WrestleMania 39* at SoFi in 2023.

A precedent had already been set in January when the NFL staged Super Bowl LV at Raymond James Stadium, after consulting with the CDC, Florida Department of Health and area hospitals and health systems about the most responsible way to bring back an annual spectacular. In that instance, all 32 NFL clubs selected a total of 7,500 vaccinated health care workers as special guests, joining some 14,500 others who pledged to adhere to health guidelines. Among those in attendance were WWE representatives, keeping close track of how safety decrees were being enforced at the largest live sporting event since the start of the pandemic.

From the time I received my second dose of the Moderna vaccine in February, I knew that I was going to *WrestleMania 37*. I kind of had to, given the topic of this book. Plus, I'd be able to double dip after hustling an assignment from *Inside the Ropes Magazine*, which had been birthed during the COVID era as a throwback to the newsstand mat publications of old. WWE's PR team was being peppered with media requests without a lot of time to prepare. So there were some anxious days when I wondered about how I was getting into the stadium. Eventually, though, my press credentials were approved, so long as I agreed to sign a waiver confirming that I acknowledged that, by attending, I was putting myself in danger of "among other things, risks of spreading or acquiring COVID-19" and that "I further recognize that COVID is extremely contagious and can lead to severe illness and death."

I knew all that. But I really wanted to go to *WrestleMania*. So, assuming that I wasn't one of the rare vaccine recipients who'd catch a deadly strain of the virus, I signed — without reading the contract a second time.

Because the 2020 WWE Hall of Fame ceremony had been postponed, the company made the decision to combine it with the 2021 event early in *WrestleMania* week. "It's frustrating that it didn't happen last year," Davey Boy Smith Jr. — who accepted the award for his father, the late British Bulldog at the 2020 portion — told me. "I've been waiting all year. First, it was supposed to happen at *SummerSlam*, then at the *Survivor Series*. But it was nobody's fault. We had to wait it out."

Although certain majestic elements associated with the ceremony were included, fans were not, and a decision was made to pretape the proceedings. To compensate for the barren surroundings, audience reactions were added later. "We were told to pause at certain points, and they'd pump in some crowd noise," Smith said. "It wasn't exactly natural, but I meant what I said, and I know that the people who watched it were happy. We're not back where we need to be yet, but it's better than last year."

Scott Hall had been inducted in 2014 as Razor Ramon. Now, he was in the 2020 class as a member of the nWo, alongside Hulk Hogan, Kevin Nash and Sean "X-Pac" Waltman. "I had two gimmicks, Razor Ramon and Scott Hall," he told me when I ran into him at a very scaled-down version of WrestleCon. "And the merchandise is still selling. I make money as Razor Ramon, and I make money as Scott

Hall." Referring to his well-chronicled substance abuse issues, he added, "And now, I'm not spending $40,000 on rehab anymore, so I get to keep it."

Like every other aspect of this *WrestleMania* week, the ceremony was different from the ones that preceded it. But since he'd barely left his home for the past year, he was happy to be around his friends again and receive an honor for his work in the ring and behind a microphone. "You had to be there at 8 a.m.," he said, offering me a squirt of sanitizer from the bottle on his autograph table. "Then, we had to wait around for Vince. You know how that goes? When I did the speech, they said, 'Two or three minutes.' But we all know how to cut a promo. So I just said cool shit for two or three minutes."

The Wednesday Night Wars ended with little fanfare when NXT presented its *TakeOver: Stand & Deliver* shows on April 7 and 8, the Wednesday and Thursday leading into *WrestleMania 37*. Unlike the end of WCW in 2001, when Vince McMahon shoehorned himself into his rival's show and gloated about the people he intended to fire, neither side partook in a victory dance. Both programs would still be available, albeit on different nights. Still, NXT not only scored the ratings win over AEW on the final head-to-head Wednesday, but the quality of the programming on both nights was so high that no one could accuse WWE's third brand of losing the war and shrinking away to Tuesdays.

If *NXT TakeOver: Stand & Deliver* was supposed to offer a vision into the future, that picture was distorted. On night one, Raquel González shattered Io Shirai with a Chingona Bomb — a one-armed powerbomb — to claim the NXT Women's Championship. NXT UK titlist WALTER beat Tommaso Ciampa with a suplex followed by a hard chop to the chest — enhancing interest in the European talent that been secreted on the opposite side of the Atlantic throughout the health crisis.

In the months to come, González's momentum continued, and she seemed to be getting fast-tracked toward the main roster. The same was true of WALTER, even though, the next year, the company opted to rename him Gunther after the "Austrian Anomaly" shifted his base of operations to the U.S.

On night two, Kyle O'Reilly defeated former partner Adam Cole — leader of their Undisputed Era faction — in a tumultuous unsanctioned battle. And in the co-main event, Karrion Kross — who'd been forced to surrender his previous NXT Championship because of a separated shoulder — began his second reign by toppling Finn Balor.

Kross would be wiped from the organization in the fall. Just before Christmas, Cole and O'Reilly were back together as teammates — in AEW.

Because of crowding concerns, the live match component of WrestleCon was cancelled, with no more than 320 people at a time — 20 percent of the usual capacity — permitted on the convention floor at the Westin Tampa Waterside Hotel. When I visited, the crowd was sparse, but the fans were grateful for the opportunity to spend more time than usual with the talent.

Former WWE women's champion Victoria — who, as Tara, was a five-time TNA Knockouts titlist — had been a surprise entrant in the 2021 *Royal Rumble* and went through WWE's long list of health measures before being cleared. Still, she was concerned about whether it was too early for fans to be attending *WrestleMania 37*. "I hope everyone used common sense and stayed healthy," she told me. "We waited a long time for this, and we want to go forward, not backwards."

In addition to WrestleCon, a number of other non-WWE events could be found in the general area — although nowhere near the volume generally presented during *WrestleMania* week. About an hour outside of Tampa, in Port Richey, New York's Impact Championship Wrestling (ICW) hosted an assemblage of indie promotions in a single facility, not unlike GCW's Collective, which set itself up outdoors at the site that had initially been slated for the conclave in 2020, the Cuban Club in Ybor City. A third gathering of indie leagues was organized by another GCW, this one called Generation Championship Wrestling and based in Tampa. Legends were also signing autographs at a convention dubbed Wrestlestock, situated in an American Legion post.

The Collective's offerings included Josh Barnett's Bloodsport, Effy's Big Gay Brunch and *Joey Janela's Spring Break*, along with For the Culture, a group highlighting African American performers, Allie Katch's Hot Girl Shit, a death match company called Planet Death and indies VXS, Unsanctioned Pro and No Peace Underground.

At *Joey Janela's Spring Break*, I found myself conversing with a Florida minister named Tim Sensabaugh, who — rather than attempting to witness to me — praised Vince McMahon for his decision to stage *WrestleMania 37*. "If you don't have *WrestleMania*, you don't have this," he said, gesturing toward the ring. "You can't have this many independent wrestlers in a weekend without the big draw of *WrestleMania*."

During the two days I attended The Collective, I spotted several notables backstage, including Jon Moxley, who seemed to be having fun watching the various matchups and participated in two altercations, the first a gory encounter with Josh Barnett in the Bloodsport main event, the second the next night at *Joey Janela's Spring Break*. In that instance, Nick Gage had just reclaimed the GCW World Championship from Rickey Shane Page when Mox came down the aisle to a thunderous response from the 500 or so fans. He and Gage touched foreheads and trash talked each other — with Gage's blood smearing onto his tormentor — before the former AEW World champion lifted the titlist and used a Paradigm Shift to smash him through a collection of light tubes.

Moxley would snare the GCW crown in September while still maintaining his commitments in AEW — a statement both about the flexibility Khan allowed his stars to enjoy and the expanding influence of Brett Lauderdale's dirty Jersey promotion.

During a break in the action, I took a walk around Ybor City and found a sidewalk table sponsored by a group called the Pulse Clinical Alliance — between a 7-Eleven and a tattoo parlor — where 250 vaccines a day were being dispensed to all comers. The organization's goal was inoculating the homeless and other at-risk communities. But when I explained why I'd come to Tampa, doctoral nurse Rizzy Hawkeye asked me to go back to the Cuban Club and spread the word.

"Send the wrestling people over," she said.

Once again, *WrestleMania* was split between two nights: Saturday, April 10, and Sunday, April 11. But this was different from the last, pretaped show. Although the usual contingents of Asians, Australians, Europeans and Canadians were nowhere to be found, enough fans had come to Tampa from other parts of the United States for WWE to take credit for hosting a combined 51,350 spectators over the course of the weekend.

Despite the social distancing requirements, the stadium would look full on TV, thanks to the wooden cutouts of onlookers sandwiched into empty seats. When I tried to get a figure for the number of faux fans from the WWE representatives in the press box, I was kayfabed. But a stadium employee told me that the number exceeded 30,000. Even though WWE was known to exaggerate its attendance, this meant that, for the first time since Tito Santana stepped into the ring against the masked Executioner — "Playboy" Buddy Rose under a hood — in the premiere match at *WrestleMania I*, the worked spectators outnumbered the flesh-and-blood ticket buyers.

In the crowd, I met a guy named Ray Haines, who'd traveled to *WrestleMania* from Cumberland, Maryland. Although his ultimate goal was having an enjoyable weekend after a long entertainment famine, he also wanted to honor the wrestlers who came to work when everyone else was hunkered indoors. "They risked their health for us, and I needed to be here to show my appreciation to them for helping us through this last year."

I was in an Uber on North Dale Mabry Highway about three hours before showtime when I noticed the clouds gathering in the sky. Somewhere in another part of town, I envisioned Vince McMahon peeking out his window, seeing the same thing and sending a message to the gods.

"Halt!"

Really, it didn't matter because nobody was changing plans. One year after *WrestleMania 36*, memories were still fresh of FaceTiming friends from a locked apartment while titles were changing hands in an empty Performance Center. It had been torture — well, relatively so, since being intubated in a makeshift intensive care unit was arguably worse — and the threat of waiting out a lightning storm wasn't going to send anyone scrambling back to the Econo Lodge.

So the people poured in, even as the drops fell from the tropical skies, some prepared with rain slickers and others already soaked in their t-shirts. From the press box, I looked over at the opposite side of the stadium and saw a collection of cutouts, selling nothing. Above them, hundreds of spectators had taken their seats, *woo*ing like Ric Flair and shaking their hair back and forth, '80s metal head style, as they waited for the weather to change.

Finally, things simmered down enough for Bebe Rexha to perform "America the Beautiful," and Vince to appear at the top of the entrance ramp with the entire roster. "Throughout this past year, our WWE Superstars performed tirelessly for all of you," he began in his throaty voice, "week after week, month after month. But we all knew there was something missing, something very important, the most important. That would be all of you, our fans, the WWE Universe." He paused for the crowd to cheer, sincerely happy to see the guy they occasionally bashed on the internet welcoming them home. "As we emerge from this dreadful pandemic, on behalf of our entire WWE family" — he bent forward — "we would simply like to say, 'thank you'" — he held up one finger — "and welcome you to" — he swept his hand across his body and growled — "*WrestleMania*!"

But the speech wasn't followed by the strains of entrance music for the first match. Instead, the screens around the stadium flashed a weather alert. There were still fears of lightning storms, and fans were urged to take refuge in the concourses and wait for updates.

"What's going to kill them first," another reporter joked, "lightning or getting COVID from standing too close to each other?"

On the live broadcast, WWE had to fill time. And so the company did something I hadn't seen in years. It had the talent come out and hype their matches with spontaneous promos. Without the wrestlers having time to script anything, the interviews were fun, showcasing the wrestlers' improvisational skills and personalities, a reminder of the roster's virtuosity and versatility.

Forty-four minutes after the show was supposed to begin, the first two combatants took the ring, WWE champion Bobby Lashley and Drew

McIntyre, a pair of bulls colliding and hitting hard. A year ago, McIntyre had won his first WWE Championship in the echoey Performance Center. He had all the right qualities — looks, determination, a sympathetic back story — but I hadn't seen a live crowd react to him since his big push. And though the Scottish Warrior lost — after Lashley's manager, MVP, caused a distraction — the audience stayed with him, jeering the finish and calling for a rematch.

Like the earlier version of McIntyre, Cesaro hadn't quite lived up to his potential in WWE — despite holding numerous titles. Yet, at *WrestleMania 37*, pitted against Seth Rollins, the Swiss Superman was allowed to flaunt his innumerable skills, not only scoring his first *WrestleMania* win, but trapping Rollins in the UFO Swing for 23 rotations as the fans counted along.

In his WWE debut, Nigerian-born giant Omos and partner AJ Styles challenged the New Day for the WWE *Raw* Tag Team Championship. Although in another era, Kofi Kingston and Xavier Woods might have taken some liberties with the newcomer to teach him humility, the New Day did no such thing, bouncing off the titanic newcomer until Omos won the gold for his team with a foot planted on Kofi's chest.

After capturing the WWE Universal Championship from Bill Goldberg at *WrestleMania 36*, Braun Strowman now found himself without a title and consigned to a steel cage match with Shane McMahon — the climax of a plotline in which the boss's son ridiculed the Monster Among Men for being "stupid." Even at 51 years old, Shane could bump like few others, while Strowman would have the opportunity to showcase his brute strength. Given the criteria, fans received everything they craved. At one point, McMahon was clambering down the outside of the cage when Braun tore off a slab of chain link fencing and pulled Shane in for more punishment. After hurling his tormentor to the canvas from the top of the enclosure, Strowman won the contest with a running powerslam.

As he returned to the dressing room, few could have guessed that, in less two months, the former champion would be released from the company.

At the WWE Performance Center, Bad Bunny had been regularly working out with Damian Priest, as well as trainers Norman Smiley, Drew Gulak and Adam Pearce, a former NWA World Heavyweight champion who played a company official on WWE programming. The exertion paid off. In the tag team match pitting Bunny and Priest against The Miz and John Morrison, the Grammy-winning artist gleamed from the moment he was seen entering the stadium on top of a semi-truck. Between the ropes, he delivered a splash from the top turnbuckle to the arena floor, a Canadian Destroyer — called a "Bunny Destroyer" by the WWE announcers — and a crossbody Doomsday Device to The Miz to score the pin.

According to DAZN, the sports streaming service, the night before the event, Randy Orton told Bad Bunny that he never saw a celebrity guest take a wrestling appearance as seriously. "Thank you for accepting me," the humbled rapper reportedly replied.

But Miz and Morrison were so lavish in their willingness to elevate the outsider that they exalted themselves in the process. If WWE was sports-entertainment, the tandem convinced first-time watchers that the company could put on a show like no other.

"I've gotta give John Morrison and The Miz the ultimate '10,'" observed Booker T on *The Bump*, a commentary show seen on the Peacock network. "As far as going out and being able to general that match and create something special ... The Miz is a true soldier ... We need about 50 more guys like Miz and Morrison in the business."

In November, Morrison was rewarded for his charity by getting axed.

Since the 2020 *Royal Rumble*, when NXT standout Bianca Belair entered at number two and lasted more than 33 minutes, eliminating a record eight competitors before being dispatched to the arena floor by eventual victor Charlotte Flair, it was clear that the promotion viewed her as a star of the future. At *WrestleMania 37*, those plans came to fruition when she challenged Sasha Banks for the *SmackDown* Women's Championship. The commentators were eager to point out that this was the first *WrestleMania* main event to feature two Black women, but it was really a platform for Belair to display both her strength and athletic dexterity. Fans saw her execute a standing shooting star press and 450 splash, as well as lift Banks above the shoulders on the arena floor and march The Boss up the ring steps before dumping her over the ropes.

As the action intensified, Belair used her long braid to whip Banks, raising welts on the titlist's skin. Then, the challenger put away the match — and claimed the gold — with the Kiss of Death (KOD) — an Argentinian backbreaker into a facebuster.

With her family cheering at ringside, and her husband, Street Profits member Montez Ford, boisterously hoisting her onto his shoulders, Belair cried with joy. Even Banks, selling her thrashing at ringside, couldn't resist glancing over at the new champion and her kin and smiling warmly.

When I woke up for the second day of *WrestleMania 37*, rain was beating on my window. In the hotel lobby, I looked up at a television monitor and caught a report forecasting hail, thunder and possible tornados. But weather changes, particularly in Florida. So I went to Raymond James Stadium, knowing that the show would take place.

I arrived so early that no one was there to direct me to the press box. So I wandered around the stadium, studying the fan cutouts up close and, at one point, took a wrong turn and ended up backstage. I said hello to some of the photographers I knew from the 22 years I wrote for the company's magazines, but I got the sense that I shouldn't linger where I wasn't invited. Even after the former Brother Love, Bruce Prichard — now the executive director of *Raw* and *SmackDown* — came by and shook hands, I wasn't sure if his smile read, "It's good to see you," or "I'm gonna tell." When I saw a golf cart go by, carrying a face-masked Roman Reigns, I felt actual fear, conjuring up conversations that might be transpiring behind my back.

"*What's he doing here? Fuckin' mark.*"

Imagining some guy in a suit stepping forward and yanking my press credential off my neck, as Vince McMahon hackled with approval, I backed out.

Up in the press box, I relaxed and contemplated the night's card. After being burned alive, The Fiend returned to WWE at *Fast Lane* in March. Although WWE tends to avoid intergender matches, the company had made an exception and allowed Orton to square off with Bray's possessed follower, Alexa Bliss. With a crazed, glassy look in her eyes, the former women's champ was having a good time at her rival's expense, skipping around like a little girl while a flame shot at the Viper and a lighting rig fell from the rafters. As Randy looked on, perplexed, a hand reached up through the mat and snatched his ankle. Then, a full body emerged: The Fiend, charred but still on the roster.

The rematch between Wyatt and Orton would open night two. Prior to the bell, fans were shown a video of The Fiend burning, then transmuting to his original form. When we returned to live action, the spotlight was on Bliss cranking what appeared to be a massive jack-in-the-box until Wyatt came out, leaping down from the large cube to hit a clothesline.

But Bliss's loyalties were unclear. As The Fiend tried a Sister Abigail, fire shot from the ring posts, prompting him to look over at Bliss — who was sitting on the jack-in-the-box with mysterious black goo running down her smiling face. Wyatt appeared to contemplate the scene, hesitating long enough for the Apex Predator to surge forward with an RKO, wrapping up his enemy for the win.

Bewildered, The Fiend stared at Bliss until the lights went out.

After the exhilaration of night one, the novelty of attending *WrestleMania* had worn off to the point that I heard fans booing the company for coming up with a finish they didn't like.

The celebrity guest for the second night was YouTuber Logan Paul, who accompanied Sami Zayn for his match with Kevin Owens. The pair had been wrestling each other on and off since 2003 when each was finding his way on the Montreal indies, and probably never had a lackluster match. This was no exception, even if the focus was on Paul rather than the combatants.

After Owens triumphed with the Stunner, the online star attempted to shake the winner's hand. Sami became jealous since *he*'d invited Paul to *WrestleMania*. Not appreciating his host's possessiveness, Paul shoved Zayn to the mat and raised Owens's arm — only to receive a Stunner himself.

Having recently begun speaking with a worked Nigerian accent, Apollo Crews's status in the company appeared to be changing. A talented performer, he'd been treading water in a mid-card position before a recent push. At *WrestleMania 37*, Crews — raised in Sacramento and Atlanta by parents from Nigeria's Benue State — was challenging Big E for the WWE Intercontinental Championship in what was called a Nigerian Drum Fight.

Here's how Crews described the match in an interview: "An ancient duel created by my ancestors for those that are wronged to get a chance to make it right. No rules, no limitations, just a beating so loud it sounds like a drum."

Hey, it could be worse. At least, I didn't have to write that.

Big E was on his way to retaining when an unexpected intruder entered the fray. Wearing some type of military uniform, Babatunde Aiyegbusi — the former Dabba-Kaito on *Raw* Underground — came down the aisle to smash the titlist and shift the tide of the contest to Crews, who won with a chokeslam.

Aiyegbusi would later be branded Commander Azeez and said to be affiliated with a military unit called the Nigerian Elite Guard.

Adding Omos to the equation, it would not be preposterous to conclude that, in the 2021 variation of WWE, Nigerians were becoming the new Samoans.

While not at the level of the Banks-Belair contest the night before, WWE *Raw* women's champion Asuka and Rhea Ripley had a stunning encounter — when I left the press box to get some fan reactions, I noticed the security guards in the corridors engrossed in the action on the TV monitors — with the challenger compensating for her *WrestleMania 36* loss by using her signature Riptide to snare the title.

The reaction to the main event — a three-way clash between WWE Universal kingpin Roman Reigns, *Royal Rumble* winner Edge and Daniel Bryan — was louder than anything I'd heard over the past two nights. Each of the combatants was regarded as a star, and the fans screamed for everything they did. Reigns's cousin Jey Uso took out Bryan with a superkick. Edge neutralized Uso with a DDT on the ring steps, flattened Reigns with a spear and tied him up for a near-fall. Just before the referee counted three, Bryan pulled the official out of the ring.

The Rated-R Superstar appeared to snap, blasting Bryan with a con-chair-to. Uso inserted himself into the match again, but Edge punished him with a spear. Rising to his feet, a revived Reigns took advantage of the disarray by leveling Edge with another spear, followed by a con-chair-to. Then, he stacked Edge on top of Bryan and ended the night by pinning both men.

WWE's return to live action had been a resounding success. In the press box, the other reporters were buzzing about what they'd just witnessed, and as I left the stadium and took the long walk through traffic to find an Uber, the fans I met were overjoyed.

Like the weather in Tampa, the sky wasn't exactly clear. But WWE had accomplished its mission of reassuring us that the professional wrestling we'd known and missed was coming back.

CHAPTER 30

Toward the end of *WrestleMania 37*, I noticed that some people crowded around ringside had opted to remove their masks. I knew that I'd been vaccinated but couldn't vouch for the wider community of wrestling fans. I was having too good a time to stress, but later worried that *WrestleMania 37* would turn out to be as much a super-spreader event as the Rose Garden ceremony commemorating Donald Trump's Supreme Court nomination of Amy Coney Barrett.

But it never did.

The first post–Wednesday Night Wars edition of NXT on USA drew a respectable 805,000 viewers. The next night, the unopposed episode of AEW *Dynamite* attracted 1.2 million — the most watchers since the show debuted.

Everybody was doing just fine — or so I thought anyway. Certainly, Triple H didn't seem that broken up about coming out on the short side of the rivalry. In fact, on Peter Rosenberg's *Cheap Heat* podcast, The Cerebral Assassin insisted that the Wednesday Night Wars had been "imaginary."

"People can say what they want," he asserted, "but the truth of the matter is you compete against everything . . . including sleep and time to do other things and video games and TikTok and everything else out there."

If my editor felt the same way, I'd probably *still* be rewriting this book.

With *WrestleMania* receding into the past, WWE went through several new rounds of cuts. The Iconics were sheared in April, as were Samoa Joe, Tucker, Chelsea Green, Bo Dallas and Mickie James — along with the WWE executive blamed on social media for sending Mickie her belongings in a garbage bag. In May, the names included Brandi "Skyler Story" Lauren, Curt Stallion and referee Jake Clemons — who'd all come from EVOLVE — Jessamyn Duke and Drake Wuertz, a former CZW World Heavyweight champion who'd become NXT's head ref, but reportedly did himself no favors after coming out as "an extremist for Christ." Among his alleged transgressions: missing an NXT taping to attend a school board conference, where he argued that mandated mask wearing assisted child predators; raging against wrestlers who'd received vaccinations; storming out of a meeting after Triple H mentioned religious tolerance; and using his corporate email to promote QAnon, a conspiracy theory that linked Hillary Clinton and other high-ranking Democrats to a child sex ring operating out of a DC pizzeria.

In June, the list of cuts was expanded, and Braun Strowman, Aleister Black, Lana, Ruby Riott, Buddy Murphy, Santana Garrett, Killian Dain, the Bollywood Boyz, Tony Nese, Tyler Breeze and Fandango were among those "future endeavored."

When fans tried making sense of the departures, particularly Strowman — a recent Universal titlist who, just a month earlier, had been in a Triple Threat main event with Bobby Lashley and Drew McIntyre for the WWE Championship — rumors abounded that the company needed to shave its payroll because it was about to be sold. Others countered that there were just too many wrestlers in the system, some people had grown stale and the natural ebb and flow called for talent to be moved aside for new signings.

Interestingly, Samoa Joe — who'd received high grades as a *Raw* commentator while working through injuries — was rehired in June and given a fresh role as an enforcer for NXT General Manager William Regal. In August, he'd dethrone Karrion Kross for the NXT Championship. But in the new world order of WWE, a title victory — particularly in NXT — had little to do with job security. As previously mentioned, Kross — along with his companion, Scarlett — was let go in November. Two months later, in January 2022, both Samoa Joe and Regal were terminated as well.

After a brief delay in April 2021, amid concerns about potential blood clots resulting from Johnson & Johnson's one-shot vaccine, the injections continued in the United States and Europe. U.S. officials pointed out that the rate of this rare mishap was 1.9 in one million, and the benefits far outweighed the risk.

The war against COVID-19 was now being fought with vigor. After banning all non-essential travel, the majority of European countries began planning to welcome fully vaccinated U.S. tourists again in the summer. And, in late April, Pfizer announced that trials were underway in its development of a pill that could possibly prevent the virus from replicating in the human body.

In New Zealand, which had essentially sealed its borders at the start of the pandemic, a crowd of 50,000 fans gathered — without masks or social distancing — in Auckland's Eden Park on April 24 to hear the band Six60, Drax Project and Sir Dave Dobbyn. It was the largest live performance since the start of the COVID era.

But the coronavirus hadn't gone away.

On April 26, lucha libre star Dr. Wagner Jr. traveled to the U.S. to receive his first dose of the Pfizer vaccine. Before he could get his second shot, he was diagnosed with COVID-19.

During the same period, India saw a spike of a million infections in three days. Officials blamed the emergence on new variants and mass gatherings, including the Kumbh Mela religious festival earlier in the month. Despite the world's largest vaccine maker, the Serum Institute of India, being located in the western city of Pune, the inoculation rollout had been plagued by shortages and delays, and only two percent of India's population was vaccinated. As the government launched a drone program to deliver doses to remote sections of the country, urban families scrambled to find oxygen for infected relatives after hospitals ran out.

Even in Japan, which had been so careful in ensuring that COVID didn't spread at live events, logistical issues slowed vaccine distribution, while the country grappled with its own biases. Stories about the dangers of vaccines imposed by the west were proliferated on social media. The suspicions were rooted in a measles, mumps and rubella inoculation campaign in the 1990s that some blamed for higher rates of aseptic meningitis. While medical authorities never established a definitive link, the vaccines were discontinued, and, years later, Japanese doctors no longer recommended a combined shot for the three ailments.

Either way, by May, only 2.2 percent of the Japanese population was vaccinated, a shockingly low number for such a developed country.

Reverberations were felt in the wrestling community. In May, New Japan reported that nine of its wrestlers were experiencing mild or asymptomatic effects of COVID-19. A month later, the coronavirus forced All Japan Pro Wrestling Triple Crown champion Suwama, a seven-time titlist, to vacate the belt after his 454-day reign.

Bizarrely, Kota Ibushi would miss a series of matches shortly after receiving a COVID vaccination. At first, it appeared that he was suffering from a side effect. But after he repeatedly tested negative for the coronavirus, doctors concluded that he'd developed aspiration pneumonia, and neither the vaccine nor COVID-19 played any role in his illness.

The saga aggravated the uncertainty that the country was feeling. On May 26, less than two months before the Tokyo Olympics were scheduled to begin, one of its official sponsors, the *Asahi Shimbun* newspaper, called for the games to be postponed a second time, joining other Japanese news organizations expressing concern that the country might not yet have the resources to control the virus.

Instead, Japan banned fans from attending. To minimize transmissions, athletes were placed in rooms with cardboard beds said to have been designed to collapse during sex.

The tale turned out to be a textbook example of fake news.

But on the American wrestling circuit, the momentum begun at *WrestleMania 37* continued. As the CDC relaxed its edict on mask wearing for people who'd been vaccinated, WWE, AEW, Impact, ROH, MLW and NJPW Strong made plans to resume live touring. On May 30, AEW finally filled Daily's Place to its full capacity of 5,500 for *Double or Nothing*. While the company deserved praise for the ways it had strived to generate excitement for the past 14 months, the crowd of live, howling fans reminded viewers of what had been lacking.

The Inner Circle had become babyfaces in March when MJF turned on the group that had grudgingly admitted him and formed his own unit, The Pinnacle, with Wardlow, FTR, Shawn Spears and manager Tully Blanchard. At the conclusion of *Double or Nothing*, the two factions clashed in the Stadium Stampede. Unlike the year before, AEW was able to blend cinematic and live elements so, after watching what was essentially an entertaining movie on the big screen, the fans witnessed the melee's conclusion in the center of the ring. Despite the recent signings of WWE legends, AEW still appeared to be committed to youth, so the final two gladiators the fans saw were Spears and Guevara, brawling and fighting with chairs. Finally, the 27-year-old Guevara — who'd taken the loss for his team the year before by falling from the stands in Kenny Omega's One-Winged Angel — secured the victory for the Inner Circle by stomping Spears into a chair and hitting him with a 630 senton.

It was a move Guevara rarely executed, and it stirred the audience into a frenzy. As the cheers rained over him, he thought about how, in the recent past, he'd been one of the company's most detestable villains. "The crowd had been booing me for so long, and now they loved me," he said. "These were people who'd just look at my face and say, 'Sammy's an asshole.' But I always had good matches, and I think people can recognize authentic."

As the rest of the Inner Circle rushed to the ring to celebrate, the strains of Chris Jericho's theme music blasted from the sound system. But then the fans took over, singing so loudly as the show went off the air that their voices overshadowed everything else.

"Judas in . . . Judas in my mind."

And that's when I knew that my book wasn't completed. In June — the same weekend Brazilians staged protests in 22 of the country's 26 states to decry, among other grievances, a sluggish vaccination operation, as well as a daily infection rate of 100,000 — I met with a group of friends at a large bar in Brooklyn. Everyone was vaccinated — just a few days earlier, New York State announced that 70 percent of its residents had received at least one dose of the COVID vaccine — and I noticed that no one was coming over to our section and reminding us to put on our masks. I hadn't felt this relaxed in public since the beginning of the pandemic. And when I woke up the next morning, I went online and booked another road trip.

There's a certain sensation I'll always feel when I think about Wednesday nights in Miami. It has no correlation to romance, yet everything to do with love.

I guess I need to elaborate. When I was about 10 or so, my uncle took a job as a baker at the old Beau Rivage hotel on Collins Avenue. As time passed, my grandparents began spending more and more time at the house on Garland Avenue in Surfside until, finally, when I was in my early twenties, they were living in a spare bedroom full-time while insisting that when their health got better — they were in their nineties by this point — they were going back to Brooklyn. At first, I would venture down to Florida with my parents. Then, I started going there alone. Each Wednesday night, everything else faded out, as I made the pilgrimage to Miami Beach Convention Hall to watch Championship Wrestling from Florida.

Sometimes, a rotating assortment of relatives accompanied me. More often, I took the bus by myself to watch Bob Roop, Buddy Colt, Pak Song, Bugsy McGraw and "Haitian Sensation" Tyree Pride. Some of the matches never left me: Harley Race getting his head battered into the ring post during an NWA title defense against Jack Brisco, Superstar Billy Graham traveling south to put up his WWWF title against Dusty Rhodes, former NWA and WWWF kingpins Pat O'Connor and Pedro Morales going at it in a scientific prelim match as I stood in the aisle thinking, "Does anyone else understand the historical significance of this?"

And now, on July 7, 2021, here I was, taking the bus down Collins Avenue again to catch Wednesday night wrestling — only this time, the promoter was Tony Khan instead of Eddie Graham.

For 12 months, Eddie Kingston had been on the AEW roster. Yet, this was the first time he'd actually appear on an AEW road show. After its long conservancy at Daily's Place, the company was touring again, and the first stop was a live *Dynamite* in Miami.

"It's really weird not to be in Jacksonville," Sammy Guevara told me that morning when I interviewed him for *Inside the Ropes*. "I had a routine where I knew where everything was at. I knew where all the good restaurants were. Now, I have to learn new spots."

Since the show happened to be taking place a mere two days before the final *SmackDown* in the ThunderDome, my guess was that Khan was trying to upstage Vince McMahon. The following week, WWE would go back to live touring, with a *SmackDown* in Houston, followed by a *Money in the Bank* in Fort Worth and then, a *Raw* in Dallas. But AEW was continuing its incursion into traditional WWE territory — an offensive momentarily halted by the coronavirus — with a *Dynamite* scheduled for September at Arthur Ashe Stadium in Queens, a subway ride away from Madison Square Garden.

When I stepped off the bus in downtown Miami, I had a hard time finding the entrance to the James L. Knight Center, a venue located in the same complex as the Hyatt Regency. But then, I scanned the people on the street and found the ones I wanted: guys in Bullet Club hats, Brodie Lee memorial t-shirts and Orange Cassidy shades, along with women with pink hair and bodies like Jade Cargill — or maybe I should say "in the style of" Jade Cargill, since nobody quite looks like the ex-fitness model and inaugural AEW TBS Champion — crammed into short fluorescent-colored skirts. As I followed, I noticed some fellow members of the tribe up ahead, looking back and pointing toward the doorway.

"Oh my god, dude. I'm just ecstatic," said Natalia Victoria, a Trader Joe's employee from Miami, who'd missed live wrestling so much that she'd driven five hours to Daily's Place in December with fiancé Emanuel Lovelle, spending the night at a bed and breakfast. "All I can do is giggle and breathe in the experience."

For some, the return to live wrestling was the reason to mark a special occasion. Luke Rogaski flew to Miami to commemorate his graduation from Torrey Pines High School in San Diego, while Danny Cunado and his wife, Mariana, from Los Angeles, wove the event into their Florida honeymoon.

The cross-continental journey paid off by offering the kinds of extemporaneous moments you couldn't experience from the other side of a television screen.

Before *Dynamite* began, ring announcer Justin Roberts pointed into the crowd and instructed the audience to sing "Happy Birthday" to a fan named Kevin. Later, Roberts singled out a spectator holding a sign indicating that he was from Nebraska.

"Anyone else from Nebraska?"

Not one fellow Cornhusker stepped forward.

While cutting a heel promo alongside Kenny Omega, Don Callis — who'd legitimately left his executive position at Impact, in addition to being terminated as part of an on-air storyline — was peppered with chants of "You got fired." Without even a pause, the manager quipped, "Real men don't quit. They get fired."

During a commercial break, MJF grabbed the mic and referred to Miami — a city I'd assume he actually likes — as "the biggest cesspool in America." As I pondered his sneering countenance, I regretted not booking a ticket to AEW's next show in Texas, simply to hear what Friedman would tell the fans *there*.

The purpose of MJF's appearance was a contract signing with Chris Jericho. But as Le Champion's entrance theme played, I saw a man strolling down the ramp with a grin so wide that I thought AEW was introducing a new character. It took a few seconds to grasp that I was witnessing a situation that hadn't occurred in a major promotion in quite some time: a paying fan taking it upon himself to leave his seat and insinuate himself into the show.

Ironically, he achieved his goal. Just as he was stripping down to a black tank top, dramatically hurling an item of clothing into the crowd, security piled on and dragged him away, while Jericho — microphone in hand — added a few blows.

Once again, MJF had a comment for the crowd: "I welcome any other one of you fat, white trash hicks to jump in the ring, too, so I can beat your ass."

As an acknowledgment to the locals, a lawless encounter between Cody Rhodes and QT Marshall was billed as a South Beach Strap Match — after the fashionable neighborhood at the tip of Miami Beach. The name meant little to the people at home, but, at the Knight Center, most spectators got the joke.

The confrontation was similar to the types of strap matches Cody's father engaged in during his days as a Florida headliner. Blood poured from cuts, and action spilled from the ring. Taking advantage of the novelty of having fans in the stands, Rhodes and Marshall made it a point to brawl among the masses.

At one point, the lights went out, and the fans rose in anticipation, expecting a fresh angle. Instead, the lights flickered back on, leading the crowd to assume that the impulsive Florida weather had triggered a brief outage.

No one realized that we were being swerved.

Following Cody's victory, he went back to the dressing room to shower and change. Later on in the show, he and ringside advisor Arn Anderson were being interviewed when, once again, the arena descended into darkness.

When luminosity returned, someone else was in the ring: the man formerly known as Aleister Black, who promptly laid out Cody and Anderson.

There'd been speculation that AEW would use the attention from its first *Dynamite* road show to deliver a surprise to fans — and fire a volley at WWE. And now, it was doing both, debuting a man whose WWE termination the month before — just as he was undergoing a makeover and starting a feud with Big E — had triggered a certain level of outrage.

Interestingly, most of the crowd in Miami were ready to dispense of the invader's WWE-branded identity, shouting, "Tommy" at the ring, a reference to the Dutch-born grappler's previous moniker, Tommy End.

The newest addition to the AEW roster would henceforth be known as Malakai Black.

His appearance was made possible due to a clerical error in his WWE non-compete clause, allowing him to become available sooner than anticipated.

Black was coming in as a heel. But because of the carefully orchestrated introduction, it's doubtful that AEW management expected anything less than the euphoria that greeted him.

"Life is definitely not normalized," a Miami x-ray technician named Chris Galarza told me near the concession stands. "But this is one of the steps."

After more than a year of avoiding close crowds in indoor settings, it was strange to be surrounded by the maskless hordes. But then, it felt so natural, back inside an arena, standing alongside people who couldn't stop screaming.

It almost seemed like the entire age of COVID-19 had been a bad dream, an elaborate rib played on the world in general, and the wrestling business in particular.

"I'm grateful," Sammy Guevara replied when I asked about the symbolism of it all. "Whether you're a wrestler or a fan, we went through it, and we're living another day."

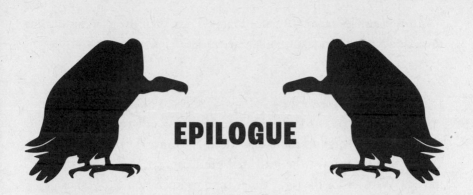

EPILOGUE

IT WASN'T OVER.

In December 2021, the Omicron variant of COVID-19 was spreading its tentacles, picking off everyone, it seemed, who'd previously managed to dodge the virus, including people who were vaccinated and boosted. By the second week of the month, Omicron had eclipsed its predecessors, shattering records and accounting for 73 percent of the new infections in the United States.

Despite New Zealand's immense success at holding off the virus, Prime Minister Jacinda Ardern warned her country to prepare for an outbreak. The Omicron transmission rate, she said, was just too high.

After nine members in a single family in Auckland were infected, the head of state not only imposed new restrictions, but postponed her own wedding.

Still, it wasn't as bad as it could have been. As a rule, the new coronavirus strain was milder than those that came before, especially among the vaccinated. While many sufferers experienced fever and discomfort, and sometimes required hospitalization, the numbers of those sent to intensive care units, as well as the morgue, were far lower than with sufferers of previous strains.

Eight weeks after the variant was first detected in South Africa, scientists there said the wave of infections were falling off as quickly as they climbed. And Hans Kluge, WHO's director for Europe, speculated that, on his continent at least, COVID-19 could very well transition from a pandemic to a controllable epidemic, like the flu.

"It is plausible," he told Agence France-Press, "that the region is moving towards a kind of pandemic end game."

In WWE, though, the scourge of layoffs showed no signs of abating.

Leaving the potential Firefly Fun House conflict with Alexa Bliss unresolved, the organization dispensed of Bray Wyatt in July 2021. "What do we do now?" the real-life Windham Rotunda asked on social media. "We wait for the right time. Then we turn Rome to Ashes."

In November, the casualties included Keith Lee, who'd been gifted — or saddled with — the nickname "Bearcat" on the main roster, presumably in honor of fellow African American Bearcat Wright, a WWE Hall of Famer. Lee's partner, Mia Yim, was also future endeavored, along with such names as Nia Jax, Ember Moon, Oney Lorcan, Lince Dorado, Gran Metalik, Eva Marie and Franky Monet, aka Taya Valkyrie.

In October, hip hop faction Hit Row appeared to be on the ascendancy, graduating from NXT to *SmackDown* as part of the 2021 WWE draft. Then, on November 4, the female member of the stable, B-Fab, was let go. Her partners, Isaiah "Swerve" Scott and Ashante "Thee" Adonis followed her 15 days later.

Seizing on the opportunity to fire another jab at Vince McMahon, Tony Khan went on *Busted Open* and remarked, "Anybody who signs a contract [with WWE] these days is not signing a real contract, in my opinion . . . It's not anything to be proud of when a company lets all those people go."

Since the conclusion of the Wednesday Night Wars, the battle between AEW and NXT had shifted — to AEW vs. WWE as a whole.

In the summer, Khan scored the biggest coup since the company's founding. When viewers tuned in to the company's new Friday night show, *Rampage*, on August 20, they were greeted with the opening riff from the Living Colour song "Cult of Personality." In the arena as well as at home, fans screamed and jumped out of their seats. Seven years after parting ways with WWE, CM Punk was returning to the ring.

And he was doing it in the city that was as much a part of his persona as his unvarnished opinions and vast collection of tattoos, in front of a sold-out United Center in Chicago.

Punk didn't wrestle on his first night back. Instead, he spoke to the crowd. Showing deference to the current crop of AEW stars, he joked that he felt like Dr. Britt Baker in her hometown of Pittsburgh. He recalled his days in Ring of Honor, and how he felt like a true professional wrestler at the time. Without mentioning the industry leader by name, he continued that the positivity ended with his decision to go to WWE in 2006.

Hence, the reason why he'd largely forsaken the business since his dismissal in 2014: "I was never going to get healthy — physically, mentally, spiritually or emotionally — staying in the same place that got me sick in the first place."

Before he ended the promo, he beseeched each spectator to pick up a free ice cream bar on the way out — compliments of him.

Later, fans would ponder two inscriptions the 42-year-old legend had made on his shoes: "CF" and "AC" — wondering if Punk was implying that two of WWE's most respected names were planning to depart. CF, it was widely believed, was Charlotte Flair, whose fiancé, Andrade El Idolo had signed with AEW earlier in the summer. AC, it was almost universally agreed, was Dr. Britt Baker's fiancé, Adam Cole.

Despite the rumors, as of June 2022, Flair — now married to Andrade — was still in a premium spot in the WWE women's division.

Cole was another story.

The former NXT Champion debuted at *All Out,* uniting with old Bullet Club confederates Kenny Omega and the Young Bucks. "It was a great feeling," Khan told *Busted Open.* "He was absolutely the person who brought us the toughest competition when there was a Wednesday Night War. It's a dream free-agency acquisition."

At the same event, the former Ruby Riott debuted as Ruby Soho, winning the women's Casino Battle Rumble. But the biggest news of the night was that Daniel Bryan — who'd main-evented at the previous *WrestleMania* — was now, as they'd say, All Elite.

WWE had worked hard to hold onto Bryan when his contract expired. In fact, Nick Khan's discussions with New Japan reportedly involved WWE cutting a special deal with the Tokyo-based company that would allow Bryan to satisfy his craving to occasionally compete there.

Unlike Punk, Bryan — who now reverted to using his birth name, Bryan Danielson — had nothing negative to say about the company where he'd met his wife, Brie Bella, and spearheaded what was known as the "Yes movement," enticing entire audiences to repeatedly thrust their fingers in the air while chanting, "Yes! Yes! Yes!" But with his time in the ring winding down, the grappler apparently wanted to be exposed to a wide range of mat styles and control the direction of his character. Whether intentional or not, the corporate framework of WWE seemed to conspire against that type of autonomy.

Danielson was the exact type of performer AEW needed when it followed through on its pre-pandemic plans to raid New York City, drawing an announced 20,177 to an event it titled *Grand Slam* at Arthur Ashe Stadium in Queens for a live *Dynamite* broadcast followed by a *Rampage* taping. It was AEW's largest crowd to date, and Danielson's championship challenge to Omega featured both men at their best. In what was arguably the premier match of 2021, the pair played off each other's strengths, making the crowd dizzy with excitement until, at the 30-minute mark, the bell sounded.

The two had given the public what was known in the business as an old-fashioned "Broadway," keeping spectators breathless until the time limit expired — a tactic that made fans hungrier to once again watch the participants tangle.

To native New Yorker Eddie Kingston, the night was a turning point — evidence that AEW had supplanted WWE as the city's preferred promotion. "To be straight up honest with you, we have bigger names," he told *Inside the Ropes*. "We have names that people want to see. . . . People want to see Kenny Omega. . . . People want to see The Bucks. People want to see Miro and people want to see Punk. We are capturing people's imaginations, and that's what makes the big difference."

Meanwhile, NXT was being taken apart and put back together again.

The first intimation of this occurred when Nick Khan announced that, starting in September, the brand would be referred to as NXT 2.0. "We are doing a complete revamp on NXT," he told BT Sport.

No longer would WWE peruse the indies as a way to stock the roster, he said: "We don't want to just keep doing the same thing. We want to look elsewhere for great, young talent."

Certainly, there'd been issues with the NXT system, particularly since the onetime indie darlings picked by the brand often floundered when they arrived on the main roster. Others remained in NXT because the power brokers in Stamford couldn't figure out where they'd fit in on *Raw* or *SmackDown*. Either way, for the better part of the last year, this meant that a lot of these folks were doomed to be penciled out during the next bloodbath.

From this point forward, it was declared, NXT was moving in a different direction. The talent would be younger and, in the case of the men, at least, larger in stature and muscle mass. No longer, it seemed, would a *Royal Rumble* winner choose to pursue the NXT title at *WrestleMania* over the *Raw*- or *SmackDown*-recognized championships. The Wednesday Night Wars were over, and NXT was back to being a developmental territory, training its talent in WWE's house style.

In fact, the NXT creative team was now being run by the front office, with *Raw* and *SmackDown* executive director and senior vice president Bruce Prichard and senior VP of creative writing operations Christine Lubrano calling the shots.

The past wasn't being completely erased, of course. Many of those already in NXT would remain. But there was definitely a new crop of headliners, among them Von Wagner, whose father had been Beau Beverly in the WWF and Wayne Bloom in the AWA, Bron Breakker, Grayson Waller (who was booked into a feud with AJ Styles to get the rub), LA Knight and Joe Gacy. On the women's side, the Toxic Attraction stable was drawing attention, with Gigi Dolin and Jacy Jayne winning the tag team gold and partner Mandy Rose experiencing a revival that included a reign as NXT women's champion to showcase her legitimate athletic skills.

The show had a completely different look, too, with more vignettes and pastel colors replacing the black and gold associated with the product built by Triple H.

Where Triple H stood in all this was a matter of conjecture. In

September, the company said, he underwent a successful medical procedure "caused by a genetic heart issue." He was expected "to make a full recovery."

Although he later said his convalescence was more trying than initially reported, hopefully, he did. But, to those who followed such things on the internet, his role within the company appeared marginalized. Rumors circulated that he was being blamed for NXT losing the Wednesday Night Wars. In January 2022, several employees described as his confidants were — to paraphrase Broken Matt Hardy — deleted.

These included onetime DX teammate "Road Dogg" Jesse James, a promo and character development instructor at the Performance Center and his brother, Scott Armstrong, NXT's sole referee coach. But William Regal's exit was the most shocking. Like Gerald Brisco, Regal — whose wrestling background dated to the Blackpool, UK, boardwalk, where he'd shoot on challengers as a teen to protect the promoter's prize money — was one of the most prolific recruiters WWE ever had, rummaging through the indies and international promotions to conscript names like Kevin Owens, Finn Balor, Shayna Baszler, Asuka, Io Shirai, Shinsuke Nakamura, Johnny Gargano and Tommaso Ciampa.

In this new landscape, the promotion that may have funneled more talent to NXT than anyplace else became one of the biggest victims of the age of COVID-19.

"Throughout the pandemic, our top priority was to keep everyone healthy and safe," read a statement released by Ring of Honor in October 2021, "and despite not producing any live events over 18 months, we were able to keep everyone fully contracted. We now find ourselves at a time where we need to make changes to our new business operations and are planning a pivot for Ring of Honor with a new mission and strategy."

After its *Final Battle* pay-per-view on December 12, the company continued, it would go on hiatus for the first quarter of 2022 — releasing most of the wrestlers from their contracts — before returning with its traditional *Supercard of Honor* on *WrestleMania* weekend.

On the morning of *Final Battle*, I caught a bus to Baltimore. "The name feels too real," former ROH ringside photographer Mary Kate Anthony told me shortly after I arrived. "Wrestling is what it is today because of Ring of Honor. My life is what it is today because of Ring of Honor."

The emergence of former ROH stalwarts Cody, the Bucks, Hangman Page — who'd captured the AEW World Championship from Omega two months before *Final Battle* — and others on TNT had come at the expense of the smaller promotion. Even so, Tony Khan agreed to help with the card, sharing talent and letting some of his top names send video greetings. The action was compelling, but the mood was bittersweet at best.

"This is the closing of a chapter," Mike Bennett told me when I interviewed him for *Inside the Ropes*. "I was hoping it would be longer. But if this is the end, this is the end."

Ring of Honor COO Joe Koff was practically in tears when he addressed the fans before the show. Then, masking up, he went into the audience and personally thanked the people who'd supported the group.

So was this it? When I caught up with Koff in the crowd, I asked if the whole thing was going away. Although I knew him to be a sincere wrestling fan who could rattle off historical trivia and loved losing himself in a match, he answered like the kind of promoter who'd put a post-pubescent William Regal in the carnival booth to stretch the marks back in Blackpool: "This is the *Final Battle* of the old Ring of Honor. But tomorrow's a new beginning."

But maybe he wasn't jiving me.

I mean, if the promotion was shutting down, why was Deonna Purrazzo — the AAA Reina de Reinas titlist and a multiple Impact champion — there as a surprise guest, challenging Rok-C for her ROH Women's World belt following a successful defense over Willow Nightingale?

And that wasn't the only outside attraction. The former Braun Strowman, Adam Scherr, showed up out of nowhere, blowing the roof off the place as he joined a faction headed by EC3. And after Mark and Jay Briscoe captured the ROH tag straps from Mike Bennett and Matt Taven, FTR stormed the ring to brawl with the new champs.

Shortly before *Final Battle*, the promotion stripped Bandido of the ROH World Championship when he was diagnosed with COVID-19, instead staging a clash for the gold pitting Jay Lethal — who'd already defected for AEW — against Jonathan Gresham. As the pair collided, the dressing room emptied, everyone surrounding and pounding on the ring, encouraging the combatants while exchanging melancholy smiles with one another.

When Gresham finally won, he took the mic and pledged to be a fighting champion. It was no idle promise. Prior to Tony Khan's March 2022 announcement that he was expanding his empire to include ROH, Gresham defended the Ring of Honor title on other promotions' cards, including his Terminus group, Impact and Game Changer Wrestling.

Even before ROH's hiatus was announced, Brett Lauderdale had big plans, going after the same niche audience that previously embraced ECW and ROH. In January 2022, GCW presented its first show in New York's Hammerstein Ballroom, where ECW appeared both when Paul Heyman was in charge and after WWE purchased the brand and decided to resurrect the glory days with its *One Night Stand* pay-per-views in 2005 and 2006. But starting in 2008, the Hammerstein was ROH's home base in New York City, and the decision to run there sent a message that GCW perceived itself as the country's number three promotion.

The pay-per-view, *The Wrld on GCW*, sold out instantly.

"There's a place and time for everybody and everything," Lio Rush told me. "It's not perfect. Ring of Honor gave people a lot of memories. But right now, GCW is the one here, giving the people what they've been waiting on a long time."

Chris Dickinson — who'd won the Ring of Honor World Tag Team Championship with Homicide in July 2021 — had been with GCW since it was called Jersey Championship Wrestling. "With Ring of Honor, I came in at an uncertain time," he explained. "Nobody knew what was going to happen there. GCW is my home promotion, a place I helped build. On the indies, passion plays a huge part. And GCW has passion."

And while ROH was admirably paying its workers while keeping them home during the pandemic, GCW was staging the social distancing match between Joey Janela and Jimmy Lloyd and holding outdoor shows in Indianapolis. "We didn't stop the machine," Dickinson said, "and now, you see where we are."

Although Tony Khan's "forbidden door" promos included no mention of GCW, Lauderdale was aggressively living the philosophy, giving talent from AEW, Impact and other promotions the luxury to express themselves in ways that wouldn't be allowed on commercial television.

Nobody embodied this better than Matt Cardona, who in GCW had become as compelling a heel as fellow Long Islander MJF.

On a Queens show that took place the same week as *Grand Slam*, the former Zack Ryder entered the ring wearing two titles, one on top of the other, a spinning "GCW Universal" belt along with the "Internet Championship" from his YouTube series. Then, he cut a promo to the counterculture crowd, insisting that GCW become more like WWE, incorporating "sports-entertainment" elements.

As the people booed, he referred to them as the "GCW Universe."

In July 2021, Cardona captured the group's championship in a death match with Nick Gage. He was showered with garbage.

While *The Wrld on GCW* lineup was extensive, featuring, among other clashes, Jon Moxley — who'd unseated Cardona for the GCW World Championship in September — beating Homicide, Ruby Soho defeating Allie Katch and 54-year-old Jeff Jarrett bashing Effy with a guitar to steal a win, the one match that truly represented the promotion's spirit was Cardona vs. Janela.

Cardona's shtick started the moment fans entered the Hammerstein and found a sanitizing wipe on each seat, a gift, according to the wrapping, from Matt; his wife, Chelsea Green; and the night's sponsor, Pabst Blue Ribbon.

Playing off the crowd's ECW ardor, the contest began with the Sandman's entrance music blaring through the speakers. Fans turned and looked everywhere, expecting the ECW legend to tear through the crowd, swigging beer and swinging his kendo stick. As it turned out, the whole thing was an obnoxious swerve. Instead of the Sandman, the audience got

Cardona splashing Pabst on observers and Chelsea swinging the Sandman's signature weapon.

Referring to internet rumors that AEW was about to let Janela go, Cardona declared, "Joey, tonight I'm going to end your career before Tony Khan can say, 'You're fired.'"

But although, as of late, Janela had been largely relegated to AEW's YouTube offerings, in GCW, he was a combination of The Rock, Ric Flair and Bruno Sammartino.

The backstory hinged on Cardona's suspicion that his recent bride had violated her vows with The Bad Boy. As the match was intensifying, fans taunted Chelsea with chants of "She fucked Joey." Selling the insults, she shrieked back, "I did not!"

Still, at one point, it appeared that the stories might be true. When Cardona lifted a chair above his shoulders to smash Janela, Green pulled it away then seemed to kick her husband in the balls. Janela shot her a quizzical glance, and she urged him to scale the ropes. But, as with Sandman's entrance music, this was yet another ruse. After Joey reached the top turnbuckle, Chelsea shook the strands, crotching him.

The bout included so much outside interference, I'll only mention the names I remember. Jade Cargill's "lawyer" from AEW, "Smart" Mark Sterling, appeared at one point to declare that Janela was legally barred from using the Internet Championship as a weapon. A guy in a Vince McMahon mask turned out to be former WWF personality Virgil. The former Hornswoggle shoved Janela into the ring post, prompting Marko Stunt — who hadn't been seen on AEW programming in four months — to come to the rescue.

The contest ended when Brian Meyers — who, as Curt Hawkins, held the WWE Tag Team Championship with Zack Ryder in 2007 — helped his friend score the victory. But the run-ins continued. Sean "X-Pac" Waltman came out to throttle the heels. He was followed to the ring by a flurry of GCW personalities: Mance Warner, Atticus Cogar, Matthew Justice and heel faction 44OH! Then, the lights went out, allowing Sabu and whistle-blowing manager Bill Alfonso to materialize and drive home the point that, in the modern era, GCW was the closest fans were going to get to Paul Heyman's ECW.

"This is different than Ring of Honor and every other place," said Bandido, who'd participated in a lucha match earlier in the show. "All the style can mix here. And one day, they have a new style. Everyone in wrestling will know GCW style."

Exactly two years to the day that the WHO requested "further information" from Chinese authorities on a troubling virus in Wuhan and my work on this book started, WWE presented a new event, *Day 1*, on January 1, 2022. All these occurrences seemed tied together and left me with a simple conclusion.

Through all its phases, pro wrestling has proven to be imperishable.

So apparently was COVID-19.

In the *Day 1* main event, Roman Reigns was supposed to defend his WWE Universal Championship against Brock Lesnar. But Reigns was diagnosed with COVID, and plans were changed. Instead, Lesnar was inserted into what had been scheduled as a Fatal Fourway, pitting WWE champion Big E against Bobby Lashley, Kevin Owens and Seth Rollins. When the show ended, it was The Beast Incarnate who left Atlanta's State Farm Arena with the belt.

It wasn't what anyone originally envisioned, but WWE responded the way it had throughout the pandemic, razing whatever obstructions had been placed on the road to *WrestleMania*.

Just as the void created by the demise of WCW was eventually filled by AEW, and the Hammerstein slot was now occupied by GCW, one variant of COVID would beget another — Alpha to Delta, Delta to Omicron and on and on. Vaccines might be adjusted, and the severity could vary. But like a Donald Trump rally, or a ref bump in a WWE title match, the reality appeared to be that this was something we'd be seeing again.

So maybe it was time to learn to live in a world where the One True Sport and the coronavirus coexisted in perpetuity.

ACKNOWLEDGMENTS

THIS BOOK WAS researched and written under trying circumstances, particularly when so many of us were locked down. During the course of this project, a number of friends and relatives were infected with COVID — in a few cases, fatally — and so I was grateful for any diversion. In addition to expressing gratitude to the art form that gave us that diversion, I want to thank the individual wrestling companies — all mentioned in the book — that granted me access to events. Throughout my lengthy career of observing and chronicling the spectacle and drama of the squared circle, I have not forgotten that it is always a privilege to be admitted into this closed society to widen perceptions of the beautiful craft that has offered me sanctuary my entire life.

Special appreciation also goes out to the podcasters, YouTubers and radio hosts who had me on their programs during this period to discuss my last book, *Too Sweet* — which happened to be released in the middle of the pandemic — the supporters who reached out on social media, the friends who dissected online gossip and storylines with me and Randy Tyson and his wife, Suzanne, who were benevolent enough to open a pro wrestling themed bar, DDT, mere walking distance from my home in Brooklyn.

I am indebted to Dante Richardson and Kenny McIntosh for launching *Inside the Ropes Wrestling Magazine* in the UK during a time when newsstand publishing was supposed to be dead — and promptly assigning me a monthly column. In the small window between the Delta and Omicron variants, I was able to venture to Glasgow for a few days, where Kenny and Stuart Innis not only put me up, but managed to wrangle numerous members of the *Inside the Ropes* crew — and several standouts of the Scottish wrestling scene — to turn up in my honor.

Since I began researching *Follow the Buzzards* while I was completing *Too Sweet*, I feel like I'm in some type of marathon with the ECW Press team. Obviously, this would not have come about if Executive Editor Michael Holmes were not sold on the concept. But so many others have helped the process go smoothly, including Co-Publisher David Caron, Managing and Development Editor Shannon Parr, Digital and Art Director Jessica Albert, Sales and Rights Director Emily Ferko, Senior Publicist Elham Ali, Publicity Manager Claire Pokorchak, Production Manager Jennifer Gallinger, Copy Editor Rachel Ironstone, Senior Editor Jen Knoch and the people at Made by Emblem, whose cover art provided the perfect packaging for this story.

KEITH ELLIOT GREENBERG is a *New York Times* bestselling author and monthly columnist for *Inside the Ropes Wrestling Magazine* in the United Kingdom. A lifetime New Yorker and third-generation wrestling fan, he wrote for WWE's publications for 22 years and co-authored the autobiographies of "Classy" Freddie Blassie, "Nature Boy" Ric Flair and Superstar Billy Graham, as well as the third and fourth editions of the *WWE Encyclopedia of Sports Entertainment*. *Follow the Buzzards* is a sequel to his last book for ECW Press, *Too Sweet: Inside the Indie Wrestling Revolution*. His vast writing credits include more than 35 other books, on topics ranging from true crime to pop culture, as well as the *Daily Beast, Men's Journal, Maxim, Playboy, Huffington Post, Bleacher Report* and *USA Today*. As a television producer, he has worked for every major U.S. television network.